Abstracts of the

TESTAMENTARY PROCEEDINGS

of the

PREROGATIVE COURT OF MARYLAND

Volume III: 1675–1677, 1703–1704

Libers: 7, 8A, 8B, 9A (1–371)

I0113087

by

V. L. Skinner, Jr.

Copyright © 2006
by Vernon L. Skinner, Jr.
All Rights Reserved.

Printed for
Clearfield Company, Inc. by
Genealogical Publishing Co., Inc.
Baltimore, Maryland
2006

International Standard Book Number: 0-8063-5289-2

Made in the United States of America

INTRODUCTION

Purpose of the Prerogative Court.

The Prerogative Court was the central point for probate for Provincial Maryland. It was mirrored after the Prerogative Court of Canterbury. There was a judge as well as clerk(s) of the court. Initially, all probate was brought directly to the Prerogative Court, located in the Provincial Capital. As the Province became more populous, all documents were still to be filed with the Prerogative Court; however, administration of probate was delegated to the various county courts. Even so, there are documents only in the Prerogative Court and not in the appropriate county, and vice versa.

Documents filed in the Prerogative Court.

The following documents were filed in the Prerogative Court: administration bond, will, inventory, administration accounts, and final balances. The testamentary proceedings contain the administration bond and the docket for the court. If the administrator is lax in filing documents, then a summons is also recorded.

Equity Court

The Prerogative Court was also the court for equity cases--resolution of disputes over the settlement and distribution of an estate. The case was brought before the judge and could take several years to resolve. Often depositions were taken and recorded in the minutes.

Notes on the Abstraction.

1. The left hand column contains the liber/folio number. The folio numbers are presented just as they appear in the actual document, e.g., 32a, 78½.

2. The right hand column contains the abstraction text.

3. Various libers specify a particular session for the Prerogative Court, e.g., 1678; or, September Court 1742. This information is presented as "Court Session:" followed by the

appropriate session. Should no session have been specified, then the phrase "no date" is used.

4. An ellipsis (...) is used to indicate a continuation of the previous information, but no relevant genealogical information is present.

5. The following symbols are used in the abstraction:

- ? difficult to read.
- # pounds of tobacco.
- ! [sic].

Abbreviations.

The following abbreviations have been used throughout this abstraction:

AA - Anne Arundel Co.
ACC - Accomac Co.
BA - Baltimore Co.
CE - Cecil Co.
CH - Charles Co.
CR - Caroline Co.
CV - Calvert Co.
dbn - de bonis non
DE - Delaware
DO - Dorchester Co.
ENG - England
FR - Frederick Co.
g - gentleman
HA - Harford Co.
IRE - Ireland
KE - Kent Co. MD
KEDE - Kent Co. DE
LaC - letters ad colligendum (for temporary collection & preservation of assets)
LoA - letters of administration
MA - Massachusetts
MD - Maryland
MO - Montgomery Co.
NE - New England
NY - New York
NYC - New York City
p - planter
PA - Pennsylvania
PG - Prince George's Co.
PoA - power of attorney
QA - Queen Anne's Co.
SM - St. Mary's Co.
SMC - St. Mary's City
SO - Somerset Co.
TA - Talbot Co.
VA - Virginia
WA - Washington Co.
WO - Worcester Co.

This volume is a continuation of the series, covering 1675 to 1677. It also includes some inventories dating 1703/4. Beginning in 1674, inventories and accounts were recorded in a separate series.

Court Session: 1675

7:1 18 June. Nathaniell Heathcote (g, AA) exhibited oath of Jane Heliard widow & administratrix of Daniell Heliard (AA), sworn 30 November 1674. Appraisers: William Cockes, Bernard Eccleston.

7:2 Capt. Thomas Howell (CE) exhibited oath of Thomas Salmon & John Cox, appraisers of estate of Capt. Thomas Tarleton (CE), sworn 17 April 1675. Inventory was exhibited.

Inventory of Robertt Lusby (AA) was exhibited, by appraisers William Harris & William Farquison (AA).

23 June. Will of Robertt Harwood (TA) was exhibited. William Stevens renounced administration.
7:3 Date: 2 June 1675. Thomas Taylor renounced administration on said estate.
7:4 John Sumner renounced administration on said estate. Date: 23 June 1675.
7:5 The judge ruled that said Robertt died as intestate; his will made the following bequests: wife plantation, son Peter Harwood 200 a. at Tuckahoe, land at King's Creek to be sold. Richard Wollman (g, TA) to prove said will.
7:6 Appraisers: Richard Royston, Thomas Vaughan.

Jacob Abrahams son & heir & one of executors of Isack Abrahams (TA) exhibited his will. Said Jacob is an infant under age 17 & other executor Elisabeth Abrahams is lately dec'd. Richard Gorsuch (g, TA) to prove said will. Inventory is to be made in presence of Sarah Reade & executor Jacob & any 2 of the creditors. Said Gorsuch to administer oath.
7:7 Said Elisabeth as widow of Isaack made her own will, naming Brien O'Maly & Thomas Taylor as executors. Witnesses were: William Allen, Margueritt Lodge. Richard Wollman (g, TA) to prove said will.

7:8 25 June. John Coxe (CE) was granted administration on estate of Francis

Barnes (CE), who died childless & unmarried, as principle creditor. Appraisers: John West, Thomas Rumsey. Abraham Wild (g, CE) to administer oath.

7:9 3 July. Francis Hopewell (CV) exhibited the renunciation of Judith Booth (Poplar Hill, SM) widow of John Booth (Poplar Hill, SM). Date: 25 June 1675. Witness: Henry Hyde.

7:10 Francis Hopewell was granted administration on said estate. Security: John Wiseman (CV), William Hemstid (SM). Appraisers: Peter Carwardine, Herberth Howman. Henry Hyde (g, SM) to administer oath.

7:11 7 July. Abr. Wilde (g, CE) exhibited will of Richard Leake (BA). Bequests: William to old man at Mr. Young, Richard Whitton. Date: 9 January 1673/4. Witnesses: Thomas Oveton, Hugh Williams.

7:12 Will proved by Thomas Overton on 9 April. Said Williams "is not in the country".

Richard Whitton (CE) executor of Richard Leake (BA) exhibited inventory.

8 July. Notice to the commissioners of AA regarding the wasting condition of the estates of Nathaniell & Thomassin Stinchecomb.

12 July. Thomas Chandler (AA) was granted administration on estate of Symon Harrison, who died childless & unmarried,

7:13 as greatest creditor. Samuell Chew, Esq. to take the bond. Appraisers: Mr. James Chilcot, Robert Connant. Samuell Chew, Esq. to administer oath.

13 July. John Stone (g, CH) exhibited will of Verlinda Stone (CH). Benjamin Rozer (g, CH) to prove said will.

7:14 Appraisers: Robertt Doyne, Mathew Stone. Benjamin Rozer to administer oath.

John Stone (g, CH) exhibited oath of John Munns & Henry Aspinall, appraisers of Robertt Prowse (CH), sworn 10

Court Session: 1675

September 1674.

19 July. John Beale (Resurrection
Hundred, CV) who married relict &
administratrix of George Reade
(Resurrection Hundred, CV) & relict &
executrix of
7:15 Robertt Tyler (Resurrection Hundred, CV)
exhibited that on 30 July 1674, his wife
as Joane Tyler made a deed of gift of
her lands, etc., to Thomas Sprigg (g,
CV).
7:16 Witnesses: John Halles, William
Hannington.
7:17 John Beale married Joane Tyler on 30
July 1674. Also, said Joane made her
will on 6 June, with said John as
executor; witnesses: Thomas Sprigg, John
Halles. Her will mentions: her natural
son Peter alias John Mounten.
7:18 Will of Joane Beale wife of John Beale.
Date: 6 June 1675. Bequests: son George
Read (under age) his estate to be
entrusted to his godfathers George
Mackall & John Wawhub, son Robertt &
daughter Elisabeth legacies left them by
my late husband
7:19 Robertt Tyler, natural son Peter alias
John Mounten 200 a. from land bequeathed
my by my late husband Robertt Tyler,
youngest son John Beale 200 a.,
goddaughter Elisabeth Coomes, Mr. John
Halles (illiterate)
7:20 100 a. Executor: husband John Beale.
Witnesses: Thomas Sprigg, John Halles.

Sarah Clarke widow of Thomas Clarke (CV)
exhibited his will. Will of Thomas
Clarke (CV). Date: 18 March 1674.
7:21 Executrix: wife Sarah.
7:22 Bequests: wife Sarah, 2 children Robertt
(son) & Sarah (daughter). Witnesses:
Thomas Sprigg, John Halles. Will proved
19 July 1675.
7:23 Said Sarah was granted administration.
Appraisers (gentlemen): Thomas Sprigg,
John Halles.

Mary Jarboe (SM) widow & administratrix
of Lt. Co. John Jarboe (SM) exhibited
inventory.

William Claw (SM) surviving executor of John Reynolds (SM) petitioned to sell "Fresh Ponneck". Walter Hall & Thomas Courtney (SM) to appraise said land.

7:24 Jonathon Sibrey (TA) exhibited will of
Seth Foster (g, Great Choptank Island,
TA). Bequests: wife Elisabeth Foster &
youngest daughter Sarah all money in
7:25 ENG which was in the hands of Mr.
Richard Owen (merchant, London, now
dec'd), son-in-law John Hawkins, wife
1/3rd, residue to 2 daughters Elisabeth
(eldest) & Sarah (youngest), wife 1/3rd
of Great Choptank Island & 1/3rd land at
Chester River & 1/3rd of land on Kent
Island, son-in-law John Hawkins "Tully's
Delight" 1000 a.
7:26 excepting his mother's 1/3rd, eldest
daughter Elisabeth Lowe Great Choptank
Island, youngest daughter Sarah
"Standish Woods" 1000 a. on Chester
River & "Green's Plantation" on Kent
Island currently in possession of Edward
Hull. Executrix: wife. Overseers: MM
William Hamelton (Miles River, TA),
son-in-law Vincent Lowe.
7:27 Date: 2 December 1674. Witnesses:
Vincent Lowe, Robertt White, Richard
Rissy, Will proved on 12 March 1674.
Elisabeth Foster (widow) was granted
administration. Jonathon Sibrey (g, TA)
exhibited oath of Mr. William Hamelton
& Edmund Webb, appraisers of Seth Foster
(TA),
7:28 sworn 24 June 1675. Inventory was
exhibited.

(N) Martin (TA) widow of Robertt Martin
(TA) was granted administration on his
estate. Vincent Lowe, Esq. (Attorney
General) to prove will. Appraisers:
James Murphy, Edward Elliot.
7:29 Said Lowe to administer oath.

Mary Bridges (TA) widow & executrix of Richard Bridges (TA) was granted administration on his estate. Vincent Lowe, Esq. to prove said will. Appraisers: Edmund Webb, Richard Gold. Said Lowe to administer oath.

Court Session: 1675

7:30 22 July. Emia Burgesse (TA) widow of John Burgesse (TA) was granted administration on his estate. Appraisers: George Watts, Cornelius Morain. Richard Gorsuch (g) to administer oath.

23 July. Mary Wright (KE) widow of John Wright (KE)
7:31 was granted administration on his estate. Tobias Wells (KE) is creditor to estate. Appraisers: MM Thomas Osborne, John Currer. John Hinson (g, KE) to administer oath.

24 July. Joane Hilliard (AA) widow & administratrix of Daniell Hilliard (AA) exhibited inventory.

7:32 26 July. Jonathon Sibrey (g, TA) exhibited accounts of Capt. Philemon Lloyd (TA) executor of Henry Hawkins (TA). Discharge was granted.

Alice Roper (AA) relict of Janus Morgan (AA) was granted administration on his estate. Appraisers: John Gray, Marin duVall. Maj. William Burgesse to administer oath.

7:33 Mary Davis (AA) widow & administratrix of Evan Davis (AA) petitioned for appraisers John Moonshott & William Sineck. Samuell Lane (g) to administer oath.

20 July. Joane Tyler (CV) widow
7:34 gave to her friend Thomas Sprigg all lands. Date: 30 July 1674.
7:35 Witnesses: John Halles, William Hannington. Thomas Sprigg (g, CV) confirmed the gift from Joane Tyler (CV) now wife of John Beale
7:36 gives same to Joane Beale.
7:37 Date: 30 July 1674. Witnesses: John Halles, William Hannington.

Samuell Hatton administrator of George Soley (chirurgeon, TA). Widow of said Soley refused administration. He was brought to court for taking chattel from estate.

7:38 Mentions: Edward Man (merchant) attorney for William Orchard (Poole, ENG) as greatest creditor to said estate.

Samuell Boston (high sheriff, BA) administrator of Capt. George Goldsmith (BA).

7:39 Estate is unadministered by Mary Boston relict & executrix of said dec'd. Said Mary is lately dec'd. Inventory for both exhibited.

Francis Hopewell (CV) administrator of John Booth (SM) exhibited inventory.

ultimate July. John Beale (CV) was granted administration on estate of his wife Joane Beale. Appraisers: John Halles (g), William Wilson. Thomas Sprigg (g) to administer oath.

Cuthbert Fenwick (g) to swear Thomas Sprigge & John Halles as appraisers of estate of Thomas Clarke (CV).

7:40 Alice Walker (CH) widow & executrix of James Walker (CV) exhibited inventory.

2 July [sic]. Jane Paine (SM) widow & administratrix of Thomas Paine died on 9 June last. Mentions: orphans of said Jane.

Jochim Guilbert (SM) administrator of Dr. Luke Barbier (SM) exhibited accounts.

7:41 Distribution: John Blomfield who married relict (1/3rd), orphans. Date: 2 August 1675. Guibert Joachim was granted discharge.

7:42 4 August. Daniell Murphy (SM) administrator of Peter Robertts (SM) exhibited renunciation of Anne Murphy his wife the relict of the dec'd. Date: 7 June 1675. Witnesses: William Rosewell, Robert Toat. Inventory was exhibited.

7:43 Clement Haly (SM) executor of John Robertts (SM) exhibited inventory.

William Harper (St. George's, SM) has taken guardianship of orphans of Jane Paine (SM).

6 August. Robertt Burle (g, AA) exhibited oath of Ralph & William Hawkins, appraisers of Quinton Parker.

7:44 George Wells (g, BA) exhibited oath of Henry Haslewood & James Ives, appraisers of estates of Capt. George Goldsmith & Mary his relict.

William Slade (AA) executor of Quinton Parker (BA) exhibited inventory.

Margueritt Bird (CV) widow & administratrix of Charles Bird (CV) exhibited inventory.

7:45 7 August. Lewis Blangey (AA) was granted administration on estate of James File (AA), who died childless & unmarried. Appraisers: John Rick, Jacob Lesby. Robertt Burle (AA) to administer oath.

10 August. Robertt Fisher (CV), as next
of blood, was granted administration on
estate of his brother Henry Fisher,
whose widow died immediately afterward,
7:46 for the orphans. Appraisers: William
Herberth, John Lawrence. Roger Brookes
(g) to administer oath.

Hanna Pott (CV) widow of John Pott (CV)
exhibited his will. Thomas Trueman,
Esq. to prove.
7:47 Appraisers: Edward Isaack, James
Williams. Said Trueman to administer
oath.

11 August. Margery Cooke (TA) widow & administratrix of John Cooke (TA) exhibited inventory.

Mary Maxewell (TA) widow & administratrix of Alexander Maxewell (TA) exhibited inventory.

7:48 12 August. William Slade (AA) executor of Quinton Parker (BA) exhibited inventory.

Thomas Overton (BA) executor of Bernard Uty (BA) exhibited inventory.

Col. Nathaniell Uty (BA) exhibited will of Quinton Parker (BA), proved by Harman Williams on 22 May 1675.

7:49 Col. Nathaniell Uty (BA) exhibited the will of Bernard Uty (BA), proved by Edward Jackson & Robertt Goodwin on 28 June 1675.

13 August. John Turpinne (BA) was granted administration on estate of William Hewett (BA), who died leaving wife & children in ENG.
7:50 Appraisers: Henry Haslewood, William Palmer. Col. Nathaniell Uty to administer oath.

16 August. Thomas Long (g, BA) exhibited will of Johanna Spry (BA). Will of Johanna Spry (widow, BA).
7:51 Bequests: Mrs. Howell wife of Thomas Howell (KE), 2 children of James Denton (BA), Mr. John Waterton, my servant Richard Ramsey, 3 grandchildren Sarah & Elisabeth & Mary Harmer,
7:52 my only child Mary Harmer (widow). Executrix: said Mary. Date: 6 October 1674. Witnesses: John Waterton, Roger Sheacock. Will proved
7:53 by Mr. John Waterton on 21 May 1675. Said Sheacock is not to be found. Mary Stansby alias Harmer executrix was granted administration.

Thomas Long (g, BA) exhibited oath of William Hollis & William Yorke, appraisers of estate of Johanna Spry. Executrix Mary Stansby
7:54 exhibited inventory.

17 August. Dr. John Stansby (BA) executor of Mary Peake (CV) widow & executrix of George Peake (CV) exhibited accounts. Distribution to: 2 orphans. Discharge was granted.

Court Session: 1675

7:55 20 August. Dianna James (SM) widow & executrix of Abell James (SM) exhibited inventory.

26 August. John Warren (SM) exhibited that Edward Cotton is dec'd, & said Edward devised his land to said John. Said devise is obscure. Capt. William Boreman to obtain testimony of John Pile regarding said devise.

7:56 William Claw (SM) sole surviving executor of John Reynolds (SM) exhibited inventory.

30 August. Samuell Lane (g, AA) exhibited LoA to Mary Davis widow of Evan Davis. Said Mary could not get security for her administration, because the amount of the estate is very little (less than 4000 pounds of tobacco). Greatest creditor: Thomas Morrise. Date: 29 August 1675. Thomas Morrice (AA) was granted administration, as greatest creditor.
7:57 Appraisers: John Moonshott, William Sinneck. John Welsh (AA) to administer oath.

Thomas Bland (AA) who married relict & executrix of Nicholas Wyatt (AA) petitioned for Samuell Chew, Esq. to examine under oath Ellen Hall, Richard & Ellen Waikfield, & John Watkins regarding the confirmation of will of dec'd.

7:58 James Boyd administrator of Anne relict of John Norwood (AA) was ordered to pay the orphans of said John & Anne their portions of said estates.

7:59 ultimate August. Margueritt Downes (CH) widow of Robertt Downes (CH) was granted administration on his estate. Appraisers: Alexander White, (N). Benjamin Rozer (high sheriff, CH) to administer oath.

1 September. Edward Roe (p, TA) exhibited that Robertt Hale (TA) died 15 months ago. His widow married William

Simson. Said William paid several debts & sold most of the land without an administration. Said William & widow have run out of the Province, or absented themselves.
7:60 Said Roe was granted administration. Security: Samuell Hatton. Appraisers: John Bricks, Thomas Phillips. Richard Gorsuch (g) to administer oath.

8 September. Richard Nash (CE) executor of Tobias Apelford (KE) exhibited accounts. Discharge was granted.

Richard Nash for his wife Anne Nash (CE) relict & executrix of Richard Blunt (KE) exhibited accounts.
7:61 Augustine Harman (g) to take oath of said Anne.

Richard Walters (TA) administrator of Richard Hacker (TA) exhibited inventory.

John Beale (CV) executor of Joane Beale (CV) exhibited inventory.

Samuell Chew, Esq. (AA) executor of John Meers (AA) exhibited inventory.

10 September. Alice Roper (AA) relict & administratrix of Janus Morgan (AA) exhibited inventory.

7:62 Richard Hill (g, AA) exhibited will of Philip Thomas (AA). Bequests: 2 sons Philip Thomas & Samuell Thomas "Beakely" 500 a. at Clifts (CV), wife Sarah Thomas "Fuller's Point" 120 a. (AA) & "The Plaines" 500 a. in Petapsco River (BA),
7:63 son Samuell Thomas, daughter Martha Thomas, grandchild Mary daughter of John Meers, 2 grandchildren Philip & Elisabeth son & daughter of William Cole, wife rents of 2 houses in Bristoll. Residue to: 5 children:
7:64 Philip, Samuell, Sarah, Elisabeth, Martha. Further bequests: poor Quakers. Executrix: wife Sarah Thomas. Date: 9 September 1674. Witnesses: John Ricks, Marmaduke Noble.
7:65 Will proved 10 July 1675.

Court Session: 1675

Richard Hill (g, AA) exhibited will of
Dorothy Bruton. (AA). Date: 19
November 1674. Bequests: eldest
daughter Elisabeth "Solomons Hills",
daughter Mary & daughter Anne, Richard
Wayd, Isabell Meeck, Elisabeth Allcock.
7:66 Mr. Sarah Homewood is guardian to
daughter Elisabeth. Mrs. Jane Haman is
guardian to daughter Anne. Executor:
Edward Gardner. Witnesses: Philip
Dawson, Richard Wayd. Will proved 7
August 1675.
7:67 Said Gardner was granted administration.

Richard Hill (AA) returned commission to prove will of John Bruton (AA), by witnesses: John Price, William Bysie. They would not swear that the will is valid, since the testator said he wanted to make changes. Date: 10 September 1675.

Elisabeth Read (AA) widow & executrix of
William Reade (AA) exhibited his will.
7:68 Richard Hill (g, AA) to prove said will
& administer oaths. Appraisers: William
Ferguson, Robertt Clarkson.

Richard Hill (g, AA) to prove the will
of John Edwards (AA). Appraisers:
Ebenezar Blackstone, Anth. Rawlins.
7:69 Said Hill to administer oaths.

11 September. Abraham Wilde (CE)
exhibited the will of Thomas Salmon
(CE). Will of Thomas Salmon (CE).
7:70 Bequests: son Peter Salmon 200 a.
plantation on Worton Creek, Elisabeth
Rayley her mother's wearing apparel,
Thomas Howell, Jr., John Howell,
Nathaniell Howell. Executor: son Peter.
Overseers: Capt. Thomas Howell, Mr.
John Vanheck, Mr. Nath. Stiles, Thomas
Howell, Jr. Date: 26 May 1675.
Witnesses: William Dunkerton, John
Dixon. Will proved by William Dunkerton
on 24 June 1675,
7:71 and by John Dixon on 29 July 1675. John
Vanheck & Nathaniell Stiles were granted
administration on behalf of Peter
Salmon.

John Coxe (CE) administrator of Francis Barnes (CE) exhibited that John West, one of the appraisers of said estate, refused to take the oath. New appraisers: William Hopkins, William Peirse. Abraham Wilde (g) to administer oath.

7:72 13 September. Richard Gorsuch (g, TA) exhibited the will of Isack Abrahams (TA). Will of Isack Abrahams. Date: 14 October 1674. Bequests: Sarah Reede chattel that was her father's, George Parett & Benjamin Parett.
7:73 Residue: wife, son (under age 19), daughter. Further bequests: sons Jacob Abraham land. Executrix: wife Elisabeth Abraham, son Jacob Abraham. Witnesses: John Stoaker, Edmund Fisher.
7:74 Will proved by John Stoaker & Edmund Fish on 28 June 1675.

Richard Wollman (g, TA) exhibited the will of Elisabeth Abrahams (TA). Will of Elisabeth Abrahams. Date: 11 May 1675.
7:75 Bequests: William Southbee, daughter of William Southbee, wife of William Southbee, son Jacob Abrahams, daughter Mary Abrahams, Elisabeth Southbee chattel which was her father's. Residue: 3 children: Jacob Abrahams, Mary Abrahams, Sarah Reed. Executors: Bryan O'Maly, Thomas Taylor.
7:76 Witnesses: William Allen, Margueritt Lodge. Will proved on 1 July 1675. Appraisers: Richard Roystone, Tho. Vaughan.

7:77 Richard Wollman (g, TA) exhibited the will of Robertt Harwood (TA). Will of Robertt Harwood. Bequests: wife, each child. Plantation is to be at wife's disposal; land at King's Creek is to be sold. Further bequests: son Peter Harwood 200 a. at Tuckahoe on Roebothom, William Southby, Samuell Harwood. Executors: Thomas Taylor, William Stevens,
7:78 John Sumner. Date: 27 May 1675. Further bequests: John Harwood chattel due from John Edmundson. Witnesses:

William Wood, George Shattenwhite. Will proved on 1 July 1675. Appraisers: Richard Roystone, Thomas Vaughan.

Jacob Abrahams (TA) sole heir & executor of Isack & Elisabeth Abrahams (TA) exhibited their inventories.

7:79 Widow of Robertt Harwood (TA) exhibited inventory.

22 September. Henry Ward (CE) was granted administration on estate of Richard Gore (merchant, Barbadoes), as principle creditor. Appraisers: John Coxe, Richard Edmunds.
7:80 Augustine Harman (g, CE) to administer oath.

25 September. John Stevens (DO) one of executors of Thomas Preston (CV) renounced administration on his estate.
7:81 Signed: John Steevens. Witness: Michael Rochford.

28 September. William Steevens, Jr. (TA) & Howell Powell (TA), the other 2 executors of Thomas Preston, have not appeared.

William Parker (CV) who married relict of Thomas Preston was granted administration his estate. Security: Dr. Henry Joles, William Parker [sic].
7:82 Appraisers: Richard Keene, John Hance. Richard Lad (g, CV) to administer oath.

Dr. John Stansbey (BA) was granted administration on estate of John Reycroft (BA), who died childless & unmarried.
7:83 Appraisers: William Yorke, Thomas Preston. John Waterton (g) to administer oath.

ultimate September. Cutbert Fenwick (g, CV) exhibited oath of Thomas Sprigge & John Halles, appraisers of Thomas Clarke (CV). Inventory was exhibited.

7:84 Alice Foster (CE) was granted administration on estate of her husband

Richard Foster. Appraisers: John Hyland, Richard Whitton. Abraham Wilde (g) to administer oath.

8 October. Timothy Goodridge (TA) administrator of George Richardson (TA) exhibited that the probate papers were burned.
7:85 Discharge was granted.

Emia Burgesse (TA) widow & administratrix of John Burgesse (TA) exhibited inventory.

12 October. Vincent Lowe (high sheriff, TA) exhibited will of Richard Briges (TA, age 47). Bequests: wife Mary Briges land & after her decease then the land at Harry Creek to
7:86 eldest son Thomas & "Dilerrit" land at Wy 500 a. to other 3 sons, 2nd son Richard, chattel to wife then to sons & daughter. Date: 30 March 1675. Witnesses: Richard Gould, William Jones. Will proved by Richard Gold on 30 September 1675. Said Mary was granted administration.

7:87 Vincent Lowe (high sheriff, TA) exhibited will of Robert Martin (p, TA). Overseers: Charles Hollinsworth, John Reynols. Bequests: wife & 2 daughters. At death of wife,
7:88 estate to Charles Hollinsworth the younger, my son Charles Hollinsworth, John Reynolds. Date: 24 June 1675. Witnesses: Humphry Devenport, John Reynolds, Elisabeth Griffith.
7:89 Will proved 19 August 1675.

Edward Roe (TA) exhibited will of Benjamin Hancock (TA). Date: 14 December 1674. Executrix: wife Sarah Hancock. Bequests: wife.
7:90 Witnesses: Benony Bishop, William Coksell, Mary Wilson. Will proved by William Coksell & Mary Wilson on 10 June. Sarah Hancock was granted administration.

Mary Briges (TA) widow & executrix of Richard Briges (TA) exhibited inventory.

7:91 Vincent Lowe (high sheriff, TA) exhibited oath of James Murphy & Edward Elliott, appraisers of Robertt Martin.

14 October. Susanna Wadswoorth (CV) widow of Richard Wadswoorth (CV) exhibited his will, proved by Richard Trewent & John Hawkins.
7:92 Will of Richard Wadsworth (p, Patuxent River, CV). Bequests: sons Richard & William, wife plantation 100 a., son Richard 200 a., son William (under age) 100 a., wife 2 servants Anne Jones & John Hawkins, son Richard 2 servants Robertt Trivett & John Paggitt (boy).
7:93 Date: 17 June 1675. Witnesses: Robertt Trewent, John Hawkins. Codicil: bequests: 2 grandchildren. Said Susanna was granted administration. Appraisers: James Thompson, Peter Archer. Tobias Norton (g) to administer oath.

7:94 25 October. Ralph Blackhall (TA) administrator of Edward Norman (TA) exhibited inventory & accounts. Discharge was granted.

Mathew Ward (g, TA) exhibited will of John Nevill (CV) & oath to Patrick Sullivant as executor. Will proved by Ralph Blackhall on 5 November 1674, and by James Bankhurst on 6 November 1674. Appraisers Henry Hosier & John Wells were sworn on 25 August 1675.

7:95 Patrick Sullivant (KE) executor of John Nevill (CV) exhibited inventory.

Richard Tilghman (TA) administrator of John Yates (TA) exhibited inventory.

30 October. William Rosewell (g, SM) was granted administration on estate of Francis Montefort (SM), who died childless & unmarried, as principle creditor. Appraisers: Robertt Perry, William Longwoorth. Capt. John Jourdain to administer oath.

7:96 Thomas Notley (merchant, SM) was granted administration on estate of his brother John Notley (SM). Appraisers: Kenelm

Cheseldyn, John Jones. Inventory was exhibited.

7:97 Henry Hosier (KE) one of executors of Walter Spencer (KE) exhibited his will. James Ringold (g, KE) to prove said will. Executors: said Hosier, Cornelius Comagies, John Bowles. Appraisers: William Larey, Thomas Warren. Said Ringold to administer oath.

Henry Hawkins (CH) exhibited will of Giles Cole
7:98 (p, CH). He was desperately wounded by Susquehanna Indians. Bequests: John Hawkins, Jr., Henry Hawkins brother to said John,
7:99 Elisabeth Hawkins sister of afsd, Thomas Hawkins, Jr., Stephen Coward, John Lemare, Joseph the shoemaker. Executor: Mr. Henry Hawkins. Date: 7 October 1675. Witnesses: Humphry Jones, Henry Neale.
7:100 Will proved by Henry Neale on 27 October 1675. Said Henry Hawkins was granted administration. Appraisers: Edmund Linsey, Archiball Wacop. Mr. Benjamin Rozer (high sheriff) to administer oath.

William Ford (DO) exhibited will of John Clements (TA). Capt. Philemon Lloyd to prove. Executors: said Ford, Thomas Tayler, Edward Roe, William Stevens, Jr.

7:101 2 November. Edward Turner (CV) exhibited will of William Singleton (CV), proved by Robertt Taylor. Will of William Singleton. Date: 25 April 1672. Testator is now bound for ENG. Bequests: Edward Turner. Mentions: bill of Samuell Taylor.
7:102 Witnesses: Robertt Tayler, William Sedbury. Said Edward was granted administration. Appraisers: Demetrius Cartwright, Robertt Tayler. Roger Brookes (g) to administer oath.

Robertt Tayler (CV) was granted administration on estate of Coniers Barbor (CV), who died childless & unmarried.
7:103 Security: Demetrius Cartwright.

Appraisers: Demetrius Cartwright, Edward Turner. Roger Brookes (g) to administer oath.

3 November. John Vanheck (g, CE) exhibited will of Capt. Thomas Powell (CE). Joseph Hopkins (g) to prove said will. Said Vanheck was granted administration on behalf of John & Nathaniell Howell executors, during their minority. Appraisers: William Chadborne, William Salesbery. Said Hopkins to administer oath.

7:104 Joseph Sears (CE) was granted administration on estate of William Sethberry (CE), who died childless & unmarried, as principle creditor. Appraisers: Richard Adams, Cornelius Arenson. John Vanheck (g) to administer oath.

7:105 John Gray (BA) exhibited will of Thomas Jones (BA). Robertt Burle (g, AA) to prove said will.

5 November. Henry Elliott (St. Inigos Hundred, SM) exhibited his partnership with William Gifford. Said Gifford was pressed as a soldier to fight against Indians. While at camp, he wrote to said Elliott, indicating that if he died all of his goods went to said Elliott. Said Gifford is since dec'd of his wounds. John Hales (SM) brought said letter to said Elliott. John DabridgeCourt wrote the letter.
7:106 Said Hales was charged to bring the letter on 21 October last. Said Elliott was granted administration. Security: Mr. Walter Hall. Appraisers: Mr. Walter Hall, John Hailes.

7:107 6 November. Joannah Farrer widow of Robertt Farrer (SM) exhibited his will, witnessed by William Kennedy & George Dundas. Said Kennedy indicated additional bequests: John Evans, Dr. John Wynne, William Greene, John Milner (alias John Yorkeshire), said Kennedy, Henry Jones. George Dundasse proved the will.

Court Session: 1675

7:108 Will of Robertt Farrer. Date: 24 August 1675.
7:109 Bequests: wife Joanna Farrer. Executrix: wife. Witnesses: William Kennedy, George Dundas.
7:110 Said Joanna was granted administration. Appraisers: John Wacop, William Kennedy.

Frances widow of Henry Hyde (g, SM) exhibited his will, proved by George Dundas, & John Pollart. Will of Henry Hyde. Date: 29 October 1675.
7:111 Bequests: daughter Anne Hyde chattel from her grandparents John & Joane Warhop, daughter Margrett Hyde chattel from her godmother Ellenor Forrest, son Robertt Hyde & wife Frances Hyde. Executrix: wife. Advisors: Mr. Thomas Dent, father John Warhope, brother Thomas Hatton. Witnesses: George Dundas, John Pollart.
7:112 Said Frances was granted administration. Appraisers: William Hatton, George Mackall. Thomas Dent (g) to administer oath.

John Macky (p, SM) was granted administration on the estate of Robertt Cutberth (merchant, Barbadoes), on a debt passed to John Newton (master of the Endeavor of Hull).
7:113 Security: Thomas Dent. Appraisers: William Kennedy, Patrick Forrest. Thomas Dent (g) to administer oath.

10 November. John Southe, John Mackeell, & Edmund Brannock (DO) executors of Alexander Roche (merchant, Barbadoes) exhibited accounts. Discharge was granted.

12 November. James Lewis (SM) executor of Benjamin Hunton (SM) petitioned for new appraisers: Thomas Potter, Constantine O'Kieff.
7:114 William Calvert, Esq. to administer oath.

Henry Hosier (KE) administrator of Lewis Stevens (KE) exhibited inventory & accounts. Discharge was granted.

Court Session: 1675

13 November. Thomas Notley (g, SM) administrator of John Notley (SM) exhibited accounts. Discharge was granted.

7:115 Capt. Richard Hill (AA) was granted administration on estate of Richard Gardner (AA) who was executor of Dorothy Bruton (AA). William Burgess to prove the will. Appraisers: Edward Dorsey, Andrew Norwood.

Capt. Richard Hill (AA) exhibited the will of John Edwards (AA). Will of John Edwards.
7:116 Bequests: wife Elisabeth. Executrix: said wife. Date: 10 May 1670. Witnesses: Samuell Withers, Robertt Lusby. Commission to prove will dated 10 September 1675. Mr. Samuell Withers wrote said will. Witnesses are both dec'd.
7:117 Elisabeth Edwards was granted administration. Date: 8 November 1675.

Capt. Richard Hill (AA) exhibited the will of William Reade (AA). Will of William Reade. Bequests: wife Elisabeth Reade. Date: 7 November 1674. Witnesses: John Merson, Margrett Merson.
7:118 Commission to prove will dated 10 September 1675, and will was proved on 8 January 1675. Elisabeth Reade was granted administration.

Edward Perrish (AA) exhibited the will of John Pecks, who was killed by Susquehanna Indians,
7:119 who died childless & unmarried. Security: Major William Burgesse. Appraisers: John Walters, Thomas Spratt. Robertt Franclin (g) to administer oath.

Major William Burgesse on behalf of Magdalene Smethwicks relict & executrix of Edmund Townehill (AA) exhibited his will dated 6 April 1661 & witnessed by John Bruer & Elisabeth Bruer (AA, both now dec'd). Probate per Maudlin Townhill (relict) & verified by Mr.
7:120 John Bruer on 10 May 1662 per A. Skinner. Sons of the dec'd are in

danger of loosing their children's portions, & are to sue Richard Snowedon who married one of the daughters of executrix. Will of Edmund Towning. Bequests: son Edmund Towning (under age 17) land on the Ridge,
7:121 wife the plantation she lives on, daughter-in-law Deborah Abbot, daughter-in-law Dorcas Abbot, servant Richard Snodon. Executrix: wife.
7:122 Date: 6 April 1661. Signed: Edmond Townill. Witnesses: John Bruer, Elisabeth Bruer. Magdalene Townill was granted administration; she is of great age & unable to travel to the Office. Major William Burgesse to administer oath.

William Roper (AA) administrator of William Hapcote (AA) exhibited accounts.

7:123 15 November. Richard Jones for his now wife Elisabeth Jones (TA) relict & administratrix of Richard Stevens (TA) exhibited accounts. Discharge was granted.

Dr. Richard Tilghman (TA) administrator of John Barnes (TA) exhibited accounts.

Richard Tilghman administrator of John Yates (TA) exhibited accounts. Discharge was granted.

16 November. Andrew Norwood for self & his brothers & sister
7:124 (he is one of the orphans of Capt. John Norwood) petitioned that James Boyd who married Anne the relict had exhibited accounts. Division of the estate was granted, but not fulfilled.
7:125 Mentions: judgement against Dr. Neale.
7:126 Said Anne received from the estate of Jacob Neale administrated by Thomas Marsh.
7:127 Suit was denied. Division is to occur by order of the County Court.

Richard Beck (CH) was granted administration on estate of his brother Lewis Beck (CH), who was childless & unmarried, as next of kin. Appraisers:

Kenelm Maclougin, Robertt Lederland. Mr. Benjamin Rozer (high sheriff, CH) to administer oath.

7:128 Thomas King (CH) was granted administration on estate of Samuell Cooper (CH), who was childless & unmarried. Appraisers: Jacob Peterson, Philip Lynes. Mr. Benjamin Rozer (high sheriff, CH) to administer oath.

Katherine Montague (TA) widow of Hugh Montague (chirurgeon, TA)
7:129 was granted administration on his estate. Edward Roe (g) to administer oath.

Margueritt Downes (CH) widow & administratrix of Robertt Downes (CH) petitioned for new appraisers: Appraisers: John Fanning, John Wright. Mr. Benjamin Rozer (high sheriff, CH) to administer oath.

7:130 Benjamin Rozer (high sheriff, CH) exhibited the will of Verlinda Stone (CH). Will of Verlanda Stone (CH). Date: 23 March 1674/5. Executor: son John Stone. Bequests: son John Stone, Benony Thomas (under age 21) "Sant Verlindas" 400 a., daughter Doyen. Residue: son John Stone.
7:131 Signed: Verlinda Stone. Witnesses: Margueritt Baggbay, Barbara Kendall. Commission to prove will dated 13 July 1675. Will proved by Margueritt Bagsbay & Barbara Kendall on 17 September 1675. John Stone was granted administration.

Benjamin Rozer (high sheriff, CH) exhibited oath of Margueritt Downes widow & administratrix of Robertt Downes,
7:132 sworn 6 September 1675. Security: Edward Price.

John Bould & John Courts (CH) administrators of Thomas Bull (CH) were granted discharge on his estate.

17 November. Thomas Morrice (AA) administrator of Evan Davis (AA)

exhibited inventory.

7:133 Henry Elliott (SM) administrator of William Gifford (SM) exhibited inventory.

Thomas Hinson (TA) was granted administration on estate of John Vyne (TA), who was childless & unmarried. Appraisers: Ralph Blackhall, Richard Jones. Mathew Ward (g) to administer oath.

7:134 Mr. Henry Stockett (high sheriff, AA) exhibited the division of estate of John Norwood (AA) to the orphans. Said orphans refuse the division without a new appraisal.

19 November. Joachim Guibert (SM) was granted administration on estate of James Trask (SM). Security: Edward Connerie. Appraisers: Edward Connerie, Thomas Carvill.

7:135 Sarah Claw (St. Jerom's, SM) widow of William Claw (SM) exhibited his will. Will of William Claw (St. Jerom's). Date: 1 October 1675. Bequests: wife Sarah Claw "Daylie Desire" at head of Sassafryes River. Witnesses: Thomas Wynne, Thomas Griffin. Will proved 16 November 1675.

7:136 Said Sarah was granted administration. Securities: Elias Beeche, William Newport. Appraisers: Mr. Walter Hall, Elias Beeche.

William Newport (SM) executor of George Walker (SM) exhibited accounts.

Samuell Hatton (TA) administrator of George Soley (TA) exhibited accounts.

Rebecca Brooke (CV) was granted administration on estate of John Brooke (CV).

7:137 Appraisers: Charles Buttler, Christopher Bayne. Baker Brooke, Esq. to administer oath.

George Parker (CV) was granted administration on estate of Lownes Eason (apotecary, CV), who has a wife & children in ENG. Appraisers: Francis Stockett (AA), Henry Joles (CV). Richard Ladd (g) to administer oath.

7:138 22 November. Richard Whitton (CE) executor of Richard Leake (BA) was granted administration on his estate. Will was proved by Abraham Wilde (g).

Roger Brooke (g, CV) exhibited will of Philip Harwood (CV). Baker Brooke, Esq. to prove said will. Said Roger was granted administration. Appraisers: Charles Buttler, Christopher Bayne. Said Baker to administer oath.

7:139 William Hollis (BA) & James Phillips (BA) were granted administration on estate of Thomas Winfield (BA), who was childless & unmarried, as principle creditors. Appraisers: William Osborne, Miles Gibson. Henry Haslewood (g) to administer oath.

Sarah Hancock (TA) widow & administratrix of Benjamin Hancock exhibited inventory.

7:140 James Denten (BA) who married the relict of Thomas Daniell exhibited that said Thomas died about 10 years ago. Said Denten was granted administration. Appraisers: Joseph Gallien, James Collier. John Walterton (g) to administer oath.

Thomas Jones (BA) exhibited the nuncupative will of John Reycroft (BA), who left all of his estate to said Jones. John Walterton (g) to prove said will.

7:141 23 November. Edward Swanson (BA) administrator of William Robisson (BA) exhibited accounts. Discharge was granted.

24 November. Samuell Cressey (CH) administrator of John Harrington (CH) exhibited accounts.

William Stevens (g, SO) exhibited will of William Morgan (wheelwright, SO). Date: 25 March 1675. Bequests: Joseph Taylor,
7:142 John Covan, Thomas Walker (g, SO) land. Executor: said Walker. Witnesses: Edm. Beauchamp, George Hasfurt. Will proved 31 August 1675. Appraisers: William Planner, Charles Hall.
7:143 Said Walker was granted administration, & exhibited inventory.

Henry Lewis (AA) exhibited the renunciation of Paul Dorrell as administrator of his uncle Thomas Turner, as advised per Mr. Burle. Said Dorrell petitioned that he & his sister first be paid the amount due from the estate of their father.
7:144 Said Lewis was granted administration. Robertt Burle to take bond. Appraisers: William Hopkins, Bernard Egelston.

Robertt Richardson (SO) exhibited the renunciation of Elisabeth Turner relict of John Tege (SO) on his estate.
7:145 Said Richardson is the only creditor. Said Tege left a small boy/son & the widow Elisabeth who has since married Richard Turner. Date: 11 September 1675. Witnesses: Richard Curtis, John Coulston. Said Richardson was granted administration. William Stevens (g) to take bond. Appraisers: Thomas Purnell, Henry Bishop, Jr.

7:146 Robertt Burle (g, AA) exhibited oath of John Ricks and Jacob Lisbie, appraisers of James File (AA), sworn 24 August 1675. Lewis Blangey was granted administration on said estate.

<u>26 November</u>. George Robins (TA) administrator of Thomas Wilmer (merchant, London) exhibited accounts.

7:147 Joanna Wadswoorth (CV) widow & administration of Richard Wadswoorth (CV) exhibited inventory.

Edward Turner (CV) executor of William Singleton (CV) exhibited inventory.

Edward Roe (g, TA) one of executors of John Clements (TA) exhibited his will. Capt. Philemon Lloyd to prove said will. Other executors: William Ford (DO), Thomas Tayler (TA), William Stevens, Jr. (TA). Appraisers: William Hambleton, Richard Gorsuch (gentlemen). Said Lloyd to administer oath.

7:148 2 December. William Russell (AA) was granted administration on estate of Thomas Chandler (AA, late of SMC). Said Russell was a partner with said Chandler, & is the greatest creditor for the children of said Chandler. Samuell Chew, Esq. (AA) to take bond. Appraisers: George Parker, John Sellers.

6 December. Thomas Gerrard (g, SM) was granted administration on estate of Marmaduke Snow (SM).
7:149 William Rosewell (g, SM) to take bond. Security: Mr. Thomas Notley. Appraisers: Capt. Gerrard Slye, Thomas Lomax. William Rosewell (g) to administer oath.

Robertt Burle (AA) exhibited oath of Mr. Richard Hill and William Slade, appraisers of John Keely (AA), sworn 6 August 1675. Inventory was exhibited.

7:150 8 December. Christopher Andrews (KI) was granted administration on estate of Robertt Carpenter (CE), who was childless & unmarried. Appraisers: Edward Skidmore, John Crouche. William Towlson (g) to administer oath.

William Dare (CV) administrator of John Parker (CV) was granted continuance.

9 December. Robertt Burle (g, AA) exhibited the will of Thomas Jones (BA).
7:151 Will of Thomas Jones (boatwright, BA). Bequests: Sarah Gray "Nashes Rest" plantation 200 a. on Patapsco River. If she dies without heirs, then to her sister Jane Gray, then to her brother Zacharia Gray, then to the other Grays. Further bequests: Sarah Gray
7:152 at James Smith on Severn & chattel at

Stephen White, John Gray, Mathias Stevenson chattel at Charles Gossage, James Martin, Zacharia Gray. Executor: John Gray. Date: 4 August 1675.
7:153 Witnesses: Mathias Stevenson, Mathew Porter, Mary Christopher. Will proved by Mathias Stevenson & Mary Christopher on 2 January 1675. John Gray was granted administration, & exhibited inventory.

Henry Lewis (AA) administrator of Thomas Turner (AA) exhibited that the said Turner was the executor of Thomassin Stinchecomb
7:154 (AA). Said Lewis was granted administration on estate of said Thomassin. Robertt Burle (g) to take bond. Appraisers: William Hopkins, Bernard Egelston. Said Burle to administer oath.

11 December. Anne Tapticoe (CV) widow of Peter Tapticoe (CV) exhibited that her husband drowned about 12 months ago. Mentions: Thomas Clagett.
7:155 Said Anne was granted administration on his estate.

13 December. Joseph Hopkins (g, CE) exhibited will of Capt. Thomas Howell (CE), proved. John Vanheck, overseer and executor during the minority of the executors, is since dec'd. One of the appraisers William Chadborne is also dec'd. John Howell is now of age at 17. Will of Thomas Howell (CE). Bequests:
7:156 wife Elisabeth Howell then to my 2 sons, son John Howell "Daletowne" plantation 700 a., son Nathaniell Howell land between "Daletowne" & Podlinton's now in the possession of Col. John Owen, daughter Sarah Vanheck plantation at Farley.
7:157 Executors: 2 sons. Overseer: son-in-law John Vanheck. Date: 5 October 1675. Witnesses: Robertt Sanders, Robertt Crooke. Will proved 28 November 1675. John Howell was granted administration for self & his brother Nathaniell Howell (minor).
7:158 Appraisers: William Galloway, William

Salesbury. Joseph Hopkins to administer oath.

Nathaniell Stiles (g, CE) exhibited that John Vanheck (g, CE) made his will on 17 November & then died, citing as executors: John & Nathaniell Howell. Said John is 17 years old & chose Nathaniell Stile as his guardian. Judge ruled that said John can be an executor. Joseph Hopkins (g, CE) to prove the will.

7:159 Appraisers: William Galloway, William Salesbury. Said Hopkins to administer oath. ["Voyage up the Bay in this winter season is dangerous."] Will of John Vanheck (g, CE). Bequests: wife Sarah Vanheck chattel from her father & Negro Franck daughter of Negro Mary (born since the testator had received the mother).

7:160 Residue to: wife (1/3rd), & child (2/3rd, if wife is pregnant); but, if no issue, then: wife (1/3rd), John & Nathaniell Howell (2/3rd, sons of Capt. Thomas Howell). Further bequests: James Simonds (under age 21), servant John Read.

7:161 ...

7:162 Executors: John & Nathaniell Howell. Overseers: Mr. Nathaniell Stiles, Mr. William Towlson. Date: 17 November 1675. Witnesses: Richard Sanders, Robert Crooke, Henry Howard.

Thomas Dent (g, SM) exhibited will of Henry Hall (SM), proved by William Hatton & George Mackall.

7:163 Will of Henry Hull. Date: 6 November 1675. Bequests: Mr. Francis Sourton, Mrs. Elisabeth Hatton wife of Mr. William Hatton (St. George's), brother Mr. Humphry Hull (Dorchester), servants of Mr. Thomas Dent,

7:164 Thomas Dent (merchant). Executor: said Dent. Witnesses: William Hatton, George Mackall. Will signed on 24 November 1675. William Hatton deposed additional bequests to: brother Humphry Hull, Rebecca wife of Thomas Dent (executor). Date: 11 December 1675.

7:165 Thomas Dent was granted administration.

Appraisers: George Mackall, Patrick Forrest. William Hatton (g) to administer oath.

Will of Richard Moy (inholder, the Vyneyard, SM).
7:166 Bequests: Chappel at SMC, Mr. Michael Foster, wife Elisabeth Moy. Executrix: wife. Further bequests: son Daniell Moy. Date: 19 February 1670. Testator desires that his son be brought up Roman Catholic.
7:167 Witnesses: Thomas Notley, Daniell Jenifer, Roger Seale. Later will of Richard Moy. Date: 9 December 1675. Bequests: wife Elisabeth Moy plantation "Vineyard" & "Kent Fort" (KE) then to son Daniell Moy,
7:168 Chappel at SMC (bequest revoked), Mr. Henry Carew, godson Richard Griffith. Witnesses: Robertt Carvile, Thomas Wynne, John Baker. Will proved by Robertt Carvile & Thomas Wynne on 15 December 1675.
7:169 Elisabeth Moy was granted administration. Appraisers: Thomas Hatton (g), Thomas Griffin (p). Robertt Carvile (g) to administer oath.

Thomas Keyting, one of the overseers of estate of Bryne O'Daly (St. Michael's Hundred) petitioned. Executor is an infant under age. Constantine O'Kieff proved the will on 9 May last; other witness Anthony Loghlin is dec'd. Said O'Kieff
7:170 wrote the will on 17 November last, to make all to his children, only Katherine St. George to have chattel & chattel to her young child. Brine O'Daly asked Katherine on 18 November if Constant had given her his will. Overseers Col. William Calvert & Thomas Keiting
7:171 were granted administration on behalf of Bryne O'Daly & his sister Andree (children of the dec'd). Appraisers: Henry Smith, William Thomas. Walter Hall (g, the Crosse) to administer oath.
7:172 Signed: Thomas Doxey, Thomas Potter. Will of Bryen Daly (SM). Bound on voyage to ENG & IRE. Executor: son Bryan Daly (under age 18). Overseers:

Col. William Calvert, Thomas Keytin, Constantine O'Kieff. Bequests: daughter Adree Daly (under age 16),
7:173 children Brien Daly & Adree Daly, son Brien land. If both children die without issue, then to brother Avelline Daly (IRE) then land to godchild Arthurtin Kieff & residue to children of Katherine St. George then to Thomas Keyting & his sister Nell Keyton, money due from Mr. Peacock (merchant) to brother Aveliff Daly & sister Elisabeth Dally & her child & my sister Margueritt (all in IRE), Katherine St. George.
7:174 Son Brien Daly is 13 August next, Adree is 10 on 7 October next. Date: 9 May 1675. Signed: Brien O'Dally. Witnesses: Constantine O'Kieffe, Anthony Loghlin. Codicil: bequest to Catherine St. George. Date: 10 May 1675.

7:175 Edward Fielding, Timothy Parker, Richard Hart, John Dudlestone, & William Hardidge (merchants, Bristoll, owners & freighters of ship Sarah & Elisabeth of Bristoll) petitioned that John Holbrooke was master in her last voyage to MD & they have PoA to Christopher Haswell (Bristoll, bound on voyage to MD) to receive from John Brooke (merchant, now resident of Patuxent) of items left by William Hardidge.
7:176 Date: 11 September 1675. Witnesses: Hen. Roacht, John Holbrooke, Samuell Hartwell, Thomas Hartwell. Will proved by John Holbrooke on 1 December 1675.

7:177 16 December. Capt. Richard Hill (AA) was granted administration on estate of James Rawbone, who died widower & childless, as creditor. Major William Burgesse to take bond. Appraisers: Andrew Norwood, Edward Dorsey. Said Burgesse to administer oath.

Sarah Hudson (AA) widow of John Hudson (AA) ws granted administration on his estate. Appraisers: Andrew Norwood, Edward Dorsey. Capt. Richard Hill to administer oath.

Court Session: 1675

7:178 Sarah Porter (AA) widow of Peter Porter (AA) was granted administration on his estate. Appraisers: Andrew Norwood, Edward Dorsey. Capt. Richard Hill (AA) to administer oath.

William Rosewell (g, SM) was granted administration on estate of Robertt Perry (SM), who was unmarried & childless.
7:179 Appraisers: William Asseter, Joseph Alvey. Capt. John Jourdain to administer oath.

William Rosewell (g, SM) exhibited that Robertt Perry, appraiser of estate of Francis Montefort, is dec'd. New appraisers: Joseph Alvey, William Longworth. Capt. John Jourdain to administer oath.

17 December. Garrett Vansweringen & John Barnes (both SM) petitioned for administration on estate of William Baker & his wife Mary, who left 1 child Mary (age 3 years).
7:180 No person of blood in the Province except the infant daughter. Daniell Clocker married Patience sister of Mary Baker & an aunt to Mary the infant daughter. Said Clocker can claim administration.

7:181 Capt. Richard Hill (AA) was granted administration on estate of Philip Dawson (Susquehanna Fort, AA).

Katherine Bartley (SM) widow of George Bartley (SM) was granted administration on his estate. Security: Patrick Forrest. Appraisers: John Mackey, Patrick Forrest.

7:182 Joseph Weecks & John Hinson (gentlemen, KE) exhibited the will of John Rodaway (TA). William Coursey (g) or Thomas Hinson (g) to prove the will. Will of John Rodaway (TA). Date: 20 October 1675.
7:183 Bequests: mother Margueritt Rodaway (widow, Bristoll) then to sister Mary Rodaway (under age 21) then to Elisabeth

Beaks wife of Richard Beaks (cordwiner, Bristoll), said Elisabeth Beaks, mother, sister Mary, Dominick Hobson (cordwiner, Bristoll),
7:184 landlord Richard Mackline, Sr., his son Robertt Mackline, Jr., Richard Mackline, landlady Margueritt Mackline, Mr. Joseph Weeks & Mr. John Hinson (gentlemen, KE). Executors: Mr. Joseph Weeks & Mr. John Hinson (gentlemen, KE). Further bequests: mother chattel shipped to London to Mathew Francis (tobacconist) at the Plume of Feather on Watline St. Signed: John Rodway. Witnesses: Richard Tilghman, Ralph Blackhall.
7:185 Said Joseph & John were granted administration. Appraisers: Ralph Blackhall, John Barkus. William Coursey or John Hinson to administer oath.

Joseph Weeks & John Hinson (gentlemen, KE) exhibited that Robertt Mackline, Sr. (KE) is dec'd, with a will. Robertt Markline, Jr. (eldest son) exhibited that his father burned his last will. In order to preserve the interest of Richard Mackline (youngest son) being joint tenant with the said Robertt Mackline, Jr., William & Henry Coursey (gentlemen) to take depositions
7:186 to prove the will, of said Robertt & Ralph Blackhall.

Joanna Farrar (SM) widow & executrix of Robertt Farrar (SM) exhibited inventory.

7:187 Elisabeth Edward (AA) widow & executrix of John Edwards (AA) exhibited inventory.

John Mackey (SM) administrator of Robertt Cutberth (merchant, Barbadoes) exhibited inventory & accounts. Discharge was granted.

Dianna James widow & executrix of Abell James petitioned.

7:188 20 December. Edward English (merchant, London) exhibited that John Allen (merchant, London) died in MD & that

John Vanheck (CE) was administrator & gave notice to the partners & principle employees of said Allen in ENG who empowered said English. Said Vanheck is since dec'd. Edward English was granted administration. Col. Samuell Chew to take bond.
7:189 Appraisers: Charles James, William Salesbury. Joseph Hopkins (g, CE) to administer oath.

Thomas Potter (SM) exhibited will of George Marshall (SM). Walter Hall (g) to prove the will. Appraisers: Thomas Doxey, Constantine Kieeff. Said Hall to administer oath.

21 December. Thomas Mathews (g, CH) was granted administration on estate of George Charlesworth (SM),
7:190 as principle creditor. Securities: Capt. William Boreman, Thomas Griffin. Appraisers: Thomas Wynne, Elias Beeche. Walter Hall (g) to administer oath.

22 December. Garrett Vansweringen (g, SM) exhibited that Daniell Clocker, Jr. would not accept the administration on estate of William Baker (SM). Therefore, said Vansweringen was granted administration, as principle creditor. Surety: Thomas Courtenay.
7:191 Appraisers: John Baker, Richard Chilman. Robert Carvile (g) to administer oath.

24 December. Richard Fetherstone (AA) was granted administration on estate of George Langlie (AA), who was childless & unmarried, as principle creditor. Appraisers: Daniell Hedge, Samuell Howard. Capt. Richard Hill to administer oath.

29 December. George Parker (CV) administrator of Lownes Eason (apotecary, CV) exhibited that Francis Stockett, one of the appraisers, has fallen sick. New appraisers: Henry Joles,
7:192 Andrew Higgs. Richard Lad (g) to administer oath.

George Young (CV) exhibited the renunciation of Henry & Thomassin Kent (p, Clifts) to administer estate of William Young (p, Clifts, CV). Said Thomassin is the mother of William Young. George Young is a natural brother. Date: 24 December 1675. Witnesses: Richard Heath, Gravier Rowse.

7:193 Said George Young was granted administration. Richard Ladd (g) to take bond. Appraisers: Francis Malding, James Mackall. Said Ladd to administer oath.

30 December. Thomas Griffin (SM) was granted administration on estate of Peter Eure (SM), as principle creditor. Security: Thomas Wynne. Appraisers: Thomas Wynne, Thomas Hatton. Thomas Dent (g) to administer oath.

7:194 3 January. Richard Chilman (SM) exhibited that John Hall (SM) made his will, making Thomas Doxey (SM) sole executor. Said Doxey has burned the will. Said Richard was granted administration. Security: John Tant. Appraisers: John Loquer, John Baker. Garrett Vansweringen (mayor of SMC) to administer oath.

Elisabeth de la Roche (SMC) widow of Charles de la Roche (inholder, SMC) was granted continuance.

7:195 William Kent (CV) was granted administration on estate of Richard Williams (CV), who was childless & unmarried, as principle creditor. Appraisers: Marke Clarke, John Dodson. Edward Keene (g) to administer oath.

Capt. John Cobreath (CV) exhibited that Richard Evans (CV) made a nuncupative will, bequeathing all to said Cobreath.

7:196 Richard Ladd (g) to prove the will. Will of Richard Evans (p, Clifts). Bequests: Capt. John Cobreath, Capt. Richard Hill, Robertt Dickson, James Holmen. Witnesses: Robertt Dickson, Elisabeth Dickson, Edy Carpenter. Said Cobreath was granted administration.

Appraisers: William Adould, William Davis. Said Ladd to administer oath.

5 January. Samuell Cressey (CH) was granted administration on estate of John Waas (CH), who died childless & unmarried, as principle creditor.
7:197 Henry Adams (g) to take bond. Appraisers: John O'Cane, John Hilmes. Said Adams to administer oath.

Thomas Corker (CH) was granted administration on estate of Clement Theobald (CH), who died a widower & with some children, for his wife Elisabeth (eldest daughter of said Theobald) & the rest of the orphans. Appraisers: Achiball Wahob, George Godfrey. Henry Adams (g) to administer oath.

7:198 Samuell Cressey (CH) was granted administration on estate of Alexander Smith (CH), who died childless & unmarried, as principle creditor. Capt. Boreman to take bond. Appraisers: James Bowlin, Richard Edlin. Capt. Boreman to administer oath.

7:199 10 January. Joseph Edly (SM) was granted administration on estate of his brother John Edly, who died at the house of Henry Ryder.

Thomas Griffin (SM) exhibited the nuncupative will of Thomas Hunt (SM), made in the presence of Thomas Bayle & Joseph Edly.

- Thomas Bayle, age 24, deposed on 10 January that on 24 December last, Thomas Hunt, servant to George Charlesworth, desired Mr. Winsore to write his will, but said Winsore was not at home. Said Hunt indicated that Thomas Griffin should have all.

7:200 ...

- Joseph Edly, age 28, deposed on 10 January that Thomas Hunt, servant to George Charlesworth, desired the widow Claw to send for Mr. Winsore. She did not. Said Hunt indicated that Thomas Griffin should have all.

Said Thomas Griffin was granted

administration.

7:201 12 January. Frances Lucas (SM) widow of William Lucas (SM) exhibited his will, proved by Thomas Bayle. Will of William Lucas (SM). Executrix: wife Frances Lucas. Bequests: wife land until son William Lucas comes of age 21. Mentions: land sold to Henry Ryder,
7:202 children (under age). Overseers: Richard Attwood, William Newport. Date: 30 November 1675. Witnesses: Alex. Winsore, Thomas O'Baile. Frances Lucas was granted administration. Appraisers: Thomas Bayle, Benjamin Neshamne.

7:203 Edward Connery (SM) exhibited will of William Bourke (SM). Capt. William Boreman to prove, & administer oaths to executors Edward Connery & Roger Digins. Appraisers: Joachim Guibert, William Sommerhill. Said Boreman to administer oath.

Col. Samuell Chew (AA) exhibited oaths of:

- Thomas Chandler & his security Dr. William Jones. Date: 31 July 1675. Appraisers never appeared.
- William Russell & his securities Jeremiah Sudenam & Robertt Connatt. Date: 13 December 1675.

7:204 ...

- George Parker & John Sollers appraisers of estate of Thomas Chandler, sworn 6 January 1675.
- Edward English & his securities Thomas Taylor, Esq. & Maior William Burgesse. Date: 24 December 1675.

17 January. Elisabeth de la Roche (SMC) widow of Charles de la Roche (SMC) was granted continuance, being very sick & unable to travel to the Office. [The judge is also sick at present & unable to attend any person.]

18 January. Lidia Pierse (SMC) widow of Thomas Pierse (SMC) was granted administration on his estate.
7:205 Security: Walter Hall. Appraisers: Walter Hall, John Thompson.

William Dorsey (DO) was granted administration on estate of John Wigfield (DO), who died childless & unmarried. Appraisers: John Dorsey, Morrice Mathews. Robertt Winsmore (g) to take bond & administer oath.

7:206 Elisabeth Uty (BA) widow of Col. Nathaniell Uty (BA) was granted administration on his estate. Securities: Capt. Samuell Boston, Henry Haslewood (g). Appraisers: Henry Haslewood, James Mills. Capt. George Wells (BA) to administer oath.

Capt. Samuell Boston (high sheriff, BA) was granted administration on estate of William Bowton (BA), who died childless & unmarried, as principle creditor.
7:207 Appraisers: Henry Haslewood, William Palmer. Capt. George Wells to administer oath.

20 January. The Judge ordered that Alexander Wismore, who lives on the plantation of Jane Paine (St. Jerom's, SM), to provide for the orphans of said Paine.

7:208 22 January. Margueritt Jolley (SM) widow of Edward Jolley (SM) was granted administration on his estate. Securities: James Lewis, Thomas Potter. Appraisers: James Lewis, Thomas Potter.

Elisabeth de la Roche (SMC) widow of Charles de la Roche (inholder, SMC) exhibited his will,
7:209 proved by Nicholas Painter. Will of Charles de la Roche (inholder, SM). Bequests: wife Elisabeth "Galloway" 50 a. & "Paris" 150 a. in SM then to my brother Peter de la Roche & Mary Burt wife of (N) Burt (chirurgeon, London), brother Peter. Executrix: wife.
7:210 Date: 16 December 1675. Witnesses: Nic. Painter, J. Lefebure. Said Elisabeth was granted administration. Appraisers: Walter Hall, Garrett Vansweringen (gentlemen).

Court Session: 1675

7:211 James Lewis (SM) executor of Benjamin Hunton (SM) exhibited inventory.

Robertt Tayler (CV) administrator of Coniers Barbier (CV) exhibited inventory.

Garrett Vansweringen (g, SM) administrator of William Baker (SM) exhibited inventory.

Robertt Carvile (recorder, SMC) exhibited oath of John Baker & Richard Chilman, appraisers of William Baker (SM), sworn 27 December 1675.

7:212 Garrett Vansweringen (g, SMC) exhibited oath of Thomas Loquer & John Baker, appraisers of estate of John Hall (SM), sworn 10 January 1675.

24 January. Mary Hailes (SM) widow of John Hailes (SM) was granted administration on his estate. Securities: Joseph Hackney, Robertt Large. Appraisers: Joseph Hackney, Robertt Large.

7:213 Anne Murphey (SM) widow of Daniell Murphey (SM) was granted administration on his estate. Security: Thomas Carvile. Appraisers: Samuell Malickson, Thomas Carvile. William Rosewell (g) to administer oath.

27 January. Anne Bigger (CV) widow of John Bigger (CV) exhibited his will, proved by James Caneday. Will of John Bigger (p, Patuxent River, CV). Date: 18 November 1675.
7:214 Bequests: eldest son John Bigger "Baiers Grove" 300 a. on west branch of Patuxent River, son James pt. of "Beall's Chance" 300 a. on west branch of Patuxent River, son Walter Bigger remainder of "Beall's Chance" & "Two Good" on Charles Branch & bounding land of Mr. Christopher Rowsby,
7:215 daughter Mary Stoakely "Mussell Shell" 200 a. on west branch of Patuxent River. Executrix: wife Anne Bigger. Wife to retain property until children are of

age. Further bequests: wife plantation & 200 a. on Fronson's Creek. Witnesses: Arthur Ludford, James Canaday.

7:216 Anne Bigger deposed that she knows of no later will. Date: 27 January 1675. Said Anne was granted administration. Appraisers: William Groome, Arthur Ludford. Francis Swanson (g) to administer oath.

29 January. John Halfhead (CV) was granted administration on estate of his father John Halfhead (CV), who died a widower, as his eldest son & heir.

7:217 Security: Joseph Edloe (SM). Appraisers: George Thompson, Joseph Edloe.

1 February. Alexander Winsore (SM) exhibited that Mary Paine (daughter of Jane Paine (dec'd)) is lately dec'd & was granted administration on her estate. Said Alexander had been empowered to provide for the orphans of said Jane.

7:218 3 February. Jasper Allen (CV) was granted administration on estate of John Martin (merchant, Barbadoes), who died with a wife & children in Barbadoes. Appraisers: Humphrey Waters, John Turner. Richard Ladd (g) to administer oath.

Anne Mackall (SM) widow of George Mackall (SM) exhibited his will.

7:219 Thomas Dent (g) or William Hatton (g) to prove the will.

4 February. Mary Hailes (SM) widow & administratrix of John Hailes (SM) exhibited inventory.

Richard Edelen (AA) exhibited will of Samuell Cressey (AA), proved by Henry Trent. Capt. John Jourdain to obtain oath of other witness Anne Steps, who got sick on the journey.

7:220 Said Edelen was granted administration. Appraisers: Thomas Baker, John Coates. Henry Adams (g) to administer oath.

Peter Watts (SM) exhibited will of John Hewett (SM), proved by Francis Hill. Will of John Hewett. Bequests: Peter Watts (SM).
7:221 Date: 28 January 1675. Witnesses: Francis Hill, Martha White. Said Watts was granted administration. Appraisers: William Hatton, Francis Hill.

7:222 Thomas Dent & William Hatton (gentlemen, SM) renounced their administration on estate of Thomas Hatton (SM), as 2 of the overseers. Witness: Michael Rochford.
7:223 Randolph Handson, the other overseer, exhibited said will, proved by Abraham Rhoads & George Dundasse. Will of Thomas Hatton (SM). Date: 27 January 1675. Bequests: sister-in-law Barbary Hanson chattel formerly belonging to my first wife, father-in-law Rand. Hanson, Robertt son of John Chevrill, 2 sisters-in-law Barbary & Elisabeth Hanson,
7:224 brother-in-law Thomas Wahop & his 2 sisters Margueritt & Rebecca Wahop, Margueritt Forrest daughter of Patrick Forrest, wife Elisabeth & only son Thomas (under age). Executrix: wife. Overseers: Mr. William Hatton, Mr. Rand. Hanson, Thomas Dent. If wife & son die without issue, then
7:225 to children of Mr. Rand. Hanson & his wife: James Johnson, Richard Handson, Thomas Handson, Timothy Handson, Barbary Handson, Elisabeth Handson. Witnesses: George Dundasse, Abraham Rhoades. Will proved 4 February 1675.
7:226 Said Hanson was granted administration, on behalf of Thomas Hatton, Jr. during his minority. Security: William Harper, Appraisers: Peter Watts, John Chevrill. Thomas Dent (g) to administer oath.

Thomas Dent (g, St. George's Hundred, SM) & William Watts (g, St. George's Hundred, SM) exhibited the will of Robertt Cager (Herring Creek, SM), & proved said will as witnesses. Peter Watts is named as one of the executors, &
7:227 requests Jonathon Clarke & Nathaniell

Fisher to prove the 2 legacies to Peter Watts, Jr. (son of said Peter) & Mary Watts (daughter of said Peter). Will of Robertt Cager (St. George's Hundred, SM).

7:228 Bequests: inhabitants of St. George's & Poplar Hill Hundreds to maintain a Protestant minister. Executors: MM Francis Sourton, George Mackall, Peter Watts. Date: 24 January 1675. Witnesses: Tho. Dent, William Watts, John Wyn.

7:229 Jonathon Clarke & Nathaniell Fisher attested to legacies to Peter Watts, Jr. & Mary Watts. Date: 4 February 1675. Francis Sourton renounced administration; George Mackall is dec'd. Date: 17 February 1675/6. Witnesses: Robertt Grahame, Henry Williams.

7:230 Peter Watts (p) was granted administration. Appraisers: William Hatton, Francis Hill. Thomas Dent (g) to administer oath.

5 February. Will of Richard Keene (inholder, Patuxent, CV). Date: 1 April 1672.

7:231 Bequests: eldest son Richard (under age 19) plantation "Richard's Mannor" patented in name of Luke Gardner 1000 a. on south side of Patuxent River & Negro Sarah,

7:232 youngest son John (under age 19) land in DO,

7:233 niece Mary Keene (daughter of Henry Keene (dec'd)), wife Mary Keene,

7:234 father Henry Keene (Wordstowne, Surrey, ENG). Executrix: wife. Overseers: MM Christopher Rowsby, George Beckwith, Francis Hutchings (CV), William Steevens the younger (TA).

7:235 Witnesses: Ri. Smith, Mordecay Hunton. Will proved by Mordecay Hunton & Richard Smith on 7 February 1675. Mary (widow) was granted administration. Appraisers: John Halles, John Pikrin.

7:236 Joseph Edloe (SM) exhibited will of William Cane (SM), proved by George Thompson (g) & John Tant (taylor). Will of William Cane (SM). Date: 25 January 1675.

7:237 Bequests: son William Cane, Jr. (under age, out of the Province) then to Jeane Edloe (under age) daughter of Joseph & Jeane Edloe. Executor: Joseph Edloe (p). Witnesses: George Thompson, John Tant.
7:238 Said Joseph was granted administration.

John Halfhead, Jr. (CV) administrator of John Halfhead (CV) exhibited inventory.

Capt. William Boreman (SM) exhibited the will of William Bourke (SM). Will of William Bourke (p, SM). Bequests: Thomas Kairtly, Edward Connery & Roger Digins.
7:239 Date: 8 January 1675. Witnesses: Joshua Guibert, Mary Poier. Will proved by Edward Connery & Roger Digins on 25 January 1675. Appraisers: Joshua Guibertt, William Sommerhill. Said Connery & Digins were granted administration.

7 February. Thomas Dent (g, SM) exhibited the will of George Mackall (SM).
7:240 Will of George Mackall (St. George's Hundred, SM). Bequests: eldest daughter Jane Mackall "Pinie Point" & Negro Fornie (boy) & Negro Kate (girl), daughter Hanna Mackall Negro William & Negro Rose, daughter Sarah Mackall Negro Philip & Negro Jane,
7:241 daughter Rachell Mackall "Hepbourne's Choice" & "Magy's Jointure" 400 a. on branches of Sassafras River (BA) & Negro Charles, wife Anne Mackall. Executrix: wife. Overseers: MM John Waghop, John Cambell, Robertt Graham, Henry Williams.
7:242 Mentions: children are under age 14.
7:243 Date: 30 September 1675. Witnesses: Francis Sourton, Richard Lloyd, William Brewerton, Christopher Williamson. Per commission of 3 February, proved by Francis Sourton (clerke), William Brewerton, & Christopher Williamson on 5 February 1675.
7:244 Said Anne Mackall was granted administration.

Thomas Morrice (AA) administrator of Evan Davis (AA) exhibited accounts. Discharge was granted.

Thomas Griffin (SM) administrator of Peter Eure (SM) exhibited that Thomas Hatton, one of the appraisers, is now dec'd. New appraisers: Thomas Wynne,
7:245 John Baker.

8 February. Thomas King (CH) exhibited will of Jinkin Jones (SM). Mr. Benjamin Rozer (high sheriff, CH) to prove will. Said King was granted administration. Appraisers: William Chandler, Philip Lynes. Said Rozer to administer oath.

Joseph Pile (SM) was granted administration on estate of his father John Pile (g, SM), who died leaving 1 son.
7:246 Security: William Rosewell (g). Appraisers: said William Rosewell, William Langwoorth. Capt. William Boreman to administer oath.

William Rosewell (g, SM) exhibited renunciation of Anastasie Rithson widow of Nicholas Rithson (SM) as administratrix. Date: 2 February 1674. Mr. William Rosewell (St. Clement's Bay, SM) was granted administration, as greatest creditor.
7:247 Security: Joseph Pile (g). Appraisers (CH): Bennett Marshigay, Kenelm Macloughlin. Mr. Benjamin Rozer (high sheriff, CH) to administer oath.

Capt. Philemon Lloyd (TA) exhibited the bond of Frances Sayer daughter & administratrix of Frances Morgan (KE) & of Henry Morgan unadministered by said Frances the widow. On 8 January 1673, Frances Morgan took oath.
7:248 Inventory was completed on 3 January 1675/6.

Mary Downes (CH) widow & administratrix of Robertt Downes (CH) exhibited inventory.

Court Session: 1675

9 February. George Parker (CV) administrator of Lownes Eason (CV) exhibited inventory.

Per Susanna Neale (AA) widow of William Neale (AA), Capt. Richard Hill is to prove his will. Said Susanna
7:249 was granted administration. Appraisers: Ralph & William Hawkins. Said Hill to administer oath.

William Parker, Jr. (CV) administrator of Thomas Preston (CV) exhibited that Richard Keene, one of the appraisers, is dec'd. New appraisers: Francis Hutchins, John Hance. Richard Ladd (g) to administer oath. [Sworn on 21 March.]

William Kent (CV) administrator of Richard Williams (CV) exhibited that Edward Keene, who was to take bond & oaths, is dec'd. Appraisers: Marke Clarke, John Dodson. Col.
7:250 Samuell Chewe (AA) to take bond & administer oaths.

Samuell Bourne (Clifts, CV) was granted administration on estate of Robertt Taverner (CV), who has no relation in the Province but brothers in ENG, for the use of said brother. Richard Ladd (g) to take bond.
7:251 Appraisers: John Hance, William Parker. Said Ladd to administer oath.

10 February. Elisabeth Skinner (DO) widow of Thomas Skinner (DO) was granted administration on his estate. Security: Henry Beckwith. Appraisers: Stephen Gary, Arthur Wright. Dr. Robertt Winsmore to administer oath.

Joseph Hopkins (g, KE) exhibited probate of will of John Vanheck (g, CE),
7:252 proved on 10 January 1675.

Joseph Hopkins (g, CE) exhibited oath of John Howell heir & administrator of Capt. Thomas Howell (CE), sworn 10 January 1675.

Jane Raven (DO) widow of John Raven was granted administration on his estate. Appraisers: Stephen Gary, John Brookes (g). Dr. Robertt Winsmore to administer oath.

7:253 11 February. Baker Brooke, Esq. exhibited oath of Charles Boteler and Christopher Baine, appraisers of John Brooke (g), sworn on 30 January 1675. Mentions: oath to Rebecca Brooke widow & administratrix. Inventory was exhibited.

Baker Brooke, Esq. (CV) exhibited will of Philip Harwood (Battle Creek, CV). Bequests: Mr. Henry Carew,
7:254 Thomas Robson 75 a., son Andrew Harwood (out of the Province) plantation. If he doesn't come to MD, then to Mr. Roger Brooke & Mr. John Brooke. Mentions: burial in the Chapple at Calvert Towne. Executors: MM Roger Brooke, John Brooke. Date: 19 April 1675. Witnesses: Richard Raxbeg, Joseph Williams. Appraisers sworn on 30 January 1675: Charles Boteler, Christopher Baine. Mr. Roger Brooke sworn on same date. Mr. John Brooke is dec'd.
7:255 Roger Brooke was granted administration.

Mary Keene (CV) widow & executrix of Richard Keene (CV) exhibited inventory.

Capt. John Jourdain (SM) exhibited will of Samuell Cressey (CH). Bequests: George Robesson. He is to be sent down to Robert Thomas his wife, so to have his head cured at the Spring of the year next.
7:256 Further bequests: 2 daughters (under age) Mary & Susanna. Executor: Richard Edelen Mentions: Capt. Paine. Date: 21 January 1675/6. Witnesses: Anne Steps, Henry Trent. Will proved by Henry Trent on 4 February 1675. Proved by Anne Stepps on 6 February 1675. Signed: Jean Jourdain.

7:257 12 February. Vincent Atcheson (KE) administrator of Thomas Snow (KE) exhibited accounts. Discharge was granted.

Joyce Shaw (TA) widow of William Shaw (TA) was granted administration on his estate. Appraisers: Andrew Skinner, Jonathon Hopkins. Capt. Philemon Lloyd to administer oath.

Mary Tilghman (TA) widow of Dr. Richard Tilghman (TA) exhibited his will. Mathew Ward (g) to prove.
7:258 Said Mary was granted administration. Appraisers: Thomas Hinson, William Bishop (gentlemen). Said Ward to administer oath.

Elisabeth Hudson (KE) widow of Richard Hudson (KE) was granted administration on his estate. Appraisers: John Bowles, William Davis. Henry Hosier (g) to administer oath. [Administratrix could not find security. Amount of the estate is inconsiderable.]

14 February. Richard Blunt (CE) was granted administration on estate of William Howard (CE), & said Richard married the widow of the dec'd.
7:259 Appraisers: Henry Ward (g), Richard Nash. Augustine Herman to administer oath.

Henry Ward (g, CE) exhibited that Abraham Coflin (CE) is dec'd & the relict & her now husband (without administration) have converted the most part of the estate to their use, whereby the creditors have sustained great loss. Said relict & her now husband have runaway to NJ. Said Ward was granted administration, as a creditor to said Coflin. Appraisers: Richard Edmunds, Henry Elldersse. Augustine Herman (g) to administer oath.

7:260 Daniell Clocker, Jr. (SM) & Peter Watts (SM) exhibited will of Daniell Clocker, Sr. (SM), proved by Kenelm Cheseldyn & William Watts. Will of Daniell Clocker. Date: 4 February 1675. Bequests: son Daniell Clocker & daughter Rebecca Clocker, grandchildren Peter Watts &

Mary Watts. Executors: Daniell Clocker, son-in-law Peter Watts. Witnesses: Kenelm Cheseldyn, William Watts.
7:261 Will proved 12 February 1675. Said Daniell & Peter were granted administration. Appraisers: Thomas Griffin, John Baker.

Ellinor Forrest (SM) exhibited will of Patrick Forrest (SM), proved by John Hepworth & Edward Fisher. Will of Patrick Forrest (St. George's Hundred, SM). Date: 31 January 1675/6.
7:262 Bequests: Ellinor Chivrall daughter of John Chivrall, son Richard Forrest plantation & 150 a., 2 daughters Anne & Margret, son George Dundasse & his wife Elisabeth 300 a. on Back River on west side of Chesapeake Bay (BA).
7:263 Executors: wife Ellinor Forrest, son George. Mentions: John Chivrall. Further bequests: daughter Margrett "Henry Leies" 50 a. (gift of Robertt & Thomas Hatton to me). Witnesses: John Hepworth, Edward Fisher. Will proved 14 February 1675. Said Ellinor Forrest & George Dundasse were granted administration.
7:264 Appraisers: Peter Watts, Francill Hill. Thomas Dent (g) to administer oath.

Robertt Mackline, Jr. (under age, TA) exhibited will of Robertt Mackline, Sr. (TA) & petitioned for Mathew Ward (g, TA) & William Bishop (g, TA) administer for said Robertt & his other brother (under age). Appraisers: Stephen Tully, Thomas Hinson. Henry Coursey (g) to administer oath.

7:265 Walter Hall (g, SM) exhibited will of George Marshall (SM). Bequests: son Adriaen Marshall. Executor: Thomas Potter. Date: 21 September 1675. Witnesses: John Hall, Morgan Jones. Will proved by John Hall on 21 December 1675. Thomas Potter was granted administration.

7:266 Anne Ewen (CV) widow of William Ewen (CV) exhibited his will, proved by John Hall & John Norman. Will of William

Ewen (Clifts, CV). Bequests: wife Anne Ewen "Worbelston" plantation on the Clifts & "Morgan's Fresh" or "Morgan's Clift" bought of John Edmundson for 212 a. & "Breake Neck" or "Mount Misery" bought of John Edmundson.

7:267 At death of wife, all 3 lands to said John Edmundson. Further bequests: wife Anne Ewen then to Mr. Richard Ladd (CV) & Mr. John Edmundson (TA), Martha Duman (alias Martha Domar) (free on 1 January next). Executrix: wife. Overseers: MM Richard Ladd, John Edmundson.

7:268 Date: 6 January 1675/6. Witnesses: John Halles, Hendry Janson, John Norman. Will proved by John Halles & John Norman on 15 February 1675. Said Anne was granted administration. Appraisers: John Halles, James Veitch. Richard Ladd (g) to administer oath.

7:269 John Waterton (g, BA) exhibited nuncupative will of John Reycroft (BA).

- James Armston, age 30, deposed on 11 December 1675 that on 20 September last, John Reycroft (at the house of Thomas Jones) desired said Jones to have all.
- Elisabeth Armston (wife of said James), age 30, deposed on 11 December, that on 20 September last, John Reycroft (at the house of Thomas Jones) desired said Jones to have all.

Before: John Waterton (BA).

7:270 Thomas Jones executor was sworn on 15 December 1675. Said Jones was granted administration. Appraisers: James Collier, Edward Rieves. John Waterton (g) to administer oath.

Richard Simes (BA) exhibited will of Roger Hill (BA). John Waterton (g) to prove. William Simes (son of said Richard, executor) is under age. Said Richard was granted administration.

7:271 Appraisers: Thomas Richardson, Richard Winley. John Waterton (g) to administer oath.

Henry Exon (CV) exhibited will of Thomas Arnold (CV), proved by William Sargeson

& Hugh Hopewell. Will of Thomas Arnold (p, Patuxent River). Bequests: landlord Henry Exon. Executor: Henry Exon. Date: 29 January 1675. Witnesses: William Sargeson, Hugh Hopewell.

7:272 Will proved by William Sargeson & Hugh Hopewell, Jr. on 15 February 1675. Henry Exon was granted administration. Appraisers: John Hales, Guy White. Thomas Sprigg (g) to administer oath.

Henry Exon (CV) exhibited nuncupative will of Thomas Cosford (CV), made in presence of Edward Crockett.

- Edward Crockett (BA) deposed that he was at the house of said Exon when Thomas Cosford desired to make his will.

7:273 ...

  Said Cosford desired said Exon to have all. Henry Exon said that he (Henry) should have what was due to him & the remainder should be sent to his father (if living). Date: 15 February 1675.

Henry Exon was granted administration. Appraisers: John Hales, Guy White. Thomas Sprigg (g) to administer oath.

Capt. William Boreman (SM) petitioned for Henry Adams (g, CH) to prove will of Thomas Mathews, Sr. (g, CH). Appraisers: Capt. William Boreman, Ignatius Causin (g). Said Adams to administer oath. [Executrix was sworn.]

7:274 Capt. William Boreman (SM) petitioned for Richard Edelen (g, SM) to prove nuncupative will of Thomas Mathews, Jr. (SM). Appraisers: James Rowlin, Robertt Greene (SM). Said Edelen to administer oath.

Elisabeth de la Roche (SMC) widow & executrix of Charles de la Roche (inholder, SMC) exhibited inventory.

Sarah Claw (SM) widow & administratrix of William Claw (SM) exhibited inventory.

Anne Mackall (SM) widow & executrix of George Mackall (SM) petitioned for appraisers: William Hatton (g), George Dundasse
7:275 (chirurgeon). Thomas Dent (g) to administer oath.

Robertt Carvile one of executors of Elisabeth Moy executrix of Richard Moy (SM) exhibited:

- Clement Hill (g, SM) & John Baker (inholder, SM) deposed that Elisabeth Moy said that her husband Richard Moy made additional bequests to: MM Robertt Carvile, Henry Carew, Thomas Griffith. Date: 14 February 1675.

7:276 Judge ruled that said devises be added as a codicil. Robert Carvile exhibited will of Elisabeth Moy, with renunciation of Clement Hill (g). Will proved by Michael Rochford. Other witness is: Thomas Wynne. Testimony of Thomas Griffin is waived because he is a legatee. Will of Elisabeth Moy (relict & executrix of Richard Moy). Date: 8 January 1675.
7:277 Bequests: Thomas & Richard Griffin sons of Thomas Griffin & his wife Elisabeth lately dec'd,
7:278 Mrs. Ellen Forrest, Mrs. Horne, Goody Attwood, goddaughter Winfield Osbaldeston daughter of William Osbaldeston, brothers & sister
7:279 Symon Turpinne & William Turpinne & Robertt Turpinne & Jane Turpinne, Mrs. Elisabeth Baker, Margueritt Wynne daughter of Thomas Wynne, Elisabeth Hatton wife of Thomas Hatton, Mrs. Elisabeth Wynne, Mrs. Rhoades, servant Mary Smith,
7:280 Grace Willen, Mrs. Ennis, MM Henry Carew & Robertt Carvile & Thomas Griffin items bequeathed them by my husband, godson Thomas Hatton, son Daniell Moy (age 6). Executors: MM Henry Carew, Robertt Carvile, Clement Hill.
7:281 Son to be of age at 18.
7:282 Witnesses: Michael Rochford, Thomas Wynne, Tho. Griffin.
7:283 Will proved by Thomas Wynne on 14 February 1675. Clement Hill renounced

executorship on 12 February 1675. Witnesses: John Blomfield, John Peerce.
7:284 Said Carvile & Henry Carew were granted administration. Appraisers: Garrett Vansweringen (maior of SMC), Walter Hall (g).

16 February. Katherine Bailley (SM) widow & administration of George Bailley petitioned for new appraisers: George Dundasse, John Chevrill. Thomas Dent (g) to administer oath.

7:285-288 <do not exist>

7:289 Rebecca Beale (SM) widow of John Beale (SM) was granted administration on his estate. Security: William Watts. Appraisers: William Watts, William Kennedy. Thomas Dent (g) to administer oath.

17 February. William Stevens (SO) was granted administration on estate of Macom Thomas (SO), who was childless & unmarried, as principle creditor.
7:290 Appraisers: Walter Powell, Edward Wale. John White (g) to administer oath.

Thomas Pinck (SM) exhibited that he was bound with Jane Paine (SM, dec'd) widow & administratrix of Thomas Paine (SM) for the balance of her account. Said Pinck was granted administration.
7:291 Securities: Walter Hall (g), John Thompson (bricklayer). Appraisers: Walter Hall (g), John Thompson (bricklayer).

18 February. Mary Hawkins (AA) widow & executrix of John Hawkins (AA) exhibited his will, proved by Thomas Hooker. Thomas Taylor, Esq. to have Alice Garland (other witness) attest to will.
7:292 Appraisers: Robertt Franclin, Walter Carre. Said Taylor to administer oath.

Richard Fetherstone (AA) administrator of George Langly (AA) exhibited inventory.

Court Session: 1675

Charles Calvert, Esq. (Governor) exhibited will of Francis Anketill (CV). Witnesses are dec'd. Will of Francis Ancktell (g, CV). Date: 2 November 1673.

7:293 Bequests: eldest son Francis Ancktell "Ancktell" of "Mannor of Little Eltonhead" 100 a. granted to Mr. William Eltonhead for 3 lives: Francis Ancktell, John Ancktell, James Ancktell. Said John & James are dec'd.

7:294 Should my son Francis die without issue, then land to George Ancktell then to youngest son Barnaby Ancktell. Further bequests: 3 sons Francis Ancktell & George Ancktell & Barnaby Ancktell 500 a. at mouth of Harris' Creek on the Choptanck. Sons to be of age at 18. Executor: Charles Calvert, Esq. (Capt. General). Witnesses: Spencer Hales, Luke Parkinson. Will proved by the Judge.

7:295 Said Charles was granted administration. Appraisers: Christopher Rowsby, George Thompson.

19 February. John Welsh who married Anne relict & administratrix of Roger Grose (AA) vs. John Grose & Richard Snoweden who married Elisabeth Grose & William Grose & Frances Grose (orphans of said Roger).

7:296 Sheriff (AA) exhibited that he could not find John Grose or Roger Grose in his bayliwick. Citation issued to sheriff (TA) & sheriff (AA) for John Grose, Roger Grose, Richard Snoweden & his wife Elisabeth, William Grose, & Frances Grose.

Ellinor Newman (SM) widow of Abraham Newman (SM) exhibited that he left "inconsiderable estate".

7:297 Said Ellinor was granted administration without a bond.

Richard Fetherstone (AA) administrator of George Langly (AA) exhibited accounts. Said Fetherstone is bound for ENG.

7:298 The balance is secured for the orphan by Commissioners of the County. Capt.

Richard Hill (AA) exhibited his commission regarding Richard Fetherstone (chirurgeon) administrator of George Langly (AA),
7:299 citing that the appraisers were sworn on 3 February 1675.

Thomas Sterling (CV) exhibited that Benjamin Brasseur (CV) made a nuncupative will. Col. Samuell Chew to prove.

7:300 James Crouche (AA) exhibited the will of William Crouche (AA). Robertt Burle (g) to prove. Said Crouche was granted administration. Appraisers: Dr. Henry Lewis, William Hawkins. Said Burle to administer oath.

Dr. Henry Lewis (AA) exhibited the will of William Slade (AA). Robertt Burle (g) to prove. Said Lewis & John Rix were granted administration. Appraisers: John Dabidge, Robertt Eagle.
7:301 Said Burle to administer oath.

Dr. Henry Lewis (AA) administrator of Thomas Turner (AA) exhibited inventory.

Dr. Henry Lewis (AA) administrator of Thomassin Stinchecomb (AA) exhibited inventory.

Robertt Burle (g, AA) exhibited commissions on estates of Thomas Turner (AA) & Nathaniell & Thomassin Stinchecomb (AA).
7:302 William Hopkins & Bernard Eglestone, appraisers of estate of Thomas Turner, were sworn on 27 December 1675. Signed: Robertt Burle.

William Hopkins & Bernard Eglestone, appraisers of Nathaniell Stinchecomb, were sworn on 27 December 1675. Signed: Robertt Burle.

7:303 Dr. John Stansbey (BA) exhibited will of Casar Prince (BA). John Waterton (g) to prove. Said Stansbey is sole surviving executor & was granted administration. Appraisers: Joseph

Gallien, William Yorke. Said Waterton to administer oath.

Thomas Hacker (BA) exhibited will of John Powell. William Towlson (g) to prove. Said Hacker was granted administration. Appraisers: William Galloway, Richard Adams. Said Towlson to administer oath.

7:304 Mary Bucknall, wife of Thomas Bucknall (AA), relict of Edward Wheelock (AA) was granted administration on his estate. Appraisers: Ralph & William Hawkins. Robertt Burle (g) to administer oath.

20 February. Rachael Towers (BA) widow of John Towers (BA) was granted administration on his estate.
7:305 Appraisers: Arthur Taylor, Thomas Richardson. John Waterton (g) to administer oath.

Abraham Stran (CE) exhibited will of George Wilson (CE). Abraham Wilde (g) to prove. Appraisers: John Coxe, Philip Alleager. Said Wilde to administer oath. [Appraisers sworn on 27 April.]

Margueritt Gittings (CV) widow of John Gittings (CV) exhibited his will. Thomas Sprigg (g) to prove.
7:306 Appraisers: David Davis, Lewis Jones. Said Sprigg to administer oath.

21 February. Elias Beeche (SM) renounced administration on estate of Thomas Loquer. Elias Beeche is brother-in-law to said Thomas. Said Beeche & Thomas Innes were executors during minority of Thomas Loquer (son of dec'd). Date: 20 February 1675. Witness: Sarah Claw.
7:307 Thomas Innes exhibited said will. Will of Thomas Loquer (SM). Bequests: son Thomas Loquer (under age). Executors: Thomas Innes, Elias Beeche.
7:308 Date: 26 January 1675. Witnesses: Mathias Woods, Nich. Painter. Thomas Innes was granted administration.
7:309 Surety: Walter Hall (g). Appraisers: Walter Hall (g), John Baker (inholder).

22 February. John Rowsby, one of attorneys of Provincial Court, exhibited PoA by Anne Allen relict & administratrix of Capt. Francis Allen (trader), attested by Charles Vaux (notary in Kingston Upon Hull) on 31 July 1675. Said Francis sometimes lived in the Libertys of St. Katherin London.
7:310 Said Anne appointed Mr. Thomas Welbourne (merchant, Accomack, VA) & Mr. John Rowsby (merchant, Patuxent River MD within the Libertys of VA) to acquire from Mr. John Edmundson, Mr. Francis Riggs, Mr. Henry Tripp (merchants or planters, VA).
7:311 Documents dated 30 June 1664.
7:312 In presence of Robert Bloome (merchant), Thomas Maister (merchant) &
7:313 Jonathon Waterland (master & mariner).

7:314 23 February. William Stevens, Esq. (SO) exhibited that Macom Thomas & his wife Elisabeth (SO) were killed by their servant. Said Stevens was granted administration, as principle creditor, for his relation in VA. Appraisers: Edward Wale, Walter Powell. John White (g) to administer oath.

7:315 26 February. Elisabeth Mackey (SM) exhibited will of John Mackey (SM), proved by Thomas Carlile & Emanuell Rateliff. Will of John Mackey (St. George's Hundred, SM). Bequests: son John Mackey plantation, son James Mackey other land, wife Elisabeth Mackey. Overseers: Thomas Dent, Patrick Forrest. Date: 27 January 1675/6. Witnesses: Thomas Carlile, Emanuell Rateliff.
7:316 Will proved 26 February 1675. Elisabeth Mackey was granted administration. Appraisers: Richard Lloyd (g), Emanuell Rateliff (taylor). Thomas Dent (g) to administer oath.

Henry Truelock (CV) was granted administration on estate of Robertt Turner (CV), who died childless & unmarried, as principle creditor.
7:317 Surety: John Muffett. Appraisers: Paul Bussy, Edward Isack. Tobias Norton (g) to administer oath.

Elisabeth Head (KE) widow & executrix of William Head (KE) exhibited accounts. James Ringold (g) to administer oath.

28 February. Mary Wells (KE) widow of Tobias Wells (KE) was granted administration on his estate.
7:318 Appraisers: Isack Winchester, Thomas Osborne. James Ringold (g) to administer oath.

1 March. Anne Burgesse (SM) widow of William Burgesse (SM) was granted administration on his estate. Sureties: Henry Exon, Robertt Ellis. Appraisers: Thomas Courtney, Thomas Price. Garrett Vansweringen (maior of SMC) to administer oath.

7:319 Anne Evan (CV) widow & executrix of William Evan (CV) exhibited inventory.

Anthony Tall (DO) was granted administration on estate of William Hambidge (DO), who died childless & unmarried, for kindred in ENG. Appraisers: John Mackiell, Edmund Brannack. Dr. Robertt Winsmore to administer oath.

7:320 2 March. Jonathon Squire (SM) administrator of Dr. John Morecroft (SM) exhibited accounts. Discharge was granted.

4 March. Morgan Jones (St. Jerom's, SM) exhibited that George Charlesworth (St. Helen's) is dec'd & Thomas Mathews (late of Portoback, CH) was granted administration, as principle creditor. Said Thomas is also dec'd, with his wife Jane as sole executrix. Said Jane has renounced administration. Said Jones was granted administration, as principle creditor.
7:321 Sureties: John Baker (inholder, SM), Robertt Large (p, St. Jerom's SM). Appraisers: William Thomas, Thomas Doxey. William Calvert, Esq. (Principle Secretary) to administer oath.

6 March. Elisabeth Head (KE) widow of William Head was granted administration on estate of her father Edward Coppedge (KE), who died leaving said Elisabeth & 2 sons under age. Appraisers: Isack Winchester, Thomas Osborne. Joseph Weecks (g) to administer oath.

7:322 Ellinor Forrest (SM) & George Dundasse (SM) executors of Patrick Forrest (SM) exhibited inventory.

Lidia Tuberfield (SM) relict & administratrix of Thomas Pierse (SM) exhibited inventory.

Thomas Pinck (SM) administrator of Jane Paine (St. Jerom's, SM) exhibited inventory.

John Browning (CE) exhibited PoA sent by Peter Quadman (merchant, Jamaica). Capt. Peter Quadman appointed
7:323 John Browning (g), bound for his maiesty's plantation of VA as attorney, to recover from Mr. John Gilbertt (merchant, "residing at Maryland in the said Countrey of VA or elsewhere").
7:324 Date: 12 August 1674. Witnesses: Nathaniell Man, Lawrence Man. Acknowledged before Thomas Linche. John Browning was granted administration on estate of John Guilbertt (merchant, CE), as attorney for said Quadman. Henry Ward (g) to take bond.
7:325 Appraisers: Richard Nash, John Poole. Said Ward to administer oath.

7 March. Isabella Swanston (CV) widow of Francis Swanston (CV) exhibited his will, proved by John Rowsby. Will of Francis Swanston (chirurgeon, CV).
7:326 Bequests: wife Isabell Swanston "Swanston's Lott" plantation 600 a. on Patuxent then to son Francis Swanston. Date: 11 April 1674. Witnesses: Chr. Rowsby, John Peerse, John Rowsby.
7:327 Will proved by John Rowsby on 6 March 1675. Isabella (widow) averred that she knows of no other will. Date: 6 March 1675. Said Isabella was granted administration. Appraisers: Lt. Ninian

Beall, Thomas Ellis. Tobias Norton (g) to administer oath.

10 March. Samuell Chewe, Esq. (AA) exhibited nuncupative will of Benjamin Brasseur (CV), proved.

7:328 Depositions by Anthony Kingsland & William Haward that said Benjamin gave to his sister Martha Brasseur all, if he died a bachelor.

- Anthony Kingsland, age 54, deposed on 3 March 1675/6 that mid-February last, he was at the house of Benjamin Brasseur in CV, Martha Brasseur being his housekeeper. Said Martha said "her time was out". Her father-in-law Mr. Sterling had come to the country. Said Benjamin called the deponent, Charles Jones, & William Haward to take note.

7:329 ...

- William Haward, age 36, deposed that Benjamin Brasseur said he would give all to his sister Martha Brasseur.

Said Martha is an infant under age of 17. Her father-in-law Thomas Sterling was granted administration, til said Martha arrive at age 17.

7:330 Appraisers: Robert Heigh, James Humbes. Said Chew to administer oath.

11 March. Marmaduke Simmes (SM) exhibited that Dianna, widow & executrix of Abell James, is lately dec'd. Said Simmes had a judgement against said Abell. Said Simmes was granted administration, as administrator de bonis non. Surety: Thomas Griffin. Appraisers: William Watts,

7:331 William Kennedy. Thomas Dent (g) to administer oath.

13 March. Thomas Clipham (merchant, CH) was granted administration on estate of John Williams (CH). Appraisers: John Wood, Kenelm Macloughlin. Benjamin Rozer (high sheriff, CH) to administer oath.

Thomas Sprigg (g, CV) exhibited will of John Gittings. (CV).

7:332 Bequests: wife & children. John Reade &

Will Libry are to work the plantation. Date: 18 January 1675. Executrix: wife. Will proved by Joane Gant & Mary Fitziarrett on 26 February 1675.

Richard Chilman (SM) administrator of John Hall (SM) exhibited inventory.

14 March. Capt. John Cammell (SM) & Randolph Hanson (SM) renounced administration on estate of Richard Hatton (SM). Date: 13 March 1675. Witnesses: Thomas Dent, William Harper.
7:333 William Hatton (g) exhibited his will, proved by John Ditchfield & Thomas Reynold. Will of Richard Hatton (Poplar Hill, SM). Bequests: Isack Booth son of widow Boothe, Richard Goodaker, servant Richard Ringe, son Richard Hatton (under age 18) land, wife Anne Hatton 100 a. for her lifetime.
7:334 If son died without issue, then land to wife & cousin Elisabeth Henson. Executrix: wife. Overseers: brother William Hatton, brother Randolph Henson, John Cammell. Date: 5 February 1675. Witnesses: John Ditchfield, Thomas Renalds. Will proved by John Ditchfield & Thomas Reynold on 14 February. Anne Hatton (widow) died immediately afterward.
7:335 Said John Cammell & Randolph Hanson, 2 of the overseers, have renounced administration. William Hatton, the other overseer, was granted administration, on behalf of Richard Hatton, Jr. (the only son & heir) during his minority. Security: Thomas Dent (g). Appraisers: Richard Lloyd, William Watts. Thomas Dent (g) to administer oath.

Edward Perrish (AA) administrator of John Beck (AA) exhibited inventory.

Inventory of Francis Anketill (CV) was exhibited.

7:336 15 March. Thomas Dent (g, SM) executor of Henry Hull (SM) exhibited that the appraisers George Mackall & Patrick Forrest are both dec'd. New appraisers:

William Hatton (g), William Harper (p). Richard Lloyd (g) to administer oath.

16 March. Jackeline Moore (CV) widow of James Moore (CV) exhibited his will, proved by Nathaniell Dawe & James Eltan.
7:337 Will of James Moore. Bequests: son James (under age 21) part of "The Gore" 100 a. bought of John Manning then to daughter Sarah Moore (under age), wife Jackeline Moore. Date: 19 February 1675/6. Witnesses: Nath. Dawe, James Eltan. Said Jackeline Moore was granted administration.
7:338 Appraisers: John Hollins, Henry Mitchell. Richard Ladd (g) to administer oath.

Arthur Taylor (BA) exhibited that John Taylor (BA) made nuncupative will in the presence of William Wesbury & John Spincks. The witnesses are unable to travel to the Office. John Waterton (g) to prove. Said Taylor was granted administration. Appraisers: James Denton, Lodowick Williams. Said Waterton to administer oath.

7:339 Thomas Preston (BA) exhibited that Thomas Armiger (BA) made a verbal will. John Waterton (g) to prove. Said Preston was granted administration. Appraisers: John Hill, William Yorke. Said Waterton to administer oath.

William Shaw (CE) who married the relict of Thomas Middlefield (CE) exhibited his nuncupative will. Joseph Hopkins (g) to prove. The relict was granted administration.
7:340 Appraisers: William Salesbury, Charles James. Said Hopkins to administer oath.

Thomas Mathews (CE) exhibited the will of John Owen. Joseph Hopkins (g) to prove. Will of John Owen (CE). Bequests: father Mr. John Owen (merchant, London) "George's Tower" 300 a., Thomas Mathews & his wife Martha. Executor: Thomas Mathews. Further bequests: George Eades,
7:341 John James. Date: 2 March 1675.

Witnesses: John Dixon, Mary Mills. Said Mathews was granted administration. Appraisers: William Salesbury, Giles Porter. Said Hopkins to administer oath.

Nicholas Shaw (CE) exhibited that his brother William Shaw (TA) is dec'd & his widow was granted administration on his estate. Then, the widow died, and there are under age children.
7:342 Said Nicholas was granted administration, on behalf of the children during their minority. Appraisers: James Scott, Andrew Skinner. Capt. Philemon Lloyd to administer oath.

Joseph Sears (merchant, CE) exhibited that John Vanheck is dec'd. Said Vanheck was security to said Sears on the estate of William Sethbery (CE). Joseph Hopkins (g) to take bond.
7:343 Appraisers: Richard Adams, Cornelius Arenson. Said Hopkins to administer oath.

John Wedge (KE) administrator of Thomas Taylor (KE) was granted discharge.

James Denton (BA) administrator of Thomas Daniell (BA) exhibited inventory.

17 March. Elisabeth Uty (BA) widow & administratrix of Col. Nathaniell Uty (BA) exhibited inventory.

William Hollis & James Phillips (BA) administrators of Thomas Winfield (BA) exhibited inventory.

7:344 Roger Brooke (g, CV) exhibited will of Edward Keene (CV), proved by Alexander Magruder & Michael Taney. Will of Edward Keene (g, CV). Bequests: wife Susan Keene & daughter Elisabeth Keene (under age 16) & daughter Martha Keene (under age 16) & wife's daughter Susan Hunt (under age 16).
7:345 Should both daughters die underage, distribution to: wife, Edward Russy, Hesekiah Bussey, Anne daughter of

brother Henry Keene (Dec'd). Executors: brother Richard Keene, brother William Berry, John Brooke, Roger Brooke. Date: 19 October 1675. Witnesses: Alexander Magruder, Michael Taney.

7:346 Will proved: 14 March. Charles Boteler deposed that he wrote the will of said Keene, on his way to Susquehanna Fort, indicating that said Keene intended to name his wife Susanna Keene as sole executrix. Signed: C. Boteler. Roger Brooke, one of the executors, was granted administration.

7:347 Appraisers: Thomas Bancks, Richard Marsham. Richard Ladd (g) to administer oath.

Richard Ladd (g, CV) exhibited that George Beckwith (CV) made his will on 25 May last, citing: executrix wife Frances, legacies to his children, overseers Christopher Rowsby (g) & said Ladd. Said Beckwith went to ENG. On return, he fell sick & on 3 November declared to Capt. Lenard Webber, that he had made a will in MD which he now felt was not fit. He now devised all to his wife. Said George is since dec'd & buried in ENG. Since his death, said Frances is also dec'd. Said children are all infants under age.

7:348 Said Ladd, one of the overseers, petitioned for administration of estates of both George & Frances. Roger Brooke (g) & the rest of the Justices of CV are bound to said Ladd. Appraisers: George Parker, John Halls.

18 March. Richard Guin (AA) exhibited that his brother Thomas Guin (AA) is dec'd & his widow died immediately thereafter. There are some children (under age). Said Richard is the only relation,

7:349 & was granted administration on behalf of the orphans. Appraisers: Stephen Burle, Richard Baylie. Robertt Burle (g) to administer oath.

George Uty (g, BA) exhibited will of John Newton ("unprofitable servant of God", BA).

7:350 Bequests: Josias White chattel on the plantation of Thomas Overton. Executor: Miles Gibson. Date: 23 September 1674. Witnesses: William Pooltney, Josias White.
7:351 Will proved 16 November 1674. Appraisers: Mr. William Hillis, James Phillips. Miles Gibson was granted administration.

William Farquisson (AA) administrator of Thomas Phelps (AA) exhibited accounts.

Marmaduke Simmes (SM) administrator of Abell James (SM) exhibited inventory.

The executrix of John Keely (AA) is lately dec'd, with several infants under age.
7:352 Robertt Burle (g, AA) to take inventory & to report names & ages of children. If any be over age 17, then administration will be granted to them.

James Mills (SO) was granted administration on estate of Robertt Maddocke (BA), on behalf of his widow in ENG.
7:353 Appraisers: Henry Haslewood, James Jues. Capt. George Wells to administer oath.

John Bird (BA) was granted administration on estate of Joseph Pierce (BA), who died childless & unmarried, as principle creditor. Appraisers: James Denton, Lodowick Williams. John Waterton (g) to administer oath.

7:354 William Stevens (g, SO) exhibited will of Richard Ackworth (SO). Said Stevens to prove. Appraisers: Christopher Nutter, Benjamin Cottman. Said Stevens to administer oath.

20 March. John Watkins (AA) petitioned for Thomas Taylor, Esq. (AA) to prove will of John Grose (AA). Appraisers: Capt. Philemon Lloyd (TA), Richard Wollman (TA). William Coursey (g) to administer oath.

Court Session: 1675

7:355 Rachell Lacey (the Clifts, CV) widow of Thomas Lacey (CV) was granted administration on his estate. Appraisers: William Kent, Walter Watkins. Col. Samuell Chewe to administer oath.

21 March. Anne Grace (SM) widow of John Grace (SM) exhibited his will, proved by Edward Bayley. Anne Breden, the other witness, deposed before William Rosewell (g, SM).
7:356 Will of John Grace (Basford Manner, SM). Date: 10 January 1675. Bequests:
7:357 wife Anne Grace. Executrix: wife. Witnesses: Edward Baylie, Anne Breden. Will proved 3 March 1675. Anne Grace was granted administration.
7:358 Appraisers: Vincent Mansfield, John Gee. William Rosewell (g) to administer oath.

22 March. Vincent Mansfield (g, SM) exhibited will of Richard Foster (St. Clement's Mannor, SM), dated 24 February last. Sara was his executrix, and she died shortly thereafter. Said Richard devised that after the deceased of his wife, his estate was to go to 2 grandchildren, Edward Mansfield & Sara Mansfield, & John Green (a child of his wife). Said George [sic] has not appeared in the Province. Said Vincent, who married daughter of Richard Foster & is the father of Edward & Sara, was granted administration.
7:359 Appraisers: John Goldsmith, Thomas Carvile. Thomas Notley (g) to administer oath.

Anne Murphy (SM) widow & administratrix of Daniell Murphey (SM) exhibited inventory.

23 March. Giles Stevens (BA) was granted administration on estate of Samuell Trasey (BA), who died unmarried & had 1 daughter (age 8), as principle creditor to William Bisse (BA), on behalf of said daughter. Security: Capt. Thomas Long.
7:360 Appraisers: John Shadwell, James Cogell. Capt. Long to administer oath.

Court Session: 1675

Sarah Clarke (BA) widow of Abraham Clarke (BA) was granted administration on his estate. Appraisers: John Eiden, William Long. Capt. Thomas Long (BA) to administer oath. [Administration was returned unaccomplished, as widow died intestate.]

Margueritt Ferrell (BA) exhibited will of her husband Richard Ferrell (BA). Will is unsigned, as the testator lost the
7:361 use of his hands. Capt. Thomas Long to prove. Will of Richard Therrell (BA). Executrix: wife Margueritt Therrell. Bequests: wife.
7:362 Mentions: debt to Capt. Thomas Long. Date: 22 September 1675. Witnesses: Miles Gibson, Thomas Long. Will proved 23 March 1675. Said Margueritt Therrell was granted administration.

7:363 Will of Francis Graile was exhibited, proved by Richard Doll & Lidia Turbervile. Will of Francis Graile (SM). Bequests: Edward Pearce & Thomas Pearce sons of Thomas Pearce (dec'd), John Pearce son of said Thomas, William Strainer, servants of Mr. Gilbert Turberfield, Mary Robinson. Executor: William Strainer. Witnesses: Richard Doll, Lidia Turberfile.
7:364 Will proved 15 March 1675.

Will of Spencer Hales (g, CV) was exhibited, proved by Christopher Rowsby (g) & Jane Halfhead (spinster). Will of Spencer Hales (g). Bequests: sister Anna Hales land in ENG. Date: 20 March 1674. Will proved 14 March 1675. Christopher Rowsby (g) wrote the will, & stated that the sister is Anna Rightty (and not Hanna Rightty).

Court Session: 1676

8A:1 last March. Robertt Goodrick (g, CH) one of the executors of his father George Goodricke was granted administration on his estate. Benjamin Rozer (g, high sheriff, CH) to prove, with oath of Ignatius Causin, who is the sole surviving witness & is sick. Appraisers: John ollard [sic], Jacob Peterson.

Frances Hyde exhibited inventory of Henry Hyde (St. George's Hundred, SM), appraised by William Hatton (g) & George Mackall (who died between time of appraisement & now).

Elisabeth Dundasse widow of George Dundasse (chirurgeon, St. George's Hundred, SM) exhibited
8A:2 that her husband made a nuncupative will, before John Hepworth & Edward Fisher. John Hepworth deposed that the will was made on 18 March instant before himself & Edward Fisher, & that he gave all to his wife. His wife & her mother, both ignorant, are to be advised by Mr. Cheseldyn. Said Fisher deposed likewise. Said Elisabeth was granted administration. Appraisers: Henry Phips (merchant), Francis Hill. William Hatton (g) to administer oath.

8A:3 Catherine Bartlett exhibited that the appraisers of estate of her husband are dec'd. New appraisers: John Chevrill, Peter Watts. William Hatton (g) to administer oath.

John Watkins (AA) exhibited that on 22 February last, John Grosse, Richard Snoweden, Elisabeth Snoweden, Roger Grosse, William Grosse, & Francis Grosse were summoned regarding accounts of John Welsh. Said John Groce is guardian to Roger Groce, William Groce, Frances Groce. Said John Groce is now dec'd. Continuance was granted.

8A:4 4 April. Thomas Potter (SM) executor of George Marshall (SM) administrator of Joseph Bruff (SM) exhibited accounts of said Bruff. Discharge was granted.

Anne Bigger (CV) widow & executrix of John Bigger exhibited inventory.

Anne Bigger (CV) exhibited will of James Stockley (Patuxent River, CV), proved by

James Rumsey & said Anne Bigger.

8A:5 Mary Stockely, who is unable to travel, was granted administration. Appraisers: James Canady, William House. Tobias Norton (g) to administer oath.

Richard Ladd has not yet given security to CV County Court nor to Roger Brooke (g) for administration on estate of George & Frances Beckwith. Said Richard to prove accounts of goods to Roger Brooke & other commissioners, John Halls (appraiser), George Parker (appraiser), John Darnall (now appraiser), Christopher Rowsby (now appraiser).

8A:6 5 April. Philip Lynes (CH) was granted administration on estate of Robertt Clarke (CH), as principle creditor. His widow died immediately afterwards. Appraisers: Thomas Corker, Thomas King. Benjamin Rozer (high sheriff, CH) to administer oath.

James Ringold (g, KE) exhibited accounts of Elisabeth Head (widow, KE) executrix of William Head.

8A:7 Thomas Potter (SM) executor of George Marshall (SM) exhibited inventory.

Anne Burgesse (SM) widow & administratrix of William Burgesse (SM) exhibited inventory.

William Towlson (g, CE) exhibited will of John Powell (CE). Thomas Hacker (CE) was granted administration. Inventory was exhibited.

Alice Foster (CE) widow & administratrix of Richard Foster (CE) exhibited inventory.

8A:8 Henry Ward (g, CE) administrator of Richard Pore (CE) exhibited inventory.

Augustine Herman (g, CE) exhibited oath of Richard Edmunds & John Cox, appraisers of Daniell Gover (CE). Said Edmunds was sworn on 16 October 1675; Said Cox on 25 October 1675. Mr. Henry

Ward was sworn on 16 October 1675 at Bohemia.

Capt. Richard Hill (AA) exhibited will of William Neale (AA). Susanna Neale (AA) widow & executrix was granted administration. Inventory was exhibited.

8A:9 John Coxe (CE) administrator of Francis Barnes (CE) exhibited that appraiser William Hopkins is not to be found. New appraisers: William Pierce, Thomas Rumsey. Abraham Wilde (g) to administer oath.

Capt. Richard Hill (AA) exhibited will of Joseph Morley (AA). Robertt Procter & John Gather executors were granted administration.

Abraham Wilde (g, CE) exhibited oath of Alice Foster widow & administratrix of Richard Foster (CE), sworn on 25 October last. Also exhibited was oath of John Hyland
8A:10 & Richard Whitton, appraisers sworn same day.

Elisabeth Mackart (SM) widow of John Mackart (SM) was granted administration on his estate. William Rosewell to prove his will. Appraisers: John Bullock, Thomas Ottaway. Said Rosewell to administer oath.

Richard Ladd (g, CV) was to deliver goods & keys of chattel of George & Frances Beckwith to MM John Darnall & John Hall.

8A:11 6 April. Elisabeth Mosse (AA) widow of Richard Mosse (AA) exhibited his will. Robertt Burle (g) to prove said will. Said Elisabeth was granted administration. Appraisers: Ralph Hawkins, William Hawkins. Said Burle to administer oath.

Mary Luffman (AA) widow of William Luffman exhibited his will. Robertt Burle (g) to prove said will.

8A:12 Said Mary was granted administration. Appraisers: Robertt Tyler, William Hopkins. Said Burle to administer oath.

Philemon Lloyd, Peter Sayer, & Richard Gorsuch (gentlemen, TA) renounced administration on estate of Edward Roe (g, TA), in favor of the widow & her daughter. Date: 31 March 1675. Mary Roe widow exhibited the will. Edward Manne (g) to prove said will.
8A:13 Said Mary was granted administration. Elisabeth Roe (daughter, other executrix) is in ENG. Appraisers: Anthony Neale, Thomas Alexander. Said Edward Man to administer oath.

Thomas Hinson (g, TA) exhibited will of John Rodaway (TA), proved. Also exhibited was oath of Joseph Weeks & John Hinson executors sworn on 27 December 1675. Richard Tilghman (one of the witnesses) was sworn on 27 December 1675. Ralph Blackhall (other witness) was sworn on 9 June 1675.

Major William Burgesse (g, AA) exhibited will of Edward Gardner (AA). Capt. Richard Hill executor was granted administration.

8A:14 Thomas Taylor, Esq. (AA) exhibited will of John Hawkins (AA). Mary Hawkins was granted administration.

Mary Bucknall (AA) relict & administratrix of Edward Wheelock (AA) exhibited inventory. Robertt Burle (g, AA) exhibited oath of Mary Bucknall, sworn 25 March 1676.
8A:15 Also exhibited was oath of Ralph Hawkins & William Hawkins, appraisers sworn same day.

Major William Burgesse (AA) exhibited oath of Edward Dorsey & Andrew Norwood, appraisers of James Rawbone (AA), sworn 1 April 1676.

John Howell (CE) executor of Capt. Thomas Howell (CE) exhibited inventory.

John Howell (CE) executor of John Vanheck (CE) exhibited inventory.

8A:16 William Parker (CV) administrator of Thomas Preston (CV) exhibited inventory.

William Kent (CV) administrator of Richard Williams (CV) exhibited inventory.

William Russell (AA) administrator of Thomas Chandler (AA) exhibited inventory.

Joachim Guibertt (SM) administrator of James Trasck exhibited inventory.

Rachell Lacey (CV) widow & administratrix of Thomas Lacey (CV) exhibited inventory.

8A:17 Peternella Carre (CE) widow of Capt. John Carre (CE) exhibited his will. Augustine Herman (g) to prove said will. Said Peternella was granted administration. Appraisers: John Hyland, Richard Whitton. Said Herman to administer oath.

Will of Richard Blunt (CE) was exhibited. Henry Ward (g) to prove said will. The widow was granted administration. Appraisers: Roger Padimore, Humphrey Nicolls. Said Ward to administer oath.

Mary Plum (KE) exhibited will of John Plum (KE). James Ringold (g) to prove said will.
8A:18 Mary Plum was granted administration. Appraisers: Thomas Parker, Thomas Warren. Said Ringold to administer oath.

Anne Jones (the Clifts, CV) widow of Meridith Jones (CV) was granted administration on his estate. Appraisers: John Russell, Walter Watkins. Samuell Bourne (g) to administer oath.

Court Session: 1676

8A:19 William Dare (CV) administrator of John Parker (CV) exhibited inventory.

7 April. Anne Sullivant (AA) exhibited will of Jeremiah Sullevant (AA). Col. Samuell Chew to prove said will. Anne Sullivant widow was granted administration. Appraisers: John Sollers, Robert Connett. Said Chew to administer oath.

8A:20 Thomas Smith (AA) renounced administration on estate of John Howerton (p, AA). His will was dated 19 March instant, & bequeathed all to Richard Deavor (AA) & Thomas Smith (AA) for use of his children. Date: 27 March 1676. Witnesses: John Daven, John Shrigley. Richard Deavor exhibited the will. Col. Samuell Chew to prove said will. Said Deavor was granted administration.
8A:21 Appraisers: Charles Bevin, James Chilcott. Said Chew to administer oath.

Benjamin Rozer (high sheriff, CH) was granted administration on estate of Edmund Lindsey (CH), as principle creditor. Appraisers: James Smallwood, Ralph Shaw. Thomas Hussy (g) to administer oath.

8A:22 George Godfrey (CH) was granted administration on estate of Richard Fowke, who died childless & unmarried. Appraisers: William Smith, Thomas Galey. Benjamin Rozer (g) to administer oath.

William Dare (CV) administrator of John Parker (CV) exhibited accounts.

8A:23 Thomas Jones (BA) who married relict of Walter Marcanallie (BA) was granted administration on his estate. Said relict died immediately after said Walter. Appraisers: James Collier, Thomas Preston. Dr. John Waterton to administer oath.

8 April. Elisabeth Morgan (CE) widow of John Morgan (CE) exhibited his will. Jonathon Sibrey (g) to prove said will.

8A:24 Appraisers: Edward Williams, Henry Ward. Said Sibrey to administer oath.

Mary Campher (TA) petitioned for Vincent Lowe, Esq. (Attorney General) to prove will of Thomas Campher (TA). Said Mary was granted administration. Appraisers: William Gaskin, John Hunt. Said Lowe to administer oath.

Mary Lorckie (TA) petitioned for Vincent Lowe, Esq. (Attorney General) to prove will of Nicholas Lorckie (TA).
8A:25 Said Mary was granted administration. Appraisers: Ralph Dawson, Hugh Cherod. Said Lowe to administer oath.

Robertt Blinckhorne (CV) exhibited will of William Cussen (CV), proved by James Veitch. Said Blinckhorne was granted administration; he is unable to travel to the Office. Roger Brooke, Esq. to administer oath. Appraisers: Jasper Allen, James Veitch.

8A:26 Joyce Hewton (TA) widow of Mathew Hewton (TA) was granted administration on his estate. Appraisers: Thomas Hinson (g), Richard Jones. Mathew Ward (g) to administer oath.

Joseph Weeks & John Hinson (gentlemen, KE) executors of John Rodoway (TA) exhibited that Ralph Blackhall, one of the appraisers, is dec'd. New appraisers: Richard Jones, James Barckhurst. William Coursey (g) to administer oath.

8A:27 10 April. Mary Goff (SM) relict & administratrix of Lt. Col. John Jarboe (SM) exhibited accounts. Continuance granted.

Margueritt Jolley (SM) widow & administratrix of Edward Jolley (SM) exhibited inventory.

Timothy Goodridge (TA) administrator of George Richardson (TA) exhibited accounts.

Court Session: 1676

Rachael Towers (BA) widow & administratrix of John Towers (BA) exhibited inventory.

Thomas Jones (BA) executor of John Reycroft (BA) exhibited inventory.

8A:28 Jasper Allen (CV) administrator of John Martin (merchant, Barbadoes) exhibited inventory.

William Dorsey (DO) administrator of John Wigfield (DO) exhibited inventory.

Meverell Hulse (CH) executor of Thomas Greenfield exhibited inventory.

Thomas Notley (g, SM) exhibited oath of Vincent Mansfield administrator of Richard Foster (SM),
8A:29 sworn 28 March 1676. Securities (SM): Justinian Gerrard, Robert Cole. Also exhibited was oath of John Goldsmith & Thomas Carvile, sworn same day.

8A:30 Dr. Robertt Winsmore (DO) exhibited the following oaths:

- John Dorsey & Morris Mathews, appraisers of John Wigfield (DO), sworn 15 February 1675. Inventory was exhibited.
- Stephen Gary & John Brookes, appraisers of John Raven (DO), sworn 20 February 1675.

8A:31 ...

- John Mackiell & Edmund Brannack, appraisers of William Hambridge (DO), sworn 11 March 1675.

Col. Samuel Chew (AA) exhibited the following oaths:

- Rachell Lacey administratrix of Thomas Lacey (AA), sworn 28 March 1676.
- Will Kent & Walter Watkins, appraisers sworn 28 March 1676.

Benjamin Rozer (g, high sheriff, CH) exhibited will of Jenkins Jones (CH), proved.
8A:32 Thomas King executor was sworn 21 February 1675.

Court Session: 1676

Benjamin Rozer exhibited the following oaths:

- Richard Beck administrator of Lewis Beck, sworn 12 January 1675. Security: Charles Heabound.

8A:33 ...

- Thomas Clipsham administrator of John Williams, sworn 17 March 1675.
- Henry Hawkins executor of Giles Cole, sworn 7 December 1675.
- Thomas King (CH) administrator of Walter Cooper, sworn 8 December 1675.

8A:34 ...

- Jacob Peterson & Philip Lynes, appraisers of Walter Cooper, sworn 16 November 1675.
- Kenelm Mackloglin & Bennett Marshigaiy, appraisers of Daniell Ritchison, sworn 6 April 1676.
- Penelope Helms administratrix of John Helmes (CH), sworn 18 April 1676. Security: John Chesson.

8A:35 ...

- Philip Lynes administrator of Robert Clarke (CH), sworn 11 April 1676.
- Jones Joanna administratrix & widow of Owen Jones (CH), sworn 18 April 1676. Security: John Hamilton.

8A:36 ...

- George Credwell administrator of Richard Fowkes (CH), sworn 9 April 1676. Bondsman: Henry Harders.

Col. Samuell Chew (AA) exhibited oath of William Kent administrator of Richard Williams (CV), sworn 26 February 1675. Securities: Marke Claie, Capt. John Cobreath.

8A:37 Marke Clare & John Dodson, appraisers sworn 26 February 1675.

Richard Simmes (BA) executor of Roger Hill (BA) exhibited inventory. John Waterton (BA) exhibited will of said Hill, proved. Commission dated: 14 February 1675. Said Simmes sworn 16 March 1675.

8A:38 John Waterton (g, BA) exhibited commission, dated 21 February 1675, to swear Rachell Towers administratrix of

John Towers.

8A:39 Mathew Ward (g, TA) exhibited oaths regarding estate of John Martin (TA):
- Thomas Norris was sworn 4 February 1675.
- William Bishop & John Chase were sworn 1 November 1675.

8A:40 11 April. Cornelius Howard (AA) was granted administration on estate of John Sampson (AA), who died childless & unmarried. Appraisers: John Hammond, Abraham Childe. Capt. Richard Hill to administer oath.

Margrett Cooper (AA) widow of Thomas Cooper (AA) was granted administration on his estate.
8A:41 Appraisers: Marin DuVall, Gabriell Parrott. Maj. William Burgesse to administer oath.

William Hatton (SM) exhibited that Thomas Dent (g, SM), who was to administer oath to appraisers of estate of Richard Hatton, is dec'd. Appraisers: William Harper, William Watts. Richard Lloyd (g) to administer oath.

Frances Lucas (SM) widow & executrix of William Lucas (SM) exhibited inventory.

12 April. Abraham Wilde (g, CE) exhibited will of George Wilson (CE), proved. William Pierce, one of the overseers, exhibited that the dec'd had appointed his sons James & Peter as executors, & that they are under age. Abraham Stran,
8A:42 Richard Thornton, & William Southbe (the other 3 overseers) are not willing to take oath of administrator. Said Pierce was granted administration, on behalf of the orphans. Abraham Wilde (g) to administer oath.

John Fanning (CH) was granted administration on estate of Seabright Meacock (CH), who died childless & unmarried, as principle creditor.

Appraisers: Francis Wyne, William Lee. Humphrey Warren (g) to administer oath.

8A:43 Alice Ginne (KI) widow of Arthur Ginne (KI) was granted administration on his estate. Appraisers: William Towlson, William Reathman. James Ringold (g) to administer oath.

Hanna Baxter (KE) widow & executrix of Thomas Baxter (KE) exhibited his will.
8A:44 Joseph Weeks (g) to prove said will. Said Hanna was granted administration. Appraisers: Thomas Southeran, Walter Kirby. Said Weeks to administer oath.

13 April. Henry Jowles (CV) was granted administration on estate of Andrew Higgs (chirurgeon, CV), who died childless but with a wife in ENG, as chief creditor. Appraisers: Symon Wotton, Charles Boteler. Samuell Bourne (g) to administer oath.

8A:45 14 April. Kesia White (SM) widow of Rowland White was granted administration on his estate. Thomas Notley (g) to take bond. Appraisers: Samuell Maddox, Thomas Carvile. Said Notley to administer oath.

15 April. Edward Turner (CV) executor of William Singleton (CV) affirmed said will.

8A:46 Thomas Bland (AA) who married the relict & executrix of Nicholas Wyatt (AA) vs. Edward Dorsey (AA) who married daughter of said dec'd. Continuance was granted.

17 April. John Jedbery who married a sister of Robertt Taylor (CV), who died leaving 1 child &
8A:47 a widow who died immediately afterward, was granted administration on his estate, on behalf of the child. Securities: Samuell Vynes, Humphrey Watersworth. Appraisers: Samuell Vynes, Francis Freeman. Richard Ladd (g) to administer oath.

Court Session: 1676

Samuell Vynes (CV) exhibited that Cornelius Jones made a nuncupative will in the presence of Richard Dury & Humphrey Watersworth.

8A:48 Said Jones bequeathed all to said Vynes & Mary his daughter. Said Samuell was granted administration on behalf of his daughter Mary during her minority. Appraisers: Robertt Tyler, Francis Freeman. Richard Ladd (g) to administer oath.

18 April. James Veitch (CV) exhibited that Mary widow of Jasper Allen (CV) was granted administration on his estate, but is sick & unable to travel to the Office.

8A:49 Appraisers: John Turner, James Veitch. Richard Ladd (g) to administer oath. Said Jasper is administrator of John Martin (Barbadoes). At the death of said Martin, said Martin had chattel of Mathew James (Barbadoes). Said widow Allen is to render separate inventory of said Martin or James.

Thomas Bennett, Jr. (Newtowne Hundred, SM, now dec'd) had in his possession chattel of William Wright (orphan). Said Wright has chosen John Cecill (Newtowne Hundred, SM) as his guardian. Mary Bennett widow of said Thomas was granted administration on his estate & is to deliver said chattel.

8A:50 Appraisers: Peter Mills, Henry Spinck. Capt. John Jourdain to administer oath.

James Tyer (CH) exhibited the will of John Bowles (CH). Benjamin Rozer (g, high sheriff, CH) to prove said will. Said Tyer was granted administration. Appraisers: Rand. Brent, William Lee. Said Rozer to administer oath.

Joanna Jones (CH) widow of Owen Jones (CH) was granted administration on his estate.

8A:51 Appraisers: John Wheeler, Robert Robins. Benjamin Rozer (g, high sheriff, CH) to administer oath.

Penelope Helms (CH) widow of John Helms (CH) was granted administration on his estate. Appraisers: Kenelm Macloghlin, John Wood. Benjamin Rozer (g) to administer oath.

Peter Watts (SM) executor of John Hewett (SM) exhibited inventory.

8A:52 19 April. Edward English (merchant) exhibited that John Allen (merchant, London) consigned goods to William Hewett (merchant, London). Said Allen is dec'd, & bequeathed goods & chattel to wife of said William Hewett. Said William came to MD to look after said goods & died intestate. John Turpinne (clerk, BA) was granted administration on estate of said William, on behalf of the widow & children in ENG. Said English is employed by the widow & was granted administration. Charles James (CE) to take bond. Appraisers: Thomas Hocker, Richard Adams. Said James to administer oath.

8A:53 Joseph Edloe (SM) executor of William Cane (SM) was granted administration on his estate. Appraisers: Christopher Rowsby, John Halfhead.

20 April. Thomas Carvile (SM) executor of Robert Hunt (SM) exhibited his will, proved by Samuell Cooksey & Robertt Bing. Said Thomas was granted administration. Appraisers: Samuell Cooksey, Robert Bing.

8A:54 21 April. Thomas Cooke (SM) exhibited the will of John Cooke (SM), proved by Peter Carwardyn & John Dugings. Said Thomas is only cited as overseer. Said Thomas was granted administration for self & his brothers & sisters. Securities: Peter Carwardyn, John Dugings. Appraisers: John Cammell, Thomas Hinton. William Hatton (g) to administer oath.

Elisabeth Mackey (SM) exhibited the nuncupative will of Elisabeth Rawlins widow of Nicholas Rawlins, proved by

Richard Weller.
8A:55 Said Mackey was granted administration on her estate. Appraisers: William Harper, Richard Weller.

Anne Mackall (SM) widow & executrix of George Mackall (SM) petitioned for new appraisers: William Hatton (g), Peter Watts (p). Richard Lloyd (g) to administer oath.

22 April. Katherine Bartlett (SM) widow & administratrix of George Bartlett (SM) exhibited inventory.

8A:56 Rebecca Dent (SM) widow & executrix of Thomas Dent (SM) exhibited his will, proved by William Hatton (g) & William Harper (p). Appraisers (SM): William Hatton (g), William Harper (p). Appraisers (CH): Nicholas Proddy, John Ward. John Stone (g) to administer oath.

24 April. Elisabeth Dundasse (SM) widow of George Dundasse (SM) & daughter of Patrick Forrest (dec'd, SM) exhibited nuncupative will of her mother Helena Forrest,
8A:57 widow of said Patrick, made in the presence of Henry Phips (merchant). Elisabeth Dundasse was granted administration on her estate. Appraisers: John Chevrill, Peter Watts. William Hatton (g) to administer oath.

25 April. Jane Thompson (CV) widow of James Thompson (CV) was granted administration on his estate. Appraisers: George Whitle, Nicholas Furnis. Samuell Bourne (g) to administer oath.

8A:58 Maj. Thomas Taylor (AA) exhibited the will of John Grose (AA), proved.

Isabella Swanston (CV) widow & executrix of Francis Swanston (CV) exhibited inventory.

Christopher Rowsby for Anne Hales was granted administration on the estate of her brother Spencer Hales.

26 April. Joyce Brummale (CV) widow & executrix of Richard Brummale (CV) exhibited his will, proved by Richard Farrow & Samuell Vynes.
8A:59 Said Joyce was granted administration. Appraisers: Henry Mitchell, James Mackall. Richard Ladd (g) to administer oath.

Tabitha Mill (CV) widow & executrix of William Mill (CV) exhibited his will, proved by Robertt Lindsey & Robertt Fowkes. Said Tabitha was granted administration.
8A:60 Appraisers: Peter Archer, Arthur Ludford. Maj. Thomas Trueman to administer oath.

Sarah Pile widow of John Pille (g, Sarum, SM) exhibited that Joseph Pille (her only surviving child by said John) was granted administration on said estate. Said Sarah is of great age. Said Joseph notified her that he had administered his father's estate. Sarah exhibited that she had not abandoned her right. Said Joseph broke the seal of the LoA & threw them into the fire. Said Sarah requests LoA & that LoA to said Joseph
8A:61 be vacated. William Rosewell was security to said Joseph. Said Sarah was granted administration. Appraisers: Thomas Simpson, Thomas Stonestreete. Maj. William Boreman to administer oath.

8A:62 1 May. Joseph Edloe (SM) executor of William Cane (SM) exhibited inventory.

Morgan Jones (SM) exhibited will of John Harrington (SM), proved by William Jarrett. Said Morgan was granted administration. Appraisers: Thomas Doxey, Thomas Keating.

8A:63 2 May. Geore Wells (g, BA) exhibited the nuncupative will of John Turpinne (clerk, BA), made in the presence of Henry Haslewood & Ruthin Garretson.

George Uty (g) to prove said will.

6 May. Rand. Hanson (SM) administrator of Thomas Hatton (SM) exhibited inventory.

8 May. Anne Mackall (SM) widow & executrix of George Mackall (SM) exhibited inventory.

Guilbert Turbervile (SM) exhibited will of Francis Graile (SM). William Strainer renounced executorship.
8A:64 Said Turbervile was granted administration. Surety: Walter Hall (g). Appraisers: said Walter Hall, John Thompson. William Calvert, Esq. to administer oath.

Jane Crouche (CE) widow & executrix of John Crouche (CE) exhibited his will. William Towlson (g) to prove said will. Said Jane was granted administration. Appraisers: Edward Skidmore, John Burridge. Said Towlson to administer oath.

8A:65 Thomas Mathews executor of John Owen (merchant, CE) exhibited that John James (CE) took chattel from the estate. Said John James summoned to exhibit reasons for his actions.

Rebecca Dent (SM) widow & executrix of Thomas Dent (SM) exhibited nuncupative will of William Dillon (merchant, London, ENG), proved by Capt. Leonard Webber. Said Rebecca was granted administration.

8A:66 9 May. Rebecca Moore (KE) widow of Richard Moore (KE) renounced administration on said Moore's estate to Isack Winchester (KE). Date: 6 May 1676. Witnesses: Robert Hood, Matt. Ereckson. Isack Winchester (KE) exhibited the will. William Lawrence (g) to prove said will. Said Winchester, one of the overseers, was granted administration on behalf of wife & children. Appraisers: Patrick Goardin, William Rawls. Said Lawrence to administer oath.

8A:67 Augustine Herman (g, CE) for Anne Nash (CE) relict & administratrix of Richard Blunt (CE) exhibited accounts.

John & Mathew Erickson (KE) were granted administration on estate of Edward Jones (KE), as greatest creditors. Appraisers: Isack Winchester, Thomas Osborne. William Lawrence (g) to administer oath.

Thomas Warren (KE) exhibited the will of Margrett Hill (KE). William Lawrence (g) to prove said will. Said Warren was granted administration. Appraisers: Michael Miller, Isack Winchester. Said Lawrence to administer oath.

8A:68 William Watts (SM) was granted administration on estate of Thomas Cager (SM), who died childless & unmarried, as principle creditor. Surety: Peter Watts. Appraisers: William Canady, Peter Watts. William Hatton (g) to administer oath.

15 May. Henry Hooper (DO) was granted administration on estate of his father Henry Hooper (DO), as sole surviving son.
8A:69 Appraisers (CV): William Hill, John Cooper. Appraisers (DO): Joseph Hanaway, Lewis Griffin. William Francis to administer oath.

16 May. Mary the widow of Edward Connery (SM) was granted administration on his estate. Appraisers: Clement Haly, Darby Donway. Joseph Pile (g, Sarum, SM) to administer oath. Said Mary is "a stranger in these parts."

8A:70 18 May. Richard Hall (CV) renounced administration on estate of Thomas Coxe (CV). George Langam (CV) exhibited the will of said Coxe. Tobias Norton (g) to prove said will. Appraisers: William Jenkins, Francis Spencer. Said Norton to administer oath.

Court Session: 1676

8A:71 Joanne Dunne (KE) exhibited the will of Robertt Dunne (KE). Henry Hosier (g) to prove said will. Said Joanne was granted administration. Appraisers: Desboro Bennett, Morgan Williams. Said Hosier to administer oath.

19 May. John Larkin (AA) administrator of William Powell (BA) exhibited inventory
8A:72 & accounts.

John Waterton (g, BA) exhibited nuncupative will of John Taylor (BA), proved. Arthur Taylor (BA) executor of John Taylor (BA) exhibited inventory.

Thomas Casey (CH) exhibited verbal will of Patrick Farlum (CH), made in the presence of Thomas Brien & Barbary Hall. He bequeathed all to said Casey. Benjamin Rozer (g, high sheriff, CH) to take depositions.
8A:73 Appraisers: John Weather, John Wood. Said Rozer to administer oath.

Elisabeth Skinner (DO) widow & administratrix of Thomas Skinner (DO) exhibited inventory.

Sara Poole (CE) exhibited will of John Poole. Augustine Herman (g) to prove said will. Said Sarah was granted administration. Appraisers: John Browning, William Brocas. Said Herman to administer oath.

8A:74 Martha Morgan (CE) exhibited the will of William Morgan (CE). Joseph Hopkins (g) to prove said will. Said Martha was granted administration. Appraisers: Thomas Parker, Richard Adams. Said Hopkins to administer oath.

Dr. Henry Lewis (AA) exhibited that Robertt Burle (AA) is dec'd, who was to prove will of William Slade (AA). Capt. Richard Hill now to prove said will. Said Lewis & John Ricks were granted administration.
8A:75 Appraisers: Robert Davidge, Ralph Hawkins. Said Hill to administer oath.

20 May. Edward Dorsey (AA) who married a daughter of Nicholas Wyatt (dec'd, AA) vs. Thomas Bland who married relict & executrix of said Wyatt. Libel exhibited.

Robertt Franclin, Sr. (AA) exhibited the will of William Collier (AA). Samuell Lane (g) to prove said will. Robert Franclin, Jr. was granted administration (if he is of 17 years of age). Appraisers: Robertt Loukwood, John Walters. Said Lane to administer oath.

8A:76 22 May. John Medley (Newtowne, SM) exhibited that his brother George Medley (SM) made a nuncupative will, in the presence of Richard Gary & Joseph Harding. Said will was proved. Said John Medley was granted administration. Appraisers: Thomas Kirckly, Richard Burgett.

John Davis (TA) exhibited that William Taylor (TA) died leaving a wife & children. Said wife refused to administer his estate. Said Davis is brother-in-law to said Taylor.
8A:77 Said Davis was granted administration, on behalf of the widow & orphans. Col. Vincent Lowe to take bond. Appraisers: William Lydes, John Newman. Said Lowe to administer oath.

Tobias Norton (g, CV) exhibited the will of Thomas Coxe (CV), proved. George Lingam, one of the executors, was granted administration. Richard Hall, the other executor, renounced administration.

Mary Anderson (CV) exhibited the will of John Anderson (CV). William Groome (g) to prove said will.
8A:78 Said Mary was granted administration. Appraisers: James Rumsey, John Alewell. Said Groome to administer oath.

Elisabeth Mosse (AA) exhibited that Robert Rusle (g), who was to prove the will of Richard Mosse (AA), is dec'd. Capt. Richard Hill now to prove said will. Said Elisabeth was granted administration. Appraisers: Ralph & William Hawkins. Said Hill to administer oath.

Mary Luffman (AA) exhibited that Robert Burle (g), who was to prove will of William Luffman, is dec'd. Capt. Richard Hill now to prove said will.
8A:79 Said Mary was granted administration. Appraisers: Robert Tyler, William Hopkins. Said Hill to administer oath.

23 May. James Philips for Henerietta Swanson (BA) exhibited will of Edward Swanson (BA). Henry Haslewood (g) to prove said will. Said Henerietta was granted administration. Appraisers: William Osborne, James Philips. Said Haslewood to administer oath.

James Philips for Florence Lee (BA) widow of John Lee (BA) exhibited his will. Henry Haslewood (g) to prove said will.
8A:80 Said Florence was granted administration. Appraisers: William Osborne, James Philips. Said Haslewood to administer oath.

James Philips (BA) exhibited will of William Bisse (BA). Henry Haslewood to prove said will. Said Philips was granted administration. Appraisers: William Osborne, John Wallstone. Said Haslewood to administer oath.

Giles Stevens (BA) administrator of Samuel Tracey (BA) exhibited inventory.

8A:81 Edward Dorsey (BA) who married daughter of Nicholas Wyatt (dec'd, AA) vs. Thomas Bland who married Damaris relict of said Nicholas. Mentions: Nicholas' testament dated 10 December 1671, first commission by said Dorsey to Nathaniell Heathcote to examine witnesses, Richard Boughton (clerk, BA), 2nd commission by said Bland to Samuell Chew, Esq., chancery case by Bland vs. Dorsey.
8A:82 ...
8A:83 Petition for hearing by Da. Bland.

8A:84 ...

8A:85 24 May. Petition (cont): per oath of Cornelius Howard, said Nicholas Wyatt was not of sound mind on 10 December 1671 when he made his will. After recovering from sickness, said Nicholas declared he was not "in his senses". Mary Ennis deposed the same. The will was declared void, & LoA to Damaris Wyatt now Damaris Bland were revoked. Edward Dorsey & his wife Sarah (daughter of said Nicholas) cited exceptions to the accounts, mentioning:

8A:86 Mr. Taylor, John Browne, Capt. Burgesse, (N) Turner attorney for Capt. Connaway,

8A:87 Capt. Burgesse, (N) Stavely, (N) Parker,

8A:88 Chancellor, cause of Thomas Francis & (N) Dorsey, Mallett (servant), Morgan (servant), (N) Carpenter, (N) Porter (an orphan),

8A:89 ...

8A:90 William Wakes, Lancelott Haltett, (N) Davis, Mr. Lambert, Mr. Welsh, Thomas Francis, "Whackfield's Covenant",

8A:91 ...

8A:92 Giles Stevens (BA) administrator of Samuell Tracey (BA) exhibited accounts.

Chattel ordered by Jasper Allen to William Beck (mariner) & in hands of Charles Ascomb to be delivered to widow of said Allen.

Thomas Taylor, Esq. (AA) exhibited will of John Grose (AA), proved. John Watkins was granted administration.

8A:93 Capt. John Welsh (high sheriff, AA) vs. John Watkins executor of John Grose (AA).

25 May. John Waterton (g, BA) exhibited will of Caesar Prince (BA), proved. John Stansbey, sole surviving executor, was granted administration.

William Towlson (g, CE) exhibited will of John Crouch (CE), proved. Jane Crouch widow & executrix was granted administration.

Thomas Bland vs. Edward Dorsey.

8A:94 26 May. Thomas Bland vs. Edward Dorsey. Answer of Damaris Bland executrix of Nicholas Wyatt to exceptions of Edward Dorsey & his wife Sarah. Mentions: Mr. Taylor, (N) Browne, Capt. Burgesse per Cornelius Howard,
8A:95 (N) Turner, Capt. Burges, (N) Stavely, (N) Parker,
8A:96 Mr. Connaway, Morgan,
8A:97 ...
8A:98 Lancelott Haltett, (N) Davis, (N) Carpenter, Mr. Lambertt, Thomas Francis, (N) Wakefield, estate of (N) Pyne, Nath. Evett,
8A:99 (N) Porter, (N) Willett.

8A:100 Thomas Francis (AA) was granted administration on estate of his wife Sarah Francis formerly Sarah Shaw relict & administratrix of John Shaw (AA), & of estate of John Shaw. Surety: Thomas Taylor, Esq. Appraisers: John Watkins, Richard Tydings. Nathaniell Heathcote (g) to administer oath.

8A:101 Nehemiah Birckhead (AA) exhibited that his father Christopher Birckhead (AA) made a will in ENG. Col. Samuell Chew deposed regarding said will. Said Nehemiah was granted administration. Appraisers: Nathan Smith, John Sollers. Said Chew to administer oath.

Elisabeth Royall (SM) exhibited will of Francis Barnell, proved by Francis Sourton & Henry Williams. Said Royall was granted administration.

8A:102 Mary Noake (TA) widow of William Noake (TA) was granted administration on his estate. Appraisers: Thomas Hinson, William Bishop (gentlemen). Mathew Ward (g) to administer oath.

29 May. Judith Lee (CH) relict of James Chancelor (CH) was granted administration on his estate. Benjamin Rozer (g) to take bond of William Lee her now husband. Appraisers: Henry

Hardy, Henry Bonner. Said Rozer to administer oath.

8A:103 William Forde, Thomas Taylor, & William Stevens (3 of executors) renounced administration on estate of John Clements (merchant, TA). Edward Roe (g), other executor, is dec'd.

8A:104 Mary Clements widow was granted administration for herself & children.

8A:105 Date: 5 May 1676. Witnesses (for Forde & Stevens): Will. Phelps, William Crosse. Witnesses (for Taylor): Richard Nash, Giles Blizard. George Cowley (g) to prove said will. Appraisers: Richard Gorsuch, Anthony Maile. Said Cowley to administer oath.

8A:106 Henry Willcocks (TA) exhibited will of John Singleton (TA). William Bishop (g) to prove said will. Said Henry & Charles Hollinsworth were granted administration. Appraisers: John Elliott, William Chamberlin. Said Bishop to administer oath.

Joyce Gruns (AA) exhibited will of William Gruns (AA). Capt. Richard Hill to prove said will. Said Joyce was granted administration. Appraisers: Henry Sewell, Guy Meeke. Said Hill to administer oath.

8A:107 Emia Eagle (TA) relict & administratrix of John Burgesse (TA) exhibited accounts.

Robert Blinckhorne (CV) executor of William Cussen (CV) exhibited that Jasper Allen, one of the appraisers, is dec'd. New appraisers: James Veitch, John Hollins. Roger Brooke (g) to administer oath.

30 May. Edmund Cantwell (DE) was granted administration on estate of Daniell Macary (CE), who died childless & unmarried. Appraisers: John Hyland, Richard Whitton. Augustine Herman (g) to administer oath.

Court Session: 1676

8A:108 Elisabeth Loggins relict of John Henricks (TA) was granted administration on his estate. Appraisers: John Glover, John Backer. Richard Gorsuch (g) to administer oath.

Thomas Marsh (g, KE), sole surviving executor of Ralph Williams (AA), exhibited that Robertt Burle, joint executor, is dec'd. Appraisers: William Hopkins, Dr. Henry Lewis.
8A:109 Capt. Richard Hill to administer oath.

8A:110 Joseph Weecks (g, KE), one of executors of John Rodway (TA), petitioned for new appraisers: Nathaniell Evetts, James Barckhust. Thomas Hinson (g) to administer oath.

Capt. Richard Hill (AA) was granted administration on estate of Edward Gardner (AA) on behalf of Dorothy & Mary Bruton executrices, during their minority. Security: Edward Dorsey.

Richard Walters (TA) administrator of Richard Hacker (TA) exhibited accounts. Discharge was granted.

8A:111 31 May. Rachael Clarke (AA) was granted administration on estate of Neale Clarke (AA). Col. William Burgesse to prove said will. Appraisers: Nath. Heathcote, Henry Ridgely. Said Burgesse to administer oath.

1 June. Thomas Bland & his wife Damaris relict of Nicholas Wyatt (AA) vs. Edward Dorsey who married one of daughters of said Nicholas. Administration was granted to the widow. Col. Thomas Taylor & Col. William Burgesse to take bond of said Thomas
8A:112 & of said Edward.

Thomas Mathews executor of John Owen vs. John James. Ruling: plaintiff.

Edward Monfrett (BA) exhibited will of William Poultney (BA). Richard Bale (g) to prove said will. Said Edward was granted administration. Appraisers:

John Arden, John Boren. Said Bale to administer oath.

Marmaduke Semmes (SM) was granted administration on estate of Samuell Dickeson (SM), who died childless & unmarried, as principle creditor.
8A:113 Surety: Thomas Wynne. Appraisers: William Watts, William Canady. William Hatton (g) to administer oath.

2 June. Bennett Morgan (CE) widow of Robertt Morgan (CE) was granted administration on his estate. Appraisers: John Browning, John Cox. Abraham Wilde (g) to administer oath.

Robert Burle (g, AA) was ordered to certify the lands of John Keely (AA)
8A:114 & inventory of said John & his wife Mary. Said Robert died before the order was accomplished. Mathew Ward (TA) now to certify & take inventory, with names & ages of orphans.

8A:115 7 June. William Parker (Clifts, CV) was granted administration on estate of James Elton (CV), who died a widower with 1 child, as chief creditor. Surety: George Parker. Appraisers: John Hance, Henry Kent. Richard Ladd (g) to administer oath.

William Stevens (g, SO) administrator of Macom Thomas (SO) exhibited inventory.

Roger Brooke (CV) executor of Philip Harwood (CV) exhibited inventory.

Elisabeth Dundasse (SM) executrix of Helena Forrest (SM) exhibited inventory.

8A:116 Elisabeth Dundasse (SM) widow & executrix of George Dundasse (SM) exhibited inventory.

Rebecca Beale (SM) widow & administratrix of John Beale (SM) exhibited inventory.

Jackeline Moore (CV) widow & executrix of James Moore (CV) exhibited inventory.

Anthony Tall (DO) administrator of William Hambidge (SO) exhibited inventory.

Elisabeth Mackey (SM) widow & executrix of John Mackey (SM) exhibited inventory.

John Bird (BA) administrator of Joseph Pierce (BA) exhibited inventory

8A:117 Nicholas Shaw (CE) administrator of William Shaw (CE) exhibited inventory.

Elisabeth Mackey (SM) executrix of Elisabeth Rawlins (SM) exhibited inventory.

John Stansbey (g, BA) executor of Caesar Prince (BA) exhibited inventory.

Elisabeth Uty (BA) widow & administratrix of Col. Nathaniell Uty (BA) exhibited inventory.

Jane Raven (DO) widow & administratrix of John Raven (DO) exhibited inventory.

John Watkins (AA) executor of John Grose (AA) exhibited inventory.

8A:118 Richard Edelin (SM) executor of Samuell Cressey (CH) exhibited inventory.

Henry Hosier (KE) one of executors of Walter Spencer (KE) exhibited inventory.

Capt. John Cobreth (CV) executor of Richard Evans (CV) exhibited inventory.

Thomas Sterling (CV) administrator of Benjamin Brasseur (CV) exhibited inventory.

Thomas Gerrard (SM) administrator of Marmaduke Snow (SM) exhibited inventory.

Roger Digins (SM) executor of William Bourcke (SM) exhibited inventory.

James Crouche (AA) executor of William Crouche (AA) exhibited inventory.

Court Session: 1676

8A:119 Peter Watts (SM) executor of Robertt Cager (SM) exhibited inventory.

Elisabeth Hutson (KE) widow & administratrix of Richard Hutson (KE) exhibited inventory.

Cornelius Howard (AA) administrator of John Simpson (AA) exhibited inventory.

Jane Crouche (CE) widow & executrix of John Crouche (CE) exhibited inventory.

Mary Allen (CV) widow & administratrix of Jasper Allen (CV) exhibited inventory.

Capt. Richard Hill (AA) exhibited oaths of Cornelius Howard administrator of estate of John Sampson (AA) & the appraisers
8A:120 Abraham Childe & John Hamond, all sworn 29 April 1676.

Edward Roe (g, TA) exhibited renunciation of William Stevens (TA) & Howell Powell as administrators of estate of Thomas Preston (CV). Said Preston's will was dated 26 October 1675.
8A:121 Signed: William Stevens, Jr.

8A:122 Mathew Ward (TA) exhibited oath of:

- Joyce Hewton, sworn 22 April 1676.
- Richard Jones, one of the appraisers of Mathew Hewton, sworn same day.
- Thomas Hinson (g), the other appraiser, sworn 24 April 1676.

James Ringold (g, KE) exhibited the will of Walter Spencer (KE), proved.

Richard Ladd (g, CV) exhibited the nuncupative will of Richard Evans (CV). Also exhibited was oath of Robertt Dixon, sworn 29 January 1675. Also exhibited was oath of Edy Carpenter & Capt. John Cobreth, sworn same day.

8A:123 Col. Samuell Chew (AA) exhibited the will of John Howerton (AA), proved by Henry Bennett & George Buttler. Also exhibited was oath of Richard Deaver, sworn 22 April 1675. Also exhibited was oath of Charles Beven & James Chilcot, appraisers sworn same day.

Col. Samuell Chew (AA) exhibited will of Jeremiah Sullivant (AA), proved by Robert Pew & Richard Wells.
8A:124 Also exhibited was oath of Anne Sullivant relict of Jeremiah Sullivant, sworn 22 April 1676. Also exhibited was oath of John Sollers & Robert Connatt, appraisers sworn same day.

Benjamin Rozer (g, high sheriff, CH) exhibited will of John Bowles (CH), proved by Henry Adams & Thomas Harris on 25 April instant.
8A:125 James Tyre was sworn as executor.

Col. Samuell Chew (AA) exhibited the following dated 18 April 1676:
- Bond of Thomas Sterling on estate of Benjamin Brasseur.
- Oath of Robert Heigh & James Humbes appraisers.

Richard Deavor (AA) administrator of John Howerton (AA) exhibited inventory.

Joyce Hewton (TA) widow & administratrix of Math. Hewton (TA) exhibited inventory.

8A:126 William Parker (CV) administrator of Thomas Preston (CV) exhibited accounts. Continuance was granted.

9 June. Elisabeth Morgan (CE) exhibited will of John Morgan (CE). Capt. Jonathon Sibrey to prove said will. Appraisers: Edward Williams, Philip Holleger. Said Sibrey to administer oath.

10 June. Mary Price (TA) exhibited will of William Price (TA). Philip Stevens (g) to prove said will. Mary Price was granted administration. Appraisers: Edward Stevenson, Jonathon Davis. Said Stevens to administer oath.

Court Session: 1676

8A:127 William Hemsley (TA) exhibited will of William Sturdevant (TA). Philip Stevens (TA) to prove, by oath of Thomas Euell. Rest of witnesses are dec'd. Appraisers: Edw. Stevenson, Jonathon Davis. Said Stevens to administer oath.

13 June. Thomas Docton (AA) exhibited will of Symon Hoges (AA). Robert Franclin (g) to prove said will. Thomas Docton, Sr. was granted administration.

Sarah Barnes (CH) exhibited will of Henry Barnes (CH). Benjamin Rozer (g) to prove said will. Sara Barnes was granted administration.

8A:128 15 June. Margery Stone (CH) exhibited will of Math. Stone (CH). Benjamin Rozer (g) to prove said will. Mary Stone was granted administration. Appraisers: Nicholas Proddy, John Ward. Said Rozer to administer oath.

William Deane (CH) exhibited will of John Preene (CH). Benjamin Rozer (g) to prove said will. William Deane & William Haverd were granted administration. Appraisers (CV): George Lingon, Edward Isack. Nathaniell Trueman (g, CV) to administer oath.

16 June. Arnall Parrimore (SO) exhibited will of John Parremore (SO), proved by Alexander Younger.
8A:129 Said Arnall was granted administration. Appraisers: William Ennis, Henry Bishop. William Stevens (g) to administer oath.

Benjamin Bennett (BA) was granted administration on estate of his brother Andrew Bennett (BA). Appraisers: Samuell Boston, Dennis English. Capt. George Wells to administer oath.

Elisabeth Head (KE) administratrix of Edward Coppidge (KE) exhibited inventory.

Elisabeth Mackart (SM) executrix of John Mackart (SM) exhibited inventory.

8A:130 Joseph Weecks & John Hinson (gentlemen, KE) executors of John Rodaway (TA) were granted continuance.

Samuell Vynes (CV) executor of Cornelius Jones (CV) exhibited inventory.

Robert Tayler (CV) administrator of John Sethbery (CV) exhibited inventory.

Nehemiah Birckhead (AA) executor of Christopher Birckhead (AA) was granted continuance.

8A:131 17 June. Richard Ball (g, BA) exhibited that Robertt Wilson (BA) died intestate. Said Ball is empowered to take inventory.

Mary Stasey (CV) widow of William Stasey (CV) was granted administration on his estate. Appraisers: Thomas Kemp, Thomas Lawson. William Groome (g) to administer oath.

8A:132 20 June. Mary Pope (CH) widow of Thomas Pope (CH) was granted administration on his estate. Appraisers: Thomas Baker, Richard Dod. Benjamin Rozer (g) to administer oath.

Thomas Clipsham (CH) was granted administration on estate of Roger Rowder (SM), who died childless & unmarried, as principle creditor. Appraisers: Francis Wyne, John Fanning. Benjamin Rozer (g) to administer oath.

8A:133 Daniell Clocker & Peter Watts (SM) executors of Daniell Clocker, Sr. (SM) exhibited inventory.

26 June. Stephen Burle (AA) son & heir of Robertt Burle (AA) exhibited his will. Capt. Richard Hill to prove said will. Said Stephen was granted administration. Appraisers: Ralph & William Hawkins. Said Hill to administer oath.

27 June. Philis How (CV) widow of Thomas How was granted administration on

his estate. Appraisers: John Cooper, William Hill. William Travers (g) to administer oath.

8A:134 Anne Grace (SM) widow & executrix of John Grace (SM) exhibited inventory.

Robertt Franclin, Jr. (AA) executor of William Collier (AA) exhibited inventory. Samuell Lane (AA) exhibited will of William Collier, proved by William Webb & Stephen Sebastian. Mr. Robert Franclin was granted administration. Appraisers: John Waters, Robert Lockwood.

Marg. Gittings (CV) widow & executrix of John Gittings (CV) petitioned for new appraisers: David Davis, John Nuthall.
8A:135 Col. Thomas Brooke to administer oath.

Capt. Richard Hill (AA) exhibited will of William Slade (AA), proved. Dr. Henry Lewis & John Rix were granted administration. Date: 10 June 1676.

29 June. Walter Hall (g, Crosse Mannor, SM) exhibited that his wife Margrett presented a petition during the last assembly on behalf of Philip & John Gittings (sons of John Gittings (dec'd) by Margery (sister of said Margrett, dec'd)) that:
8A:136 John Gittings married Margery Mollings (sister of the petitioner) & had 2 sons Philip & John. Said Margery died, & said John Gittings married Margarett Reade (widow). Said John died about 5 months later, leaving just 2 sons. Said Margarett Gittings has guardianship. The children were baptized Roman Catholic, as was the religion of their father & mother. The said Margarett their mother-in-law takes them to meetings of people of a contrary judgement & persuasion. She also tells the children that they are her servants.
8A:137 The petitioner & her husband request guardianship. Ruling: the law prohibits an orphan to remain under a guardian of a contrary judgement or religion. The sons are to be delivered to Walter Hall

(Crosse Mannor, SM) & his wife Margrett (the aunt).

Samuell Abbett (TA) was granted administration on estate of Edward Varing (TA), who died leaving 3 children (all under age).
8A:138 Appraisers: Thomas Alexander, William Hamstid. Richard Gorsuch (g) to administer oath.

Anne Jones (CV) widow & administratrix of Meridith Jones (CV) exhibited inventory.

Jane Thompson (CV) widow & administratrix of James Thompson (CV) exhibited inventory.

Thomas Innes (SM) administrator of Thomas Loquer (SM) exhibited inventory.

8A:139 Roger Brooke (g, CV) executor of Edward Keene (CV) exhibited inventory.

Lidia Solley (SM) widow & administratrix of Benjamin Solley (SM) exhibited accounts.

Sarah Pile (SM) widow & administratrix of John Pile (SM) exhibited inventory & accounts. Said Sarah petitioned for Benjamin Rozer (g, high sheriff, CH) to examine Henry Adams regarding his bill. Joseph Pile (heir) has liberty to cross-examine.

8A:140 Mary Hawkins (AA) widow & executrix of John Hawkins (AA) exhibited inventory.

3 July. Robertt Franclin (g, AA) exhibited will of Symon Hoges, proved. Thomas Docton, Sr. was granted administration.

4 July. Hanna Pott widow of John Pott (CV) exhibited that on 10 August 1675, she exhibited his will & Thomas Trueman, Esq. was to prove said will. Said Trueman was also to swear Edward Iack & James Williams as appraisers. Soon after said 10 August, she was chased

from her plantation by Indians & she came down with a dangerous sickness. Said will has now been proved by Francis Swinfen & James Williams.
8A:141 Said Hanna was granted administration. New appraisers: Ringam Bell, James Williams. Tobias Norton (g) to administer oath.

Mary Hamsted (SM) widow of William Hamsted (SM) was granted administration on his estate. Surety: Arthur Hert. Appraisers: Thomas Courtney, Francis Miles. Col. William Calvert to administer oath.

Nathaniell Stiles (g, CE) administrator of Thomas Salmon (CE) exhibited inventory.

Joseph Edly (SM) executor of William Cane (SM) exhibited inventory.

8A:142 5 July. William Yorke (BA) exhibited that pursuant to ultimate March 1674, the Commissioners of BA have taken into their custody the estate of the orphans of Capt. John Collier (BA). Said Yorke is administrator of the estate of said Collier. At the County Court on 7 June, said Yorke complained of being molested by Lodowick Williams regarding the said estate. A restraining order is sought against said Williams.
8A:143 Signed: George Utie, John Waterton, Tho. Hedge. Date: 19 June 1676. Said Yorke was granted said order.

Kenelm Cheseldyn & Robertt Ridgely for William King vs. William Dare administrator of John Parcker (merchant).
8A:144 Said Dare is ready to depart the Province in ship of Capt. John Body. Exceptions were exhibited. Mentions: bill of John Pitts,
8A:145 & charges regarding ship John of Waymouth.
8A:146 Signed: William King. Exceptions mention:
8A:147 Thomas Notley, Richard Moy, Thomas Bincks, Roger Baker, Thomas Clagett,

Christopher Rowsby, Richard Bayley (seaman's wages), John Edmundson,
8A:148 William Twisse & Co., George Thompson, Francis Pine, Thomas Knighton.
8A:149 ...

8A:150 John Waterton (g, BA) exhibited will of Thomas Arminger (BA), proved. Thomas Preston (BA) executor of Thomas Arminger (BA) exhibited inventory.

Thomas Jones (BA) administrator of Walter Mackenell (BA) exhibited inventory.

10 July. William King vs. William Dare administrator of John Parker.
8A:151 Answer to exceptions. Mentions: Joseph Baker, Mr. Carvill, John Pitt, ship John of Weymouth owned by Mr. Eadoth Ryatt (Weymouth) & Mr. John West (Dorchester), Mr. Robert Carvile,
8A:152 Mr. Ridgely & Mordecai Hunton.
8A:153 Answer to accounts. Mentions: William Berry executor of John Parker, Mr. Thomas Notley & Mr. Moy & Thomas Clegett,
8A:154 Mr. Roger Baker, Thomas Bincks,
8A:155 (N) Bayley for the seamen of the John of Weymouth, Mr. Robert Carvile, John Edmundson, (N) Twisse & Co.,
8A:156 Geore Thompson, widow Pine, Tobias Wells administrator of (N) Pines,
8A:157 Mr. Knighton (who was sued in AA), Mr. Royston. Signed: William Dare.
8A:158 Robertt Ridgely procurator of said King petitioned for a copy & that said Dare be restricted from leaving the Province. Ruling: there were sufficient assets for said King's debt, as well as a judgement obtained by John Grammer in CV County Court. Thomas Wynne to serve writ.

8A:159 11 July. William Dare exhibited bond by Richard Ladd (g, CV).

Thomas Docton (AA) was granted administration on estate of William Pagett (AA), who died childless & unmarried & having no relations in the Province but the wife of said Docton. Appraisers: Thomas Forde, John Wilson.

Samuell Lane (g) to administer oath.

17 June [sic]. Diana Fitting (AA) widow of Robert Fitting (AA) was granted administration on his estate.
8A:160 Appraisers: Robert Franclin, Walter Carre. Lt. Col. Thomas Taylor (also Thomas Taillor) to administer oath.

Arthur Wright (KE) was granted administration on estate of Richard Pierce (KE). Surety: Michael Miller. Appraisers: Thomas Wright, Peter Evans. William Lawrence (g) to administer oath.

8A:161 19 July. Thomas Docton (AA) administrator of William Pagett exhibited that the appraisers Thomas Foord & John Wilson refused to take the oath. New appraisers: Thomas Knighton, Patrick Hall. Samuell Lane (g) to administer oath.

20 July. John Coode (g, SM) exhibited the will of Thomas Ceely (SM), proved by William West. Peter Ceely brother & executor of said Thomas is currently in ENG. John Coode, overseer, was granted administration, on behalf of said Peter. Appraisers: William Watts, Justinian Gerrard. William Rosewell (g) to administer oath.

8A:162 Col. Jesse Wharton (Deputy Governor) exhibited PoA from William Leigh (Parish of Christ's Church, Barbadoes) & his wife Sarah relict of Edward Oistine (g, Barbadoes). Said William & Sarah are administrators of said Oistine, per Sir Jonathon Atkins, Knight, Capt. General & Chief Governor of Barbadoes. Said Wharton to receive of Wenlock Christenson 3 Negroes: Negro Ned, Negro Joley, Negro Jack.
8A:163 Date: 20 March 1675. Witnesses: Edward Leach, Thomas Peighim, John Westcott. Confirmation by Sir Jonathon Atkins.
8A:164 Date: 18 March 1675. Witness: Edwyn Slede. William Leigh & his wife Sarah obtained LoA in 1671.
8A:165 Securities: Capt. John Gasely, Capt. Thomas Odrane. Date: 18 March 1675.

Witness: Edwyn Slede. Said Wharton was granted administration on estate of Edward Oistine.

8A:166 22 July. Kenelm Cheseldyn (g, SM) exhibited bond of John Brewer & Francis Holland (AA) on said Brewer's administration of John Hatton (merchant).
8A:167 Signed: John Bruer, Francis Holland. Date: 14 July 1676. Witness: William Bretton.

Capt. George Wells (BA) exhibited will of James Ogdon (AA). Col. Samuell Chew to prove said will. Appraisers: John Sollers, Henry Archer. Said Chew to administer oath.

8A:168 Benjamin Rozer (g, high sheriff, CH) exhibited nuncupative will of Patrick Farlum, proved. Thomas Carey was granted administration. Appraisers: Nicholas Cooper, Edmund Taylor. Said Rozer to administer oath.

Henry Exon (CV) executor of Thomas Cosford (CV) exhibited inventory.

Henry Exon (CV) executor of Thomas Arnold (CV) exhibited inventory.

1 August. Elisabeth Wharton widow of Jesse Wharton (Deputy Lt.) was granted administration on his estate.
8A:169 Securities: Thomas Notley (Deputy Lt.), Benjamin Rozer (g). Appraisers (CH): William Chandler (g), Thomas Hussey (g). Benjamin Rozer (g) to administer oath. Appraisers (CV): Christopher Rowsby (g), Capt. John Pierce.

7 August. Col. Vincent Lowe (high sheriff, TA) exhibited will of Humphrey Archer (TA), proved. Appraisers: William Gaskins, Henry Clay. Said Lowe to administer oath.

8 August. John Ireland (BA) exhibited will of Margrett Penroy (CE). Capt. George Wells to prove said will.
8A:170 Anthony Copman sole heir & executor per

will is dec'd & left no heirs of his body. Said Penroy has no relations in this Province. Said Ireland was granted administration, as chief creditor. Appraisers: James Jues, William Palmer. Said Wells to administer oath.

10 August. Col. William Burgesse & Lt. Col. Thomas Taillor (AA) exhibited commission to take bond of Thomas Bland on behalf of Damaris Bland relict of Nicholas Wyatt
8A:171 (AA) & on their refusal to take bond of Edward Dorsey who married a daughter of the dec'd. Date: 10 July 1676. Thomas Bland & Damaris Bland refused to give bond. Edward Dorsey gave bond. Said Edward was granted administration. Appraisers: Cornelius Howard, Mathew Howard. Capt. Richard Hill to administer oath.

12 August. Mary Blackfan (CH) relict of Thomas Stone (CH) exhibited his will. Benjamin Rozer (g) to prove said will. Said Blackfan was granted administration. Appraisers: Edward Price, Thomas Crackson. Said Rozer to administer oath.

8A:172 Notice to Commissioners of CV County Court to take into their care the lands of George Beckwith (CV, dec'd) for his orphans & to exhibit an inventory.

8A:173 14 August. Lewis Blangey (AA) administrator of James Hill (AA) exhibited inventory & accounts.

15 August. Mary Jones (SM) relict & executrix of John Davis (SM) exhibited accounts.

16 August. Andrew Robertts (AA) exhibited will of Charles Lawrence (AA). Lt. Col. Thomas Taylor to prove said will. Said Roberts was granted administration. Appraisers: Thomas Francis, Ferdinando Baty. Said Taylor to administer oath.

8A:174 Mr. John Wells (high sheriff, AA) for Alice Roper (AA) relict & administratrix of Jervis Morgan (AA) was granted administration on his estate. She is unable to travel to the Office. Lt. Col. Thomas Taylor to administer oath.

19 August. Anne Medley (SM) widow of John Medley (SM) was granted administration on his estate. Sureties: John Warren, Ignatius Warren. Appraisers: Richard Gary, Peter Mills. John Warren (g) to administer oath.

William Stevens, Jr. (TA) one of the executors of Nicholas Homes (TA) renounced administration on said estate.
8A:175 Samuell Abbott exhibited will of said dec'd. Richard Gorsuch (g) to prove said will. Said Abbott was granted administration. Appraisers: Henry Alexander, Thomas Martin. Said Gorsuch to administer oath.

8A:176 21 August. William Barton, Jr. & Robertt Roelants (CH) executors of Richard Smoote (CH) exhibited his will. Benjamin Rozer (g, high sheriff, CH) to prove said will. Said Barton & Roelants were granted administration. Appraisers: John Cage, George Creodwell. Said Rozer to administer oath.

23 August. Hester Ennis (CV) widow of William Ennis (CV) was granted administration on his estate. Appraisers: Thomas Sprigg, Guy White. Cuttbert Fenwick (g) to administer oath.

8A:177 25 August. Margrett Gregory (SM) widow of Charles Gregory (SM) was granted administration on his estate. Appraisers: Thomas Simpson, Richard Edelen. Capt. Joshua Doyne to administer oath.

Mary Clements (TA) widow & administratrix of John Clements (TA) exhibited inventory.

Mary Roe (TA) widow & executrix of Edward Roe (TA) exhibited inventory.

Edward Manne (g, TA) exhibited will of Capt. Edward Roe, proved. Appraisers: Anthony Male, Thomas Alexander.
8A:178 Date: 3 July 1676. Signed: Edward Man. Mary Roe one of the executors was granted administration.

George Cowley (g, TA) exhibited will of John Clements (TA), proved. Appraisers: Richard Gorsuch, Anthony Maile. Mary Clements widow & relict was granted administration. Bondsman: William Forde (merchant).

8A:179 Wenlock Christenson (TA) & his wife Elisabeth relict of Robert Harwood renounced administration on his estate, and recommended that Edward Man (merchant) have administration. Date: 31 July 1676. Witness: Ri. Gorsuch. John Edmundson releases his caveat against the estate. Date: July 1676. Witness: Phi. Lloyd. Briant O'maly on behalf of James Holland & Luther Willmore cite a caveat against said estate.
8A:180 Edward Man was granted administration on said estate. Sureties: Richard Gorsuch (g), Richard Swettnam (carpenter). Appraisers: George Cowley, Thomas Alexander. Richard Gorsuch (g) to administer oath.

31 August. Richard Beard (AA) exhibited will of Daniell Taylor (AA). Col. William Burgesse to prove said will. Appraisers: William Jones, Henry Ridgely. Said Burgesse to administer oath.

8A:181 4 September. James Coursey (g, TA) exhibited the renunciation of Margrett Scott widow of John Scott (p, TA) on administration of his estate, per Kenelm Cheseldyn & John Blomfield. Mr. James Coursey, creditor, was recommended as administrator.
8A:182 Date: 22 May 1676. Witnesses: Arthur Emery, James Moore, John Eillittson. Said Coursey was granted administration. Appraisers: Arthur Emery, Robertt Roelants. William Coursey (g) to

administer oath.

Arthur Emery (TA) exhibited will of John Wright (TA). William Coursey (g) to prove said will.

8A:183 Arthur Emery married Catherine widow of said Wright, & she is now dec'd intestate, leaving 2 orphans by said Wright, with said Emery. Arthur Emery was granted administration, on behalf of said orphans. Appraisers: Robert Ellis, Thrustram Thomas. Said Coursey to administer oath.

William Hemsley (TA) exhibited renunciation of Mary Price as administratrix of estate of William Price (TA).

8A:184 She appointed Mathew Ward & Peter Sayer as PoA, & recommended said Hemsley, one of the creditors, as administrator. Date: 1 July 1676.

8A:185 Witnesses: James Clayland, Mary Clayland. Said Hemsley was granted administration. Appraisers: Edward Stevenson, Arthur Emery. Philip Stevens (g) to administer oath.

William Lawrence (g, KE) exhibited will of Richard Moore (KE), proved.

8A:186 Joseph Hopkins (g, CE) exhibited will of William Morgan (CE), proved.

William Rosewell (g, SM) exhibited will of John Mackort (SM), proved.

William Lawrence (g, KE) exhibited will of Margrett Hill (KE), proved.

Col. William Burgesse (g, AA) exhibited will of Neale Clarke, proved.

7 September. William Bishop (g, TA) exhibited will of John Singleton (TA), proved.

Inventory of George & Frances Beckwith was exhibited.

8A:187 William Rosewell (g, SM) exhibited inventory of Robertt Perry (SM).

Mary Allen (CV) widow & administratrix of Jasper Allen (CV) exhibited inventory of said Allen & accounts of John Martin (merchant, Barbadoes, said Jasper was administrator).

Casea White (SM) widow & administratrix of Rowland White (SM) exhibited inventory.

Margrett Gittings (CV) widow of John Gittings (CV) exhibited inventory.

Rebecca Dent (SM) widow & executrix of Thomas Dent (SM) exhibited inventory.

Mary Hamstid (SM) widow & administratrix of William Hamstid (SM) exhibited inventory.

8A:188 9 September. Vincent Mansfield (SM) administrator of Richard Foster & his wife Sarah (SM) exhibited inventory.

Rebecca Dent (SM) widow & executrix of Thomas Dent (SM) who was executor of Henry Hull exhibited inventory of said Hull.

Guilbert Turbervile (SM) administrator of Francis Graile (SM) exhibited inventory.

Joseph Sears (CE) administrator of William Sethbery (CE) exhibited inventory.

Thomas Mathews (CE) executor of John Owen (CE) exhibited inventory.

Mary Wells (KE) widow & administratrix of Tobias Wells (KE) exhibited inventory.

8A:189 Samuell Bourne (CV) administrator of Robertt Taverner (CV) exhibited inventory.

Anne Medley (SM) widow & administratrix of John Medley (SM) who was executor of George Medley (SM) exhibited inventory of said George.

Philis How (CV) widow & administratrix of Thomas How (CV) exhibited inventory.

Elisabeth Royall (SM) executrix of Francis Barnell (SM) exhibited inventory.

John Davis (TA) administrator of William Taylor (TA) exhibited inventory.

Thomas Casey (CH) executor of Patrick Farloe (CH) exhibited inventory.

8A:190 Mary Connery (SM) widow & administratrix of Edward Connery (SM) exhibited inventory.

Henry Hooper, Jr. (CV) administrator of Henry Hooper, Sr. (CV) exhibited inventory.

Isack Winchester (KE) administrator of Richard Moore (KE) exhibited inventory.

Tabitha Mill (CV) widow & executrix of William Mill (CV) exhibited inventory.

Hanna Baxter (KE) executrix of Thomas Baxter (KE) exhibited inventory.

Anne Rye (KE) widow & administratrix of John Rye (KE) exhibited inventory.

Alice Ginne (KE) widow & executrix of Arthur Ginne (KE) exhibited inventory.

8A:191 William Hatton (g, SM) administrator of Richard Hatton (SM) exhibited inventory.

Anne Sudevant (AA) widow & executrix of Jeremiah Sudevant (AA) exhibited inventory.

Samuell Abbott (TA) administrator of Edward Vearing (TA) exhibited inventory.

Martha Morgan (CE) widow & executrix of William Morgan (CE) exhibited inventory.

Thomas Coke (SM) administrator of John Coke (SM) exhibited inventory.

Margrett Cooper (AA) widow & administratrix of Thomas Cooper (AA) exhibited inventory.

Thomas Marsh (high sheriff, KE) sole surviving executor of Ralph Williams (AA) exhibited accounts. Robert Burle (AA) co-executor is dec'd.

8A:192 William Stevens (g, SO) exhibited will of Richard Ackworth (SO), proved. Anne Ackworth administratrix was granted administration.

William Hatton (g, SM) exhibited the oaths of the following appraisers:

- estate of Helena Forrest sworn on 12 May 1676.
- estate of George Dundasse sworn on 1 June 1676.
- estate of Thomas Cager sworn on 21 June 1676.
- Peter Watts & John Chevrill appraisers for estate of George Bartlett sworn on 1 April 1676.
- for estate of Samuell Dickeson sworn on 19 June.

8A:193 Col. Vincent Lowe (TA) exhibited oaths of appraisers for estate of William Taylor (TA) sworn on 17 June 1676.

Nathaniell Heathcote (g, AA) exhibited oaths of appraisers for estate of Sara Francis (AA) & John Shaw (AA) sworn on 1 August 1676.

James Ringold (g, KE) exhibited oath of Mary Wells administratrix of Tobias Wells (KE), sworn 10 March 1675/6.
8A:194 Also exhibited was oath of Isack Winchester & Thomas Osborne, appraisers sworn same day.

Said James Ringold exhibited oath of Anne Rye administratrix of John Rye (KE), sworn 19 June 1676. Also exhibited oath of William Towlson & William Rathman, appraisers sworn same day.

William Rosewell (g, SM) exhibited oaths of the following appraisers:

- estate of Daniell Murphy sworn on 15 April 1676.
- 4 estate of John Groce sworn on 6 September 1676.

8A:195 ...

- estate of Marmaduke Snow sworn on 4 March 1675.

Richard Lad (g, CV) exhibited oath of Samuell Bourne administrator of Robertt Taverner, sworn 15 February 1675.

Richard Gorsuch (g, TA) exhibited oaths of:

- Thomas Alexander & Clement Yaile, appraisers of Edward Varing (TA) sworn 10 July 1676.
- John Glover & John Barker, appraisers of John Hendricks sworn 21 June 1676.

8A:196 John White (g, SO) exhibited oath of William Stevens (g) administrator of Maccom Thomas. Also exhibited oath of Edward Wale & Walter Powell, appraisers.

Capt. Leonard Webber deposed on 13 March 1675, that George Beckwith on 3 November last told he that the deponent made a will before he came from MD, which he thought was not fit & desired to leave all to his wife.

8A:197 Joseph Hopkins (g, CE) exhibited will of John Owen (CE), proved.

- Thomas Mathews (p, CE) executor was sworn 6 June 1676.
- William Salsbury & Giles Porter, appraisers were sworn on 6 June 1676.

Joseph Hopkins exhibited oath of Joseph Sears (merchant, CE) administrator of William Sethbery (CE), sworn 12 May 1676. Also exhibited oath of Richard Adams & Cornelius Arenson, appraisers sworn 17 April 1676.

<u>10 September</u>. Robertt Blinckhorne (CV) executor of William Cussen (CV)

exhibited inventory.

8A:198 Henry Ward (CE) administrator of Abraham Coffin (CE) exhibited inventory.

Thomas Francis (AA) administrator of Sara Francis late Sarah Shaw & of John Shaw (AA) exhibited both inventories.

Mathew Ward (TA) & William Bishop (TA) administrators Robertt Mackline (TA) exhibited inventory.

Joseph Hopkins (g, CE) exhibited nuncupative will of Thomas Middlefield (CE). Martha Shaw relict was granted administration.

8A:199 13 September. John Blackfan (CH) was granted administration on estate of Richard Owen (CH), for the use of the orphans. Appraisers: Richard Way, Christopher Wardner. John Stone (g) to administer oath.

John Stone (g, CH) executor of Verlinda Stone (CH) exhibited that one of the appraisers, his brother Mathew Stone, is dec'd. New appraisers: Richard Migley, Simon Stevens. Benjamin Rozer (g) to administer oath.

8A:200 16 September. Mary Young (CV) relict & administratrix of William Stacey (CV) exhibited inventory.

William Hatton (g, SM) & Robertt Graham (p, SM) 2 of executors of John Cunningham (SM) renounced administration on said estate.

8A:201 ...

8A:202 Thomas Carlisle exhibited will of said John Cunningham, proved by John Wynne (chirurgeon). Thomas Carlisle & John Wattson executors were granted administration. Appraisers: John Wachop, William Canady. Richard Ladd (g) to administer oath.

18 September. Accounts of estate of George & Frances Beckwith (CV) was exhibited to John Hall for use of

children & servants.

8A:203 William Watts (SM) administrator of Thomas Cager (SM) exhibited inventory.

George Young (CV) administrator of William Young (CV) exhibited inventory.

23 September. Margrett Gregory (SM) widow of Charles Gregory (SM) renounced administration on his estate. Date: 15 September 1676. Witnesses: Richard Edelen, Robertt Browne.
8A:204 John Cage (CH) was granted administration on said estate, as greatest creditor. Appraisers: John Coles, John Clarke. John Fanning (g) to administer oath.

25 September. William Groome (g, CV) exhibited will of John Anderson, proved by William Head & Henry Norman on 17 July 1676.
8A:205 Mary Anderson executrix was sworn same day. Said John devised to said Mary & child she goes with, & said child was not then on "rerum natura". James Rumsey & John Aldwell, appraisers sworn same day.

26 September. George Parker procurator for Samuell Bourne (g, CV) exhibited that Levin Johnson (cooper, CV) made a will at the house of John Hance (Clifts, CV)
8A:206 & said will was proved. Said will is since lost. Said Bourne was granted administration, on behalf of the devisees Thomas & Elisabeth Billingsly (children of Thomas Billingsly (dec'd)). Appraisers: John Hance, William Bennett. Robertt Heigh to administer oath.

Samuell Bourne (CV) was empowered on 13 April last to take bond & swear Henry Jowles (g, CV)
8A:207 as administrator of Andrew Higgs. Said Jowles has not yet provided bond. Continuance granted.

Thomas Bancks (CV) exhibited LoA to has as administrator of George Beckwith

(CV).

8A:208 Appraisers: William Travers, John Hall. Col. Thomas Brooke to administer oath.

Hanna Pott exhibited inventory of her husband John Pott, by appraisers Ninian Beale & James Williams.

8A:209 Inventory of James Elton (CV) was exhibited, by appraisers Henry Kent & John Hance.

Richard Johns (CV) who married relict of Thomas Sparrow (AA) exhibited his wife's renunciation of administration. Other executor is Salmon Sparrow, who has neither accepted nor renounced. Said Salmon was summoned. Appraisers (AA): Thomas Francis, Richard Tydings. Lt. Col. Thomas Taylor to administer oath.

8A:210 James Rigby (AA) exhibited will of William Drury (AA). Capt. Richard Hill to prove said will. Appraisers: Robert Davage, Ralph Hawkins. Said Hill to administer oath.

Thomas Bland (AA) on behalf of his wife Damaris Bland relict of Nich. Wyatt exhibited accounts on estate of said Wyatt.

Henry Adams (g, CH) exhibited will of Thomas Mathews (CH), proved.

8A:211 Jane Mathews (CH) executrix was granted administration. Also exhibited oath of Capt. William Boreman & Ignatius Caussin, appraisers sworn 11 March 1675. Said Jane exhibited inventory.

28 September. John Welsh vs. Robertt Carvile procurator for John Watkins (AA) executor of John Grose (AA) on behalf of Richard Snoden & his wife Elisabeth (daughter of Roger Grose (dec'd)) & rest of orphans. Answer exhibited.

8A:212 Mentions other children (all infants, under age 21): Roger Grose, William Grose, & Frances Grose. Guardian is said Watkins. Anne widow of Roger Grose was granted administration on estate of said Roger & then married libellant.

8A:213 John Groce (dec'd) is eldest son of said Roger, being of age & guardian to his younger brothers, endeavored to obtain the estates of his siblings. Said John is now dec'd & nothing has been done.
8A:214 On 19 October 1672, John Groce was appointed guardian of his younger brothers & sisters. MM Thomas Taylor, Robertt Franclin, Richard Ewen, & John Watkins to take account of the orphans' estate,
8A:215 & to made division of estate. Said John Welsh did deliver accordingly. Mentions: Thomas Bradely (convicted of felony & transported out of Province).
8A:216 ...
8A:217 Signed: Robert Carvile (for the defendants). John Welsh (high sheriff, AA) by his attorney Robertt Ridgely was given a copy of the answer.

John Rowsby who married Barbara (one of daughters of Henry & Frances Morgan (dec'd, KE)) vs. Peter Sayer who married Frances (other daughter & administratrix of dec'd). Plaintiffs exhibited
8A:218 that said Frances was granted administration on 8 January 1673. Afterwards, she married Peter Sayers. On 18 May 1675, she exhibited an imperfect inventory.
8A:219 Mentions: sales of portions of estate to Langden Foster & Thompson, John Deery.
8A:220 Signed: Robert Carvile.

8A:221 Augustine Herman (g, CE) exhibited will of John Poole (CE), proved. Date: 19 July 1676.

Abraham Wilde (g) exhibited oath of Bennett Morgan administratrix of Robertt Morgan (CE), sworn 18 July. Also exhibited oath of John Cock appraiser sworn same day, & John Browning appraiser sworn 22 July. Inventory was exhibited.
8A:222 Augustine Herman (g, CE) exhibited oath of Capt. Edmund Cantwell administrator of Daniell Makary. Inventory dated 19 July was exhibited, by appraisers John Hyland & Richard Witthan.

Sarah Poole (CE) executrix of John Poole (CE) exhibited inventory.

Catherine Montegue (DO) widow & administratrix of Henry Montegue (TA) exhibited inventory.

8A:223 Edward Dorsey (AA) administrator of Nicholas Wyatt (AA) exhibited inventory.

2 October. Edward Manne (merchant, TA) was granted administration on estate of Thomas Read (TA), who died childless & unmarried, as principle creditor. Anthony Maile (g) to take bond of Edward Man. Appraisers: George Horlock, Henry Parker. Said Mayle to administer oath.

Thomas Loggins (TA) was granted administration on estate of Richard Walters (TA).
8A:224 Appraisers: John Whittington, Samuell Farmer. Richard Gorsuch (g) to administer oath.

Cornelius Howard (AA) exhibited will of William Carpenser (AA). Capt. Richard Hill to prove said will. Said Howard was granted administration.
8A:225 Appraisers: John Hammon, Abraham Child. Said Hill to administer oath.

Augustine Herman (g, CE) exhibited will of John Carre (CE), proved. Peternella Oldfield relict & executrix was granted administration.

Dr. Henry Lewis & John Rix (AA) executors of William Slade exhibited inventory.

3 October. John Rowsby who married Barbara (one of daughters of Henry & Frances Morgan (dec'd)) vs. Peter Sayers (TA) on behalf of self & his wife Frances (other daughter & administratrix of dec'd). Col. Henry Coursey or Capt. Philemon Lloyd to take oath of said Frances regarding her answer
8A:226 & her accounts.

Emia Eagle (TA) relict & administratrix of John Burgesse was granted discharge.

4 October. Thomas Mathews (CE) executor of John Owen (CE) exhibited accounts.
8A:227 Notice given to creditors.

Mary Whetstone (KE) exhibited will of Stephen Whetstone (KE). Maj. Joseph Weeks to prove said will. Said Mary was granted administration.
8A:228 Appraisers: Robertt Parck, Bennett Steers. Said Weeks to administer oath.

Benjamin Rozer (g, high sheriff, CH) exhibited oath of Thomas Clipsham administrator of Roger Rowder, sworn 10 July. Bondsman: Mathew Hill.
8A:229 Also exhibited oath of John Fanning & Francis Wynne, appraisers sworn 25 August 1676.

Benjamin Rozer (g, CH) exhibited oath of Thomas King (CH) administrator of Samuell Sherrill (CH), sworn 24 July. Bondsman: John Hamelton.
8A:230 Also exhibited oath of John Wheeler & Nich. Prody, appraisers sworn 17 July 1676.

Benjamin Rozer (g, high sheriff, CH) exhibited oath of Mary Pope (CH) widow & administratrix of Thomas Pope (CH), sworn 28 June 1676. Bondsmen (CH): Robert Ware, Philip Lynes. Also exhibited oath of Thomas Baker & Richard Dod, appraisers sworn 21 July 1676.
8A:231 Inventory was exhibited.

Margery Stone (CH) widow & executrix of Mathew Stone (CH) exhibited inventory.

Thomas King (CH) administrator of Samuell Cooper (CH) exhibited inventory.

Richard Beck (CH) administrator of Lewis Beck (CH) exhibited inventory.

Joyce Brummale (CV) executrix of Richard Brumale (CV) exhibited inventory.

Court Session: 1676

CV County Court at Calverton in Patuxent on 20 March 1676.

8A:232 Commissioners: Maj. Tho. Brooke, Mr. Cuthb. Fenwick, Mr. Sam. Borne, Mr. Rich. Ladd, Mr. Rog. Brooke, Mr. William Travers.

- Richard Brommall proved himself of full age & petitioned for his estate.
- Coward Cowdry, age 45, deposed that said Richard was born 21 years ago.
- Thomas Rowdell & William Turner summoned.

John Watkins (AA) executor of John Grose exhibited that Jonas Kinsey (dec'd, TA) was indebted to said Grose. Said Watkins was granted administration on estate of said Kinsey.
8A:233 Bondsman: John Welsh (high sheriff, AA). Appraisers: John Davis, Francis Brookes. Capt. Philemon Lloyd to administer oath.

John Edmundson for Catherine Montegue (DO) exhibited accounts of Henry Montegue (TA). Dr. Robertt Winsmore to prove accounts.

John Edmundson for Elisabeth Loggins (TA) relict & administratrix of John Henricks (TA) exhibited accounts. Richard Gorsuch (g) to prove accounts.

8A:234 Edward English (merchant, CE) administrator of William Hewett was granted continuance.

Capt. Jonathon Sibrey (high sheriff, CE) exhibited will of John Morgan, proved. Elisabeth Morgan executrix was granted administration.
8A:235 Inventory was exhibited.

Rachell Clerk (AA) widow & executrix of Neale Clerke (AA) exhibited inventory.

Peternella Oldfield (CE) relict & executrix of Capt. John Carre (CE) exhibited inventory.

Court Session: 1676

Bennett Morgan (CE) widow & administratrix of Robert Morgan (CE) exhibited inventory.

Col. William Burgesse (AA) exhibited will of Daniell Taylor (AA), proved on 14 September 1676.
8A:236 Peter Barnett & Richard Beard, Jr. were granted administration. Also exhibited was oath of William Jones & Henry Ridgely, appraisers sworn 18 September 1676. Inventory was exhibited.

8A:237 Benjamin Rozer (high sheriff, CH) exhibited will of George Goodrick (CH), proved on 9 September 1676. Robert Goodrick & Francis Goodrick were granted administration. Also exhibited was oath of John Alward & Jacob Peterson, appraisers sworn same day.

Benjamin Rozer (high sheriff, CH) exhibited will of John Greene (CH),
8A:238 proved on 27 September 1676. William Deane & William Stannard were granted administration.

Benjamin Rozer (high sheriff, CH) exhibited will of Thomas Stone (CH), proved on 25 September 1676.
8A:239 Mary Blackfan relict was granted administration. Appraisers: Edward Price, Thomas Craxon.

Benjamin Rozer (high sheriff, CH) exhibited will of Henry Barnes (CH), proved on 12 August 1676.
8A:240 Sarah Barnes executrix was granted administration. Appraisers: Robert Robins, William Standover.

Benjamin Rozer (high sheriff, CH) exhibited will of Mathew Stone (CH), proved on 7 August 1676.
8A:241 Margery Stone executrix was granted administration. Appraisers: Nicholas Proddy, John Ward.

Benjamin Rozer (high sheriff, CH) exhibited the following oaths:

- William Chandler & Thomas Hussey, appraisers of Jesse Wharton sworn 15

August 1676.

8A:242 ...

- Robert Robins & John Wheeler appraisers of Owen Jones sworn 13 August 1676.
- Thomas Galey & William Smith appraisers of Richard Fowkes sworn 15 August 1676.

6 October. Capt. John Cood (SM) administrator of Thomas Ceely (SM) exhibited inventory.

Francis & Henry Stockett (AA) executors of Thomas Stockett (AA) exhibited accounts.

8A:243 Col. Vincent Lowe (high sheriff, TA) exhibited will of Humphrey Archer (TA), proved. Ralph Dawson executor was granted administration.

Thomas Bancks (CV) administrator of George & Frances Beckwith (CV) exhibited that William Travers, one of the appraisers, would not take the oath. New appraisers: John Halls, William Hill.

William Rosewell (g, SM) administrator of Nicholas Ritcheson (SM) exhibited that Bennet Marshegay, one of the appraisers, has gone to ENG. New appraisers: John Woodward, Kenelm Macloughlin. Benjamin Rozer to administer oath.

8A:244 William Wells (CH) was granted administration on estate of David Maddox (CH), who died childless & unmarried, as chief creditor. Appraisers: Archibald Wahop, George Godfrey. Benjamin Rozer (high sheriff, CH) to administer oath.

12 October. Henry Boston, Jr. (SO) was granted administration on estate of his father Henry Boston, Sr. (SO).
8A:245 Appraisers: Stephen Horsy, Charles Halls. William Stevens (g) to administer oath.

Court Session: 1676

13 October. William Parker (g, CV) administrator of James Elton (CV) exhibited accounts. Discharge was granted.

Thomas Bancks (CV) administrator of George Beckwith exhibited that appraisers John Halls & William Hill
8A:246 refused to take the oath. New appraisers: Thomas Sprigg, John Griggs.

Henry Haslewood (g, BA) exhibited will of John Lee (BA), proved. Florence Lee executrix was granted administration.

The widow Shills (SO) exhibited will of Thomas Shills (SO). William Stevens (g) to prove said will. Said widow executrix was granted administration. Appraisers: Nicholas Rice, Thomas Holebrooke. Said Stevens to administer oath.

8A:247 14 October. Catherine Shadwell (BA) was granted administration on estate of John Shadwell (BA). Appraisers: Thomas Jones, James Collier. Capt. John Waterton to administer oath.

Richard Leake (CE) exhibited that Thomas Ward & his wife Margrett are both dec'd, leaving 4 small children &
8A:248 leaving a small estate.
8A:249 Inventory exhibited for said Ward.

Mathew & John Erickson (KE) administrators of Edward Jones (KE) exhibited inventory.

Michael Miller for Mary Eaton (KE) exhibited will of Jeremiah Eaton (KE). Desboro Bennett (g) to prove said will. Said Mary was granted administration. Appraisers: Michael Miller, Mathew Erickson. Said Bennett to administer oath.

8A:250 16 October. Elisabeth Rawls (KE) relict & executrix of William Head (KE) was granted discharge.

18 October. Richard Fenwick (CV) was granted administration on estate of his brother Cutberth Fenwick (CV). Appraisers: Robert Clarke, David Davis. Col. Thomas Brooke to administer oath.

8A:251 Thomas Marsh (high sheriff, KE) surviving executor of Ralph Williams (AA) exhibited an additional inventory.

24 October. William Travers (g, CV) exhibited that Richard Roberts (CV) is dec'd, leaving no relations except 1 boy who is infirm by sickness. Said Travers is empowered to take an inventory & to collect debts. Appraisers: Capt. Thomas Clegett, Mr. William Hill. Richard Ladd to administer oath.

8A:252 ultimate October. Jonathon Sibrey (high sheriff, CE) exhibited that Joseph Sears (merchant, CE) is dec'd, leaving a wife in ENG. Said Sibrey was granted administration, on behalf of the widow. Appraisers: George Gunnell, Edward Gunnell. Capt. Joseph Hopkins to administer oath.

8A:253 James Sedgewick (TA) exhibited that he did not know that his kinsman Miles Cooke was dec'd intestate.

4 November. Raymond Stapleford (DO) was granted administration on estate of Richard Robertts (smith, CV), who died unmarried, as principle creditor. William Travers (g, CV) is empowered to take inventory. Bondsman: Garrett Vansweringen (g).
8A:254 Appraisers: John Griggs, John Halls. William Travers (g) to administer oath.

John Rowsby who married Barbara (one of daughters of Henry & Frances Morgan (dec'd)) vs. Peter Sayer who married Frances (other daughter & administratrix of said dec'd). Col. Henry Coursey (TA) exhibited commission & answer of said Sayers,
8A:255 sworn on 30 October 1676. Mentions: said Frances was given LoA before her marriage to Capt. Peter Sayer,

Court Session: 1676

8A:256 Philemon Lloyd & Richard Wollman are appraisers,
8A:257 John Deery,
8A:258 Capt. Jonathon Sibrey who married Frances relict of said Henry Morgan.
8A:259-260 ...
8A:261 John Rowsby by his attorney Robertt Carvile was granted a copy of the answer.

8A:262 Richard Gorsuch (g, TA) exhibited oath of George Cowley & Thomas Alexander, appraisers of Robertt Harwood (TA) sworn 2 September 1676. Inventory was exhibited.

6 November. Jane Gray (SM) was granted administration on estate of Alexander Winson (SM), who died single, unmarried, & childless, as principle creditor.
8A:263 Bondsmen: Benjamin Ryder, William Guither. Appraisers: Nicholas Guither, Thomas Griffin. Col. William Calvert to administer oath.

7 November. George Parker procurator for John Hance (Clifts, CV) was granted administration on estate of James Marum (p, Clifts, CV), as principle creditor.
8A:264 Appraisers: Nicholas Furnace, William Barnett. William Parker (g) to administer oath.

George Parker procurator for Henry Barnes & Francis Malden (Clifts, CV) executors of Owen Griffith (chirurgeon, Clifts) exhibited his will. William Parker (g) to prove said will. Said Barnes & Malden were granted administration. Appraisers: Maj. Henry Jowles, James Mackall. Said William Parker to administer oath.

George Parker (CV) was granted copy of exceptions to inventory of John Parker
8A:265 exhibited by William King.

John Rowsby (CV) procurator for Stephen Jefferson (merchant, City of Yorke) was granted administration on estate of Therlagh O'Brian (Broad Creek, TA), as principle creditor. Anthony Maile (g) to administer oath. Inventory consists only of tobacco debts.

8A:266 Robertt Heigh (g, CV) exhibited oath of John Hance & William Barnett, appraisers of Levin Johnson (cooper, CV), sworn 6 October 1676. Samuell Bourne (g, CV) administrator exhibited inventory. Robertt Heigh (g, CV) exhibited bond of said Bourne. Sureties: John Hance, William Barnett.

11 November. Miles Gibson (BA) exhibited that Sarah Clarke widow & administratrix of Abraham Clarke
8A:267 (BA) is dec'd intestate, before administration was complete. Said Miles was granted administration, on behalf of orphans. Appraisers: John Arding, John Rowring. Capt. Thomas Long (high sheriff, BA) to administer oath.

14 November. Dr. John Ireland (BA) administrator of Margrett Penroy (CE) exhibited inventory.

8A:268 Kenelm Cheseldyn procurator for William King (CV) vs. William Dare administrator of John Parker. Petition that exceptions to accounts be admitted.

John Rowsby who married Barbara (one of daughters of Henry & Frances Morgan (dec'd)) vs. Peter Sayer who married Frances (other daughter & administratrix of dec'd). Plaintiff exhibited their exceptions to the answer by defendant.
8A:269-278 ...
8A:279 Signed: John Rowsby.
8A:280 Peter Sayer (TA) was granted a copy of exceptions.

16 November. William Heather & John Davis (KE) executors of Thomas Curry (KE) exhibited his will. Thomas Marsh (g, high sheriff, KE) to prove said will. Said Heather & Davis were granted administration. Appraisers: Peter Evans, Francis Ashbury. Said Marsh to administer oath.

8A:281 18 November. Anne Cole (SM) relict & administratrix of John Medley (SM) exhibited inventory.

20 November. Thomas Bancks (CV) administrator of George & Frances Beckwith (CV) exhibited inventory.

Philip Lynes for Archibald Walkup (CH) was granted administration on estate of Edward Fox (CH), who died childless & unmarried, as principle creditor.
8A:282 Appraisers: Philip Hoskins, Hugh Thomas. Henry Adams (g) to administer oath.

21 November. Sarah White (CV) widow & executrix of Guy White (CV) exhibited his will, proved by John Halls & William King (witnesses).
8A:283 Said Sarah was granted administration. Appraisers: John Halls, William King.

Thomas Gilbertt (DO) exhibited that William Worgan (DO) made a nuncupative will, in the presence of John Tyler, Grace Tyler, & Philip Sutton. William Stevens (g) to prove said will. Appraisers: Daniell Clerke, Bartholomew Enolds. Said Stevens to administer oath.

8A:284 William King (CV) exhibited citation to summon William Dare (CV) on administration of estate of John Parker. Said Dare could not be found, & notice was given to his procurator, who responded: Mr. Carvile is managing that & I know nothing. I have no instructions from Mr. Dare. Mentions: Mr. Twisse. Signed: George Parker at Clifts on 18 November 1676.

8A:285 22 November. Elias Beeche (SM) exhibited summons to Thomas Griffin, Thomas Bale, & Grace Willen regarding estate of Richard Cole (SM).

- Thomas Griffin, age 40, deposed that about 20 September last, Richard Cole (dec'd, St. Jerom's) was on the march to Whorekill in pursuit of William Davis. Said Cole came to house of said Griffin, & then to house of William Guither. Sarah Younger (mother of said Richard) came there also. She desired an end to the difference between her & her son, about his child's part of his father's estate. An argument ensued.

8A:286 ...

Said Richard left & went to house of Nicholas Guither, and then to house of Thomas Courtney, where he made his will. The deponent further said that he heard from Sarah Beech that her brother Richard Cole desired, in his sickness, to have Richard Chilman come & make his will, per Mary Jones (servant to said Younger).

- Thomas Bale, age 24, deposed that he was with Richard Cole (dec'd, St. Jerom's) on the march to Whorekill, & asked said Richard what he & his mother argued about at the house of William Guither. Richard replied that he didn't know, unless his mother feared that he would make his will & leave her nothing.

8A:287 ...

- Grace Willen, age 19, deposed that Richard Cole was on the march to Whorekill when he went to house of Thomas Griffin & was invited in. When said Richard saw his mother Sarah Younger coming, he left. She told him that she would follow him & be his death, because said Richard had abused her & her husband Younger.

The Judge issued a summons to: Thomas Courtney, William Guither, & Mary Jones.

8A:288 24 November. John Darnell (merchant, SM) exhibited PoA from Ralph Poole & John Robinson (merchants, City of Chester, ENG) to recover from William Ratcliff. Said Ratcliff (of Chester) coming to the Province, died at sea. Mentions: Ralph Poole (wooldraper, Chester), John Robinson (ironmonger, Chester),

8A:289 will of said Ratcliff made on 23 November 1675. Date: 14 September 1676.

Witnesses: John Holford, Ben. Ratcliff, Peter Bennett. Said John Darnell was granted administration, on behalf of Ralph Poole & John Robinson.
8A:290 Appraisers: William Rosewell (g), William Langworth. Joseph Pile (g) to administer oath.

Lt. Col. Thomas Taylor (AA) exhibited will of Charles Lawrence (AA), proved on 19 September 1676.
8A:291 Andrew Robertts was granted administration. Said Taylor exhibited oaths of the appraisers sworn on 15 October 1676.

Lt. Col. Thomas Taylor exhibited oath of Alice Roper relict & administratrix of Jarvis Morgan, sworn on 9 October 1675. Accounts were exhibited.

8A:292 Lt. Col. Thomas Taylor (AA) exhibited oath of Thomas Francis & Richard Tydings, appraisers of Thomas Sparrow, sworn 26 October 1676. Signed: Thomas Taillor.

Col. Samuell Chew (AA) exhibited will of James Ogden (AA), proved by William Russell, Jeremiah Cox, & Robertt Conant on 2 November 1676. Also exhibited was oath of John Sollers & Henry Archer, appraisers sworn 2 November 1676.
8A:293 Capt. George Wells (BA) executor in said will was granted administration.

25 November. John Rowlan (CV) exhibited that Thomas Ignett (CV) made a nuncupative will, in presence of Benjamin Webb & Hester. He devised all to his brother, living in ENG. Tobias Norton (g) to prove said will. Appraisers: John Chetham Alexander Magouder. Said Norton to administer oath.

8A:294 27 November. Depositions regarding the estate of Richard Cole (St. Jerom's):

- Sarah (mother of said Richard) wife of Alexander Younger & Sarah Beeche (sister of said Richard) wife of Elias Beeche exhibited that William

Thomas (dec'd, St. Jerom's) who was going to war with Capt. William Stone (late Governor) made his will & bequeathed all to children of William Cole. Said Cole was killed in his Lordship's Service shortly thereafter. William Cole had children: Richard Cole (now dec'd), Elisabeth Cole (now dec'd) wife of Thomas Griffin, Sarah wife of Elias Beeche. Last September, said Richard Cole, while marching to the Whorekill in pursuit of William Davis & his accomplices, made

8A:295 ...

a nuncupative will & gave to his sister (among others) a legacy. He declared he would have made a will at house of William Guither, but his mother hindered him. Said Sarah deposed that she never got anything from the estate of her father, nor from her mother Sarah Younger. By the depositions of Thomas Bale & William Guither, it appeared to the Judge that said Richard intended to make a will & not to leave anything to his mother. By deposition of Thomas Courtney, Said Cole disposed of his goods amongst his other relations, in case he didn't return from DE alive.

8A:296 ...

- William Guither, age 22, deposed on 25 September that in going to DE with Richard Cole, the deponent asked him if he had made a will. Said Cole replied no, & that his mother desired his death, & that she would get nothing.
- Mary Jones, age 20, deposed that about 1 November, Richard Cole was sick at the house of his mother Mrs. Younger, when the deponent heard him say that Mr. Winsore was dec'd, & wondered if Mr. Chilman could put his affairs in order.

8A:297 ...

- Thomas Courtney, age 35, deposed on 7 December that on the day that the soldiers were to rendez-vous at Matapony to pursue William Davis &

his accomplices, Richard Cole came to the deponent's house, to have him to get his things settled. Said Cole replied that his mother followed him to house of (N) Guither, scolding him. Said Cole desired: chattel to the child of his brother (N) Griffin, chattel to Elias Beeche, to Elias his child

8A:298 ...

the servant due from his father's estate, land to his 2 brothers, chattel to Grace Willen.

Said Sarah Beeche was granted administration on estate of Richard Cole.

8A:299 Bond by Elias Beeche. Sureties: Thomas Innes, Thomas Griffin. Appraisers: Nicholas Guither, William Guither.

27 November. William King vs. William Dare administrator of John Parker (merchant). Said King desires judgement obtained against John Parker, to redeem himself out of prison.

8A:300 Said Dare had gotten agreement from divers creditors for lesser amounts to their bills. Said Dare charged the whole debt in the inventory. Mentions debts of: Mr. Thomas Notley, Mr. Christopher Rowsby, Mr. Thomas Clegett, Capt. Roger Baker, Thomas Bincks, & seamen of the John of Weymouth. Mentions: Twisse & Co. Said Dare can satisfy said King's debt.

8A:301 Elisabeth Bennett (BA) exhibited that her husband Richard Bennett (BA) made a nuncupative will, in presence of Martha Tippin & Isabella Hope. Dr. Henry Lewis to prove said will. Said Elisabeth was granted administration. Appraisers: Ralph Hawkins, William Hawkins. Said Lewis to administer oath.

John Peasly (AA) exhibited that Richard Mosse (AA) made a will, constituting his wife Elisabeth Mosse as executrix. Said Elisabeth is now dec'd, before the probate of the will.

8A:302 John Peasly, who married a daughter of the dec'd, was granted administration, for the orphans. Appraisers: William Hopkins, William Jones. Dr. Henry Lewis to administer oath.

Henry Stockett (AA) exhibited will of Nathaniell Stiles (CE). William Towlson (g) to prove said will. Executor
8A:303 is currently in ENG. Said Stockett & James Stavely (overseers) were granted administration, on behalf of the executor. Said overseers live in different counties. Col. William Burgesse to take bond of said Stockett. Said Towlson to take bond of said Stavely. Appraisers (CE): John Dickson, William Salsbury.
8A:304 Said Towlson to administer oath.

29 November. Capt. George Wells (AA) exhibited will of Margrett Penroy (CE), proved by John Mahram & Richard Harney on 16 August 1676.

William Pierce (CE) administrator of George Wilson (CE) exhibited inventory.

8A:305 William Lee (CH) who married Judith relict of James Chancelor (CH) exhibited that said Judith is now dec'd. Said Lee was granted administration on estate of said Chancelor. Henry Adams (g) to take bond of said James Lee. Appraisers: Randolph Brandt, Thomas Buttler. Said Adams to administer oath.

John Cornish (CH) was granted administration on estate of Stephen Champ (CH), who died childless &
8A:306 unmarried, as principle creditor. Appraisers: Randolph Brandt, Thomas Buttler. Henry Adams (g) to administer oath.

Hugh Magruiger (CE) exhibited will of James Magruiger (CE). Augustine Herman (g) to prove said will.
8A:307 Said Hugh Magriger was granted administration. Appraisers: John Browning, Hugh Fouche. Said Herman to administer oath.

John Hanson & Elisabeth Midgely (CH) exhibited will of Richard Midgely (CH). John Stone (g) to prove said will. Said Hanson & Midgely were granted administration. Appraisers: John Wright, Edward Price. Said Stone to administer oath.

Anne O'Briant (DO) was granted administration on estate of Dennis O'Briant (DO).
8A:308 Appraisers: Thomas Pattison, John Steward. Mr. Thomas Taylor (high sheriff, DO) to administer oath.

30 November. Cornelius Howard (AA) administrator of John Sanson (AA) exhibited accounts. Notice to commissioners of AA County Court to take security for residue
8A:309 due to the orphans.

Richard Rawlins (AA) administrator of John Venall (AA) exhibited accounts.
8A:310 Discharge was granted.

John Hance (CV) exhibited will of Francis Leigh (CV). William Parker (g) to prove said will. Said Hance was granted administration. Appraisers: William Parker Fitzgeorge, William Martin. Said Parker to administer oath.

Sarah Hambleton (TA) widow & executrix of William Hambleton (TA) exhibited his will. Col. Vincent Lowe (high sheriff, TA)
8A:311 to prove said will. Said Sarah was granted administration. Appraisers: Edward Elliott, John Poore. Said Lowe to administer oath.

The widow Graves (TA) was granted administration on estate of her husband Richard Graves (TA). Appraisers: Capt. George Cowley, Capt. Henry Alexander. Col. Vincent Lowe to administer oath.

8A:312 Col. John Douglasse (CH) petitioned for Maj. Benjamin Rozer (high sheriff, CH) to prove will of Samuell Clerke (CH). Said Douglasse was granted administration.

Peter Carre (CH) petitioned for Maj. Benjamin Rozer (high sheriff, CH) to prove will of Elisabeth Lilly (CH). Said Carre was granted administration.

John Wood (CH) was granted administration on estate of Philip Browne (CH), who died childless & unmarried, as
8A:313 principle creditor. Appraisers: George Langam, Garrett Sinnot. Maj. Benjamin Rozer to administer oath.

Anne Corner (CH) exhibited will of Jobe Corner (CH). Maj. Benjamin Rozer to prove said will. Said Anne executrix was granted administration.

8A:314 Richard Bale (g, BA) was granted administration on estate of Robertt Wilson (BA), who died leaving wife in ENG, as chief creditor, on behalf of said widow. Appraisers: William Crommwell, Francis Watkins. Capt. Thomas Long (high sheriff) to administer oath.

8A:315 Henry Stockett (AA) exhibited will of Nathaniell Stiles (CE). Said Stockett & James Stavely (CE) overseers were granted administration. Said Stiles was administrator of Thomas Salmon. Said Stockett & said Stavely were granted administration on estate of Thomas Salmon, during minority of Thomas Howell, Jr. (surviving overseer of said Salmon), on behalf of Peter Salmon only son & heir of dec'd. Col. William Burgess to take bond of said Stockett. William Towlson (g) to take bond of said Stavely.
8A:316 Appraisers: John Dickson, William Salsbury. Said Towlson to administer oath.

William Stevens (g, SO) exhibited oath of Henry Boston, Jr. administrator of Henry Boston, Sr., sworn 10 November 1676.
8A:317 Also exhibited was oath of Stephen

Horsey & Charles Hall, appraisers sworn same day.

William Stevens (g, SO) exhibited will of Thomas Shiles (SO), proved by Thomas Bloise & Edward Davis on 15 November 1676. Also exhibited was oath of Nicholas Rice & Thomas Holebrook, appraisers sworn 18 November 1676.
8A:318 Since no executor was cited in the will, widow Alice Shiles was granted administration.

Capt. Richard Hill (AA) exhibited will of William Drewry, proved by James Martin & Joshua Merrikin on 26 October 1676. James Rigby executor was granted administration.
8A:319 Also exhibited was oath of Robert Davis & Ralph Hawkins, appraisers sworn 26 October 1676.

William Parker (g, CV) exhibited will of Owen Griffith (CV), proved by George Young & William Overy on 20 November 1676.
8A:320 Henry Bennett & Francis Malden executors were sworn on 20 November 1676. Henry Jowles & James Mascall appraisers were sworn on 20 November 1676.

8A:321 William Parker (g, CV) exhibited oath of John Hance administrator of James Maram, sworn 27 November 1676. Also exhibited was oath of Nicholas Furnes & William Barnett, appraisers sworn 27 November 1676.

Dr. Henry Lewis (AA) & John Ricks (AA) executors William Slade (AA) executor of Quinton Parker (BA) exhibited accounts of said Parker. Discharge was granted.

8A:322 Henry Hosier (KE) on behalf of self, Cornelius Acomagies, & John Bowles executors of Walter Spencer (KE) petitioned for Maj. Joseph Weeks to examine accounts & administer oath. Residue due to the orphans.

John Cage (CH) administrator of Charles Gregory (SM) exhibited inventory.

Court Session: 1676

8A:323 William Yorcke (BA) administrator of John Collier (BA) exhibited inventory.

Richard Bale (BA) exhibited will of William Poultney (BA), proved by John Leakings & Margrett Leakings (BA) on 1 November 1676. Edward Monfrett was granted administration. Appraisers
8A:324 were sworn on 1 November 1676.

2 December. Rachell Lacey (CV) widow & administratrix of Thomas Lacey (CV) exhibited accounts. Discharge was granted.

Catherine Winsmore (DO) exhibited will of Dr. Robert Winsmore (DO). William Stevens (g) to prove said will. Said Catherine was granted administration. Appraisers: Henry Tripp, John Brookes. Said Stevens to administer oath.

8A:325 Richard Wollman (g, TA) exhibited will of Thomas Henfrey (TA). Capt. Philemon Lloyd to prove said will. Said Wollman & Henry Costin executors were granted administration. Appraisers: William Hemsley, William Jones. Said Lloyd to administer oath.

4 December. George Parker (CV) exhibited renunciation of Salomon Sparrow (AA) as executor of Thomas Sparrow (AA)
8A:326 on 10 September 1676. Witnesses: Thomas Taylor, Thomas Francis. Said Parker
8A:327 was granted administration, on behalf of widow & orphans. Inventory exhibited.

Martha Shaw (CE) relict & executrix of Thomas Middlefield (CE) exhibited inventory.

Richard Deavor (AA) administrator of John Howerton (AA) exhibited accounts. Residue: orphans.
8A:328 ...
8A:329 Discharge was granted.

Dr. Henry Lewis (AA) one of executors of William Slade (AA) exhibited that the other executor is "insufficient to make good the estate of the dec'd now in his hands." Capt. Richard Hill to take bond of said John Ricks.

8A:330 5 December. Elias Beeche (SM) on behalf of his wife Sarah sister of Richard Cole (dec'd, SM) petitioned for administration on estate of dec'd. Mentions: caveat by Alexander Younger & his wife Sarah mother of dec'd. Said Alexander was summoned.

Dr. Henry Lewis (AA) administrator of Thomas Turner (AA)
8A:331 petitioned AA County Court to examine accounts & administer oath.

Mathew Erickson (KE) petitioned for Desboro Bennett (g) to prove will of Thomas Barnes (CE). Francis Barns, Mathew Erickson, & Rebecca Moore executors were granted administration. Michael Miller entered a caveat
8A:332 against the probate of said will. Appraisers: John Erickson, John Winchester. Said Bennett to administer oath.

Stephen Murty (SM) exhibited renunciation of Henry Carew (g) as administrator of John Bayley (SM).
8A:333 Said Murty was granted administration. Bondsmen: Edw. Russell, Thomas Simpson.

5 December. Judge ordered bond of Frances Morgan (alias Frances Sayer), William Coursey, & Peter Sayer unto John Rowsby to be given to His Lordship's Attorney.

8A:334 6 December. John Yeo (clerk, CV) exhibited will of James Varloe (CV), proved by Robertt Blinckhorne & Humphrey Watersworth. Said Yeo executor was granted administration. Appraisers: Robertt Blinckhorne, Humphrey Watersworth.

8A:335 Thomas Gaunt (CV) was granted administration on estate of Patrick Craford (CV), who died childless & unmarried, as principle creditor.

Surety: Robert Taylor. Appraisers: Thomas Tasker, Robert Taylor. Roger Brooke (g) to administer oath.

7 December. Tobias Norton (g, CV) exhibited nuncupative will of Thomas Ignett (CV), proved.
8A:336 John Rowland was granted administration, on behalf of dec'd's brother living in ENG. Sureties: Henry Cole, Thomas Gaunt. Inventory was exhibited.

George Lingam (CV) executor of Thomas Coxe (CV) exhibited inventory & accounts.

8A:337 Anthony Maile (g, TA) exhibited bond of Stephen Jefferson (merchant, City of Yorcke) administrator of Turlogh O'Briant (TA).

Richard Ladd (g, CV) exhibited oath of appraisers of estate of Richard Robertts, sworn on 3 November 1676.

8A:338 9 December. Henry Haslewood (g, BA) exhibited will of William Bisse (BA), proved by John Walstone & William Osborne. James Philips executor was granted administration. Inventory was exhibited.

8A:339 George Robins (TA) was granted administration on estate of Peter Underwood (TA), as chief creditor. Surety: Thomas Alexander. Appraisers: William Watson, William Willoby. Stephen Gary (g) to administer oath. Mentions: widow.

11 December. Joseph Chew for Elisabeth West (CE) was granted administration on estate of her husband Francis Bellows.
8A:340 Appraisers: Joseph Chew, Richard Edmunds. William Piece (g) to administer oath.

Catherine Morris (CE) widow of Peter Johnson was granted administration on his estate. Appraisers: Joseph Chew, Richard Edmunds. James Frisby (g) to administer oath.

Court Session: 1676

8A:341 Bond of Richard Fenwick (CV) administrator of Cutberth Fenwick (CV) was exhibited. Surety: John Fenwick. Col. Brooke died before he could complete his commission to swear said Richard.

George Uty (g, BA) exhibited nuncupative will of John Turpinne (BA), proved by Henry Haslewood & Rutten Garrettson. Capt. George Wells was granted administration. Appraisers: Henry Haslewood, Rutten Garrettson. Said Uty to administer oath.

8A:342 The widow Smith (TA) widow of John Smith (TA) was granted administration on his estate. Appraisers: Thomas Hinson, Stephen Tully. Mathew Ward (g) to administer oath.

John Fenwick (CV) exhibited the verbal will of Robertt Fenwick (CV). Col. Baker Brooke to prove said will.

8A:343 Mathew Ward (g, TA) exhibited will of Dr. Richard Tilghman, proved by Thomas Bruff on 6 March 1675. Mary Tilghman widow was granted administration. Also exhibited was oath of Thomas Hinson & William Bishop, appraiser sworn 28 August 1676.

8A:344 13 December. Peter Watts (SM) executor of John Hewett (SM) exhibited additional inventory & accounts. Discharge was granted.

Robertt Ridgely procurator for Alexander Younger & his wife Sarah (SM) were granted continuance to give security for estates of the orphans of William Cole.

8A:345 15 December. Marck Cordea (SM) was granted continuance on estate of John Bayley.

John Gouge (CH) exhibited will of Enoch Field (CH), proved by John Nuby & Briant Brockett. Said Gouge was granted administration.

8A:346 Capt. George Wells (BA) executor of James Ogdon (AA) exhibited inventory.

Thomas Carlisle & John Watson (SM) executors of John Cunningham (SM) exhibited inventory.

19 December. William Palmer (changed to Cadwalleder Palmer, DO) exhibited that the estate of William Worgan (innholder, DO) is indebted by Thomas Gilbert (said Worgan's bookkeeper), who altered several bills & accounts, to great loss of the creditors & orphans.
8A:347 Said Palmer is chief creditor. William Stevens & John Brooke (gentlemen) to oversee the appraisal of estate. Sheriff (DO) to summon Thomas Gilbert to appear with nuncupative will.

Jane Gray (SM) administratrix of Alexander Winsmore (SM) exhibited inventory.

8A:348 Thomas Hinson (TA) administrator of John Vine (TA) exhibited that Ralph Blackhall, one of the appraisers, has run out of the Province. New appraisers: William Bishop, Richard Jones. Mathew Ward (g) to administer oath.

James Phillips (BA) was empowered to take inventory of estate of Shelton Berry (BA), who died childless, unmarried, & relationless.

8A:349 21 December. Evan Davis, age 36, deposed on 30 November that George Beckwith bestowed chattel on Lord Baltimore, and Lord Baltimore bestowed chattel on said George, who assigned it to his daughter Mary. Thomas Bancks administrator of George Beckwith is ordered to deliver said chattel to Mary Miles (daughter of the dec'd).

29 December. Michael Rochford for Mary Goffe (SM) relict & administratrix of Lt. Col. John Jarboe (SM)
8A:350 was granted continuance.

Court Session: 1676

Elinor Brooke (CV) widow & executrix of Col. Thomas Brooke (CV) exhibited his will, proved by Richard Gardner & Thomas Herbert.

8A:351 Baker Brooke & Roger Brooke, 2 of executors, have renounced administration. Said Elinor was granted administration. Appraisers: Charles Boteler, (N). Col. Baker Brooke to administer oath.

30 December. William Adams (Topsham, ENG) exhibited will of John Shepheard (NE), part owner & master of the Jamaica (ship in Wiccocomico River). Thomas Gerard & John Lluellyn (gentlemen, SM) to prove said will. Said Adams was granted administration, on behalf of his daughter Elisabeth Adams executrix, who is in ENG. Appraisers: Capt. Thomas Shawe, Richard Angell.

8A:352 Thomas Bowdle (CV) exhibited that John Martin (Barbadoes) died intestate & that Jasper Allen (CV) had LoA, on behalf of his wife & children. Sureties: said Bowdle, Demetrius Cartwright. Soon afterwards, said Jasper died, and then said Cartwright.

8A:353 Said Bowdle was granted administration on estate of said Martin, on behalf of his wife & children. Appraisers: John Hollins, Edward Turner. Roger Brooke (g, CV) to administer oath.

William King & John Grammar vs.
8A:354 William Dare administrator of John Parker. Plaintiffs were allocated costs.

Henry Cole (CV) petitioned for sheriff (SM) to summon George Lingan (SM) executor of Thomas Cox (SM) to surrender the residue of the dec'd's estate, on behalf of the widow.

Court Session: 1676/7

8A:355 1 January. Thomas Browne (CV) who married Mary relict of William Stacey (CV) petitioned to have Maj. Thomas Trueman (CV) release her son Bazill

Stacey.

2 January. Alexander Ray (TA) exhibited that his father Alexander Ray
8A:356 made his will dated 13 September last, making his wife Joane Ray executrix during her life, & after her decease, said son Alexander (being made of age at decease of said wife). Said Joane is since dec'd, & said Alexander is over age 17. Anthony Mayle (g, TA) to prove said will. Appraisers: Thomas Vaughan, Patrick Word. Said Mayle to administer oath. Mentions: Joane is the mother of said Alexander.

8A:357 William Parker (g, CV) exhibited will of Francis Leigh (CV), proved.
8A:358 John Hance (CV) executor was granted administration, & sworn 18 December 1676. Also exhibited was oath of William Parker & William Martin, appraisers sworn 18 December 1676.

8A:359 Tomlin wife of Francis Heyden (SM) was granted administration on estate of her brother Thomas Buttler (CH). Appraisers (CH): Col. John Dowglass, Thomas Gibson. Thomas Gerard (g, SM) or John Lluellin (g, SM) to administer oath.

8A:360 3 January. Thomas Docton (AA) administrator of William Paget (AA) exhibited that the personal estate of the dec'd was embezzled by George Paschall (AA), uncle & elected guardian of dec'd. Said Paschall has fled out of the Province. Said Docton was granted continuance.

8A:361 Mary Gittings (CV) widow & executrix of John Gittings (CV) exhibited additional inventory.

8 January. David Powell & Robert Wheeler (CH) exhibited will of Henry Fletcher (CH). Zachary Wade (g, CH) to prove said will. Appraisers: Nicholas Proddy (g), Roger Dickison. Said Wade to administer oath.

8A:362 Peter Stokes (DO) was granted administration on estate of George Bolton, who died single, unmarried, & childless, as principle creditor. Appraisers: James Egg, Edmund Brennock. Stephen Gary (g, DO) to administer oath.

8A:363 William Stephens & John Brooke exhibited the inventory of William Worgan (DO). Said Stephens & Brooke are to examine the depositions of John Taylor & his wife Grace, and that of Philip Sutton, both taken 25-27 November, with cross-examinations taken 28 December. Also the depositions of: William Hanman, Cadwallader Palmer, Ann Mason.
8A:364 Mentions: children of said Worgan,
8A:365 ...
8A:366 Thomas Gilbert. Witness: Fran. Seares.
8A:367

- Deposition of William Hanman, age 37, taken on 28 December 1676. Mentions: Anne Mason, Elisabeth Hambleton.

8A:368 ...

- Deposition of Cadwallader Palmer, age 21, concerning William Worgan (innholder, DO), on 28 December 1676.

8A:369 ...

- Deposition of Anne Mason,

8A:370 ...
age 26, on 28 December 1676. Mentions: Betty Hamleton (Patuxent), Thomas Gilbert (Mr. Worgan's bookkeeper).
8A:371 ...
8A:372 Ruling: said Worgan died intestate.

8A:373 <u>9 January</u>. Judge wrote a letter to Commissioners of DO, regarding estate of (N) Worgan.
8A:374 ...
8A:375 Mentions: debt to Cadwallader Palmer. Signed: Philip Calvert.

Thomas Alwell (CV) was granted administration on estate of his brother John Alwell (CV), on behalf of the orphans.
8A:376 Mentions: said John Alwell died 26th instant, while crossing on ice on

Swansen Creek. He was a widower, with 2 small, sickly children. His estate is small.
8A:377 Surety: Thomas Lawson. Appraisers: Thomas Lawson, Samuell Ramsley. William Groome (g) to administer oath.

Robert Ridgely procurator for Cadwallader Jones & Samuell Leadbeater (merchants, City of Chester, ENG) vs. Thomas Carlisle &
8A:378 John Watson executors of John Cunningham (merchant, City of Chester). Complaint exhibited. Said Jones employed said Leadbeater & Cunningham as his factors & assigns for the ship Anne of Chester.
8A:379 Said Cunningham died, leaving a will appointing as executors Thomas Carlisle, William Watson, Robert Guines, & William Hatton. Said Hatton & Guines have renounced executorship.
8A:380 Said Thomas Carlile & John Watson to give security.

10 January. Thomas Carlile petitioned for proof from Samuell Leadbeater.

8A:381 John Fanning (g, CH) exhibited oath of John Cage administrator of Charles Gregory, sworn 29 September 1676.

Marmaduke Semms (SM) administrator of Abell James (SM) exhibited accounts
8A:382 & list of debts. Continuance was granted.

Marmaduke Semms (SM) administrator of Samuell Dickeson (SM) exhibited inventory.

12 January. Mary Rowe (TA)
8A:383 exhibited will of her son Thomas Duncombe (TA). Edward Man (g, TA) to prove said will. Appraisers: Thomas Alexander, Thomas Martin. Said Man to administer oath.

8A:384 James Sedgwick (TA) was granted administration on estate of his kinsman Capt. Miles Cooke (mariner, Surrey, ENG), on behalf of his wife & children in ENG.

8A:385 Appraisers: William Crosse, William Combes. Edward Man (g, TA) to administer oath.

William Traverse (g, CV) exhibited oath of MM John Griggs & John Halls, appraisers of Richard Roberts (CV), sworn 8 January 1676. Raymond Stapleford (CV) administrator exhibited inventory.

8A:386 Alice Graves (CV) on behalf of self & Susanna Floyd (CV) exhibited will of Demetrius Cartwright (doctor of physick, CV), proved by Edward Armstrong & Henry Hollis. Said Floyd is unable to travel to the Office.

8A:387 Said Graves & Floyd were granted administration. Appraisers: John Hollins, John Turner. Richard Ladd (g, CV) to administer oath.

15 January. Elisabeth Benson (CV) widow

8A:388 of John Benson (CV) exhibited his will. She is unable to travel this hard winter. Col. Samuell Chewe to prove said will. Appraisers: Paul Bewsy, Robert Conante. [Judge cites that other documents have been lost due to hard winter.] Said Chewe to administer oath.

8A:389 John Cable (CH) petitioned for administration on estate of Luke Greene & appraisers Nicholas Proddy & John Ward. Ruling: said Cable needs to establish his right. If valid, then Maj. Benjamin Rozer to administer oath.

Thomas Hargnesse (CH) petitioned that the will of

8A:390 Walter Russell (CH) be proved by witnesses John Cassocke & Charles Russell. Sheriff (CH) to summon said witnesses.

Capt. Philemon Lloyd (TA) exhibited oath of John Davis & Francis Brookes, appraisers of Jonas Kinsey (TA), sworn 2 November 1676. John Watkins (AA) administrator exhibited inventory.

8A:391 18 January. John Cousens (CV) exhibited will of John Ramsey, Sr. (CV). Tobias Norton (g, CV) to prove said will. Said Cousens, as overseer, was granted administration, during minority of John Ramsey (son of dec'd).
8A:392 Appraisers: Richard Edwards, Robert Anderson. Said Norton to administer oath.

19 January. Richard Fenwick (CV) administrator of his brother Cuthbert Fenwick (CV) exhibited inventory. Continuance was granted.

8A:393 24 January. Summons issued to John Fen, Elisabeth Harges, & Anne wife of Charles Russell regarding will of Walter Russell.

Robert Carvile (recorder of SMC) one of executors of Elisabeth Moy executrix of Richard Moy (Vinyard, SM) exhibited inventory of said Richard.
8A:394 Continuance was granted.

8A:395 John Browne (SM) was granted administration on estate of John Thomas, who died single, unmarried, childless, & having no relation in Province, as principle creditor. Surety: John Blomfield. Appraisers: John Cecill, Robert Beard.
8A:396 Capt. John Jourdain to administer oath.

Stephen Gary (g, DO) exhibited bond of Peter Stokes administrator of George Bolton (DO). Said Stokes was granted administration.
8A:397 Appraisers: James Egg, Edmund Brennock.

26 January. Henry Adams (g) exhibited oath of John Cornish (CH) administrator of Stephen Champ (CH), sworn 29 November past. Sureties: William Lee, Thomas Helgar.
8A:398 Also exhibited was oath of Rando. Brandt & Thomas Butler, appraisers sworn the same day.

Henry Adams (g, CH) exhibited oath to William Lee (CH) administrator of James

Chancelor, sworn 13 December last. Sureties: Thomas Butler, Thomas Helgar. Also exhibited was oath of Rando. Brandt & Thomas Butler, appraisers sworn same day.

8A:399 William Lee (g, CH) administrator of James Chancelour (CH) exhibited that appraiser Thomas Butler is dec'd. New appraisers: Thomas Helgar, Rando. Brandt. Said Adams to administer oath.

John Cornish (CH) administrator of Stephen Champ (CH) exhibited that appraiser Thomas Butler
8A:400 is dec'd. New appraisers: Thomas Helgar, Randolph Brandt. Henry Adams (g, CH) to administer oath.

John Wright (CH) executor of Thomas Gayley (CH) exhibited his will. Zachary Wade (CH) to prove said will.
8A:401 Said Wright was granted administration. Appraisers: Nicholas Proddy, William Smith. Said Wade to administer oath.

Henry Aspinall & his wife Mary (CH) executors of William Wilkinson (CH) exhibited his will. Zachary Wade (g, CH) to prove said will. Appraisers: Edward Maddock, John Munn.
8A:402 Said Henry & Mary were granted administration. Said Wade to administer oath.

Charles Cullis (CH) executor of Edmund Taylor (CH) exhibited his will. John Stone
8A:403 (g, CH) to prove said will. Said Cullis was granted administration. Appraisers: George Langham, Richard Chapman. Said Stone to administer oath.

29 January. John Halfehead (CV) administrator of his father John Halfehead
8A:404 exhibited accounts. Mentions: no other children of dec'd living to whom any part of the residue may pertain. Discharge was granted.

Francis Lucas executrix of William Lucas
(St. Jerom's, SM) exhibited accounts.
8A:405 Notice to be given to creditors.

William Heather & John Davis (KE)
executors of Thomas Curry (KE) exhibited
inventory. Thomas Marsh (high sheriff,
KE) exhibited oath of William Heather &
John Davis, executors of Thomas Curry
(KE), sworn
8A:406 23 December last. Also exhibited was
oath of Peter Evans & Francis Hershbury,
appraisers sworn same day. Said Marsh
exhibited will of said Curry (KI),
proved by Edward Hall & Matthias Smith
on 18 December 1676.
8A:407 Said Heather & Davis were granted
administration.

3 February. John Cable (CH) was granted
administration on estate of Luke Greene
(CH), who departed from the Province,
died single, unmarried, & childless & no
relation living in the Province. Said
Greene made PoA to said Cable.
8A:408 Benjamin Rozer (CH) to administer oath.

5 February. James Mills (BA) exhibited
will of Samuell Boston (BA). Dr. John
Stanesby renounced executorship
8A:409 on 19 January 1676/7. Witnesses: Will.
Burwell, Israell Shelton. Dr. John
Stanesby to prove said will.
Appraisers: Dr. John Ireland, James
Ives. Said Stanesby to administer oath.

8A:410 Will of Lewis Bryen (BA) was exhibited.
Richard Ball (g, BA) to prove said will.
Elisabeth Bowing executrix is an infant
not above age 5. Overseers Jonas Bowing
her father & Nicholas Corbin were
granted administration, during the
minority of said Elisabeth.
8A:411 Appraisers: John Harden, Nicholas
Ruxston.

James Phillips (BA) was granted
administration on estate of James Cogell
(BA), as greatest creditor. Said
Phillips lives remote from the Office.
Appraisers: John Harden, Giles Stephens.
Richard Ball (BA) to administer oath.

Court Session: 1676/7

8A:412 6 February. Daniell Clocker (SM) one of executors of his father Daniell Clocker (SM) exhibited accounts. Discharge withheld until said Daniell pays his sister Rebecca her portion.

7 February. Giles Steevens for Elisabeth Dorman executrix of James Cogill (BA) exhibited his will, proved by said Steevens (one of witnesses).
8A:413 Dec'd was also known as James Covill. Said Steevens signed as Joyles Steavens. Other witness (& author of will) was Oliver Haile. Richard Ball (g, BA) to summon said Haile to testify. Said Elisabeth was granted administration, revoking same to James Phillips. Appraisers: John Arden, Giles Steevens. Said Ball to administer oath.

8A:414 John Arden (BA) exhibited will of John Barrett (BA). Richard Ball (g, BA) to prove said will. Said Arden was granted administration. Appraisers: Giles Steevens, John Boren. Said Ball to administer oath.

8A:415 John Arden (BA) exhibited that he & Edward Smith (BA) purchased "Walton's Neck" on 28 December 1671. Articles of agreement between John Harding & Edward Smith (Back River, BA).
8A:416 Witnesses: Roger Sidwells, Tho. Mather. Said Arden further exhibited that said Smith is dec'd, childless & unmarried.
8A:417 Said Arden was granted administration on Smith's estate. Surety: Giles Steevens. Appraisers: John Boren, Giles Steevens. Richard Ball (g, BA) to administer oath.

8 February. John Steevens (BA) administrator of Samuell Tracey (BA) exhibited accounts. Discharge was granted.

8A:418 Margaret Ward (SM) widow of Andrew Ward (SM) was granted administration on his estate. Appraisers: Thomas Simpson, Thomas Stonestreete. Joseph Pile (g) to administer oath.

Zachary Wade (g, CH) exhibited will of Henry Fletcher,
8A:419 proved by Peter demasse de Masso & Thomas Atkinson on 15 January 1676. David Towell & Robert Wheeler executors were granted administration, sworn
8A:420 20 January 1676. Also exhibited was oath of Mr. Nicholas Proddy & Roger Dickenson, appraisers sworn 15 January 1676. Inventory was exhibited.

9 February. Joseph Fowler (SM) was granted administration on estate of William George (SM),
8A:421 who was possessed of a very inconsiderable estate. [Total is #1150.] Appraisers: William Watts, Coline Mackenzie. Said Fowler is principle creditor.

Will of Stephen White (AA) was exhibited. Capt. Richard Hill (AA) to prove said will. Anne White
8A:422 widow & executrix was granted administration. Appraisers: Ralph Hawkins, Ralph Duncastle. Said Hill to administer oath.

10 February. Anthony Demontadire (BA) & Henry Howard (AA) overseers of estate of Thomas Cole (BA) exhibited his will. Richard Ball (g,
8A:423 BA) to prove said will. Sarah Cole (daughter of dec'd) is cited as executrix, and is an infant under age. Said Demontadire & Howard were granted administration, on behalf of said Sarah. Appraisers: Edward Mumford, Nicholas Ruxstone. Said Ball to administer oath.

8A:424 George Lingan (CV) one of executors of Thomas Cox (CV) exhibited additional accounts.

Raymond Stapleford (CV) administrator of Richard Roberts (CV) exhibited second inventory.

12 February. Edward English (merchant) administrator of William Hewet (merchant, London) exhibited PoA from Timothy Harmor & Peter Devett, made

before Anthony Wright (notary,
8A:425 London). Timothy Harmer & Peter de Witt (merchants, London) constituted Edward Inglish (merchant, MD) as attorney, to recover from widow or executor of John Vanheck or items in hands of said Van Heck by John Allen (merchant, dec'd).
8A:426 Said Timothy also empowered said attorney to recover from William Hewet (merchant, dec'd) or John Turpin (g, dec'd).
8A:427 Signed: Timo. Harmer, Peter Devet. Witnesses: John Herne, John Randall. Date: 21 August 1676. Appraisers (of said Hewet) Thomas Hooker & Richard Adams
8A:428 were both illiterate men. New appraisers: John Dickson, Robert Neves. William Towlson to administer oath.

Edward Inglish administrator of John Allen (merchant, London) exhibited PoA from Timothy Harmer & Francis Harmer executors of John Allen & letters testimonial of Rt. Rev. Lord Archbishop of Canterbury & Rt. Hon. Sir Joseph Sheldon Lord Mayor of London. On 25 August 1676 before Anthony Wright (notary, London), Timothy Harmer & Francis Harmer
8A:429 (merchants, London) executors of John Allen (merchant) for selves & Paul Wheeler the other executor constituted to Edward Inglish a PoA to recover from the estate of John Van Heck.
8A:430 ...
8A:431 Signed: Timo. Harmer, Fran. Harmer. Witnesses: Josi. Jones, J. Randall. [Paragraph in Latin regarding Gilbert Archbishop of Canterbury.]
8A:432 Signed: Marcus Cottle. Witness: Josi. Jones. Sir Joseph Sheldon Knight Lord Mayor & Alderman or Senator of
8A:433 London certified that Anthony Wright signed the preceding documents & that Josiah Jones witnessed them. Further Roger Thorpe (merchant, London) consigned goods to said Allen for which said Allen consigned to Timothy & Francis Harmer.
8A:434 Said Thorpe is indebted to said Inglish & said Timothy & said Francis & said

Thorpe is since dec'd per letters of Francis Harmer dated 13 September last & of Timothy Harmer dated 14 September last. Appraisers: John Dickson, (N) Hodson. Said Inglish was granted administration on estate of Roger Thorpe.

8A:435 Richard Hill (AA) administrator of James Rawbone (AA) exhibited inventory & accounts.

Capt. Richard Hill (AA) was granted administration on estate of David Griffith, who died unmarried, as greatest creditor.
8A:436 Appraisers: Robert Proctor, Robert Clarkeson. Dr. Henry Lewis to administer oath.

John Hammond (aa) was granted administration on estate of Richard Russell (AA), who died unmarried. Appraisers: Samuell Howard, Abraham Child. Capt. Richard Hill to administer oath.

13 February. Robert Tyler one of the appraisers of estate
8A:437 of William Luffman (AA) has run away. Matthew Howard is appointed in his place.

Edward English administrator of William Hewet petitioned that John Turpin (BA) administrator of William Hewet (CE) has not exhibited inventory & has received most of the debts due said estate, but has not discharged the estate. Said English petitions for the bonds of security
8A:438 to be assigned to him. Ruling: bond of said Turpin with securities John Ireland & Samuell Boston be delivered to said English.

8A:439 To: Commissioners of AA County Court. An order of said Court instructed Capt. Richard Hill to take bond of Richard Fetherston for estate of orphans of George Langley. Said Fetherston has left this country. Also, the lands of

John Killey (dec'd) have been let lie waste.

8A:440 Court of AA County, at the Ridge. 14 March 1675/6. Attendees: Tho. Taylor, Esq., Maj. William Burgesse, Robert Burle, Robert Francklin. Notice for Capt. Richard Hill to take bond of security of Richard Fetherston administrator of George Langley for the orphans of said Langley. Signed: Ri. Broughton.

14 February. Diana Hollaway (AA) widow of Oliver Hollaway (AA) was granted administration on his estate.
8A:441 Appraisers: Robert Franklin (g), Richard Walter. Col. William Burgesse to administer oath.

Judith Cumber (AA) widow of John Cumber (AA) exhibited his will. Lt. Col. Thomas Taylor to prove said will. Said Judith executrix was granted administration.

8A:442 Will of John Blower (TA) was exhibited. George Cowley (g) to prove said will. John Paddison executor was granted administration. Appraisers: Thomas Martin, Henry Alexander. Said Cowley to administer oath.

15 February. Joseph Pile (g, SM) exhibited oath of William Rosewell & William Langworth, appraisers of William Ratcliffe (SM), sworn 8 December 1676.

8A:443 Maj. Henry Jowles (CV) was granted administration on estate of Andrew Higgs (chirurgeon, CV), who died leaving a wife in ENG, but no relations in this Province. Said Jowles was granted as principle creditor, for the widow. Appraisers: Charles Boteler, Simon Wootton. Roger Brooke (g) oath.

Will of Abraham Dawson (AA) was exhibited. Dr. Henry Lewis to
8A:444 prove said will. The widow was granted administration. Appraisers: Matthew Howard, William Hopkins. Said Lewis to administer oath.

Dr. Henry Lewis (AA) exhibited the nuncupative will of Richard Bennet (AA). Elisabeth Bennet widow was granted administration. Said Lewis to administer oath.

8A:445 16 February. Abigail Wright (DO) widow of Arthur Wright (DO) exhibited that he made a will. Said will was lost by (N) Douglas (the late executed Malefactor) & his accomplices. The witnesses are still living in the Province. John Brooke (g) to take depositions of witnesses. Said widow was granted administration.

Francis Barnes & Matthew Erickson (KE) exhibited that Disborough Bennet (g) was empowered to
8A:446 prove will of Thomas Barnes (KE). Said will has not been proved because: one witness has not been heard from; and, said Bennet is since dec'd. Said Barnes' estate is wasting to the detriment of the orphans. Said Francis & said Erickson were granted administration. Appraisers: John Winchester, Morgan Williams. William Lawrence (g) to administer oath.

8A:447 John Ireland (BA) administrator of Margaret Penroy (BA) exhibited accounts.

Elisabeth Bennet (AA) widow of Richard Bennet (AA) exhibited inventory.

Richard Moss (AA) son of Richard Moss, Sr. (AA) exhibited his renunciation of administration of his father's estate. Said Richard Sr. constituted his wife Elisabeth as executrix. Capt. Richard Hill (AA)
8A:448 was to prove will. Said Elisabeth is since dec'd. Said Richard has renounced administration on estates of his father & mother, & assigns to his brother-in-law John Peasly. Date: 1 January 1676. Witnesses: John Peasly, James Orurke.
8A:449 John Peasly (AA) administrator of Richard Mosse, Sr. (AA) exhibited inventory.

Court Session: 1676/7

Dr. Henry Lewis (AA) exhibited oath of Ralph Hawkins & William Hawkins, appraisers of Richard Bennet (AA), sworn 16 January 1676/7.

Henry Lewis (g, AA) exhibited oath of Mr. William Hopkins & William Jones, appraisers of Richard Moss, Sr. (AA), sworn 9 January 1676/7.

8A:450 Capt. Richard Hill (AA) exhibited will of Richard Moss, Sr., proved by John Peasly on 22 May 1676. The other witness John Andrews has left the Province, but before departing made oath before Richard Burle. Elisabeth Moss executrix was sworn on 5 July 1676.

8A:451 Capt. Richard Hill exhibited the renunciation of Cornelius Howard (AA) as executor of William Carpenter (AA). Date: 6 February 1676/7.

Capt. Richard Hill (AA) exhibited will of William Luffman (AA) proved by
8A:452 Joseph Freene (AA) on 15 July 1676. The other witness John Andrew has left for ENG. Mary Luffman was granted administration. Date: 15 July 1676.

Capt. Richard Hill (AA) exhibited the bond of Sarah Porter widow & administratrix of Peter Porter (AA), dated 1 August 1676.
8A:453 Inventory was exhibited.

Capt. Richard Hill (AA) exhibited will of William Grimes (AA), proved by Joseph Winders & Benjamin Stringer on 23 November 1676.

Richard Hill (g, AA) exhibited oath of Joyce Grimes widow & executrix of William Grimes.
8A:454 Said Joyce refused administration. She is lately married & agrees to pay all debts. Date: 24 August 1676.

Richard Hill (g, AA) exhibited oath of William Hopkins & Dr. Henry Lewis, appraisers of Ralph Williams (AA), sworn 16 July last.

Thomazin wife of Francis Heyden (SM) administratrix of her brother Thomas Butler (CH) exhibited inventory.

8A:455 Stephen Jefferson (TA) administrator of Therlagh O'Brian (TA) exhibited inventory.

Robert Burle (g, AA) exhibited oath of Stephen Burle & Richard Bayly, appraisers of Thomas Guinn (AA), sworn 13 April 1676. Richard Guinn (AA) exhibited inventory of estate of his brother Thomas Guinn (AA).

Capt. Richard Hill (AA) exhibited oath of Cornelius Howard & Matthew, appraisers of Nicholas Wyatt (AA), sworn 10 August.

8A:456 Richard Hill (g, AA) exhibited will of Robert Burle (g, AA), proved by Josias Hall (AA) on 27 June 1676. The other witness (being alive) is Mr. Thomas Marsh (KI). Stephen Burle executor was granted administration.
8A:457 Said Burle exhibited inventory of his father Robert Burle (AA).

From: Commissioners of DO County. John Brooke was granted administration on estate of William Worgan on 7 February 1676. Thomas Gilbert (Mr. Worgan's bookkeeper) replied in an obstinate manner that he would not or could not prove the accounts.
8A:458 Signed: William Stephens, Henry Bradle, John Offley. New appraisers: William Stephens, John Offley. Henry Tripp (g) to administer oath.

Col. Samuell Chew (AA) exhibited will of John Benson (CV), proved by Samuell Lane & John Bowen on 20 January 1676/7.
8A:459 Also exhibited was oath of Paul Bewsy & Robert Conante, appraisers sworn 20 January 1676/7. Also exhibited was oath to Elisabeth widow & executrix of said Benson, sworn same day.

8A:460 Thomas Gerrard & John Llewellin (gentlemen, SM) exhibited bond of

Francis Heyden for his wife Thomazin administratrix of Thomas Butler (CH). Also exhibited was oath of Col. John Dowglass & Thomas Gibson, appraisers sworn 25 January last.

8A:461 Capt. Richard Hill (AA) exhibited the commission to take bond of Sarah Hudson sister to John Hudson (AA). She requested additional time, during which she married a second husband. Bond & LoA were returned unsigned. Date: 10 February 1676/7.

Lt. Col. Thomas Taylor (AA) exhibited oath to Robert Francklin & Walter Carr, appraiser of Robert Fitting (AA), sworn 23 September 1676.

8A:462 16 February. The widow Keene relict of William Hunt exhibited inventory.

Capt. Richard Hill (AA) exhibited oath of Ralph & William Hawkins, appraisers of Robert Burle (g, AA), sworn 9 July last.

Richard Hill (g, AA) exhibited oath to Andrew Norwood & Edward Dorsey, appraisers of Peter Porter (AA), sworn 1 August 1676.

William Towlson (g, CE) exhibited will of
8A:463 Nathaniell Stiles (CE), proved by Jacob Singleton on 2 January 1676.

Capt. Richard Hill (AA) exhibited oath of Ralph & William Hawkins, appraisers of Richard Mosse, Sr. (AA), sworn 9 July.

William Towlson (g, CE) exhibited:
8A:464 ...

- Will of Nath. Stiles proved by Jacob Singleton on 2 January 1676.
- Oath of John Dickson & William Salsbury, appraisers sworn same day.
- Oath of Thomas Salmon sworn 8 January 1676.
- Oath of James Stavely administrator sworn 16 January.

Inventory of Edward Gardner (AA) was exhibited.

Inventory of Charles Lawrence (AA) was exhibited.

17 February. Thomas Pattison (DO) gave security to Commissioners of DO County Court for portions due orphans of William Kilman (DO).
8A:465 Said Pattison was instructed by the County Court.
8A:466 Signed: Edward Sauvage (clerk). Said Pattison was granted administration on said estate, & exhibited inventory.

Stephen Gary (DO) exhibited oath to
8A:467 William Watson & William Willoughby, appraisers of Peter Underwood (DO), sworn 10 February 1676/7.

Joane Dunn (KE) executrix & widow of Robert Dunn (KE) exhibited that one of the appraisers is dec'd. New appraisers: Henry Carter, Alexander Waters. William Lawrence (g) to administer oath.

Mary Whetstone (KE) widow & executrix of Stephen Whetstone (KE) exhibited inventory.

8A:468 Katharine Right (KE) widow of Arthur Right (KE) exhibited that her husband made a will, but it is lost. Witnesses were Michaell Miller & Thomas Right. William Lawrence (g) to take depositions.

19 February. Mary Blackfan (CH) widow & executrix of John Blackfan (CH) exhibited his will. Robert Doyne (g) to prove said will.
8A:469 Said Mary was granted administration. Appraisers: John Stone (g), Samuell Eaton. Said Doyne to administer oath.

John Stone (g, CH) exhibited oath of John Blackfan administrator of Richard Owen & his wife sworn 20 September last. Also exhibited was oath to Richard Way & Christopher Wardener, appraisers

8A:470 sworn same day.

Elinor Sewell (CV) widow & executrix of John Sewell (CV) exhibited his will. Baker Brooke, Esq. to prove said will. Said Elinor was granted administration. Appraisers: John Lawrence, Thomas Arnold. Said Brooke to administer oath.

20 February. John Ireland
8A:471 (BA) administrator of Margaret Penroy (CE) has carried away all goods of dec'd from CE. Said Ireland is ordered to pay Capt. Jonathon Sibrey (high sheriff, CE).

Capt. Thomas Long (high sheriff, BA) exhibited bond of Miles Gibson administrator of Abraham Clarke (BA). Also exhibited was oath to administrator, sworn 11 December last. Also exhibited was
8A:472 oath to John Arding & John Boaring, appraisers sworn same day. Miles Gibson exhibited inventory.

21 February. John Addison (CH) exhibited that Nicholas Proddy (CH) made a verbal will. Maj. Benjamin Rozer to prove said will. Appraisers: John Wheeler, Thomas Shuttleworth.
8A:473 Zachary Wade (g) to administer oath.

24 February. Maj. Benjamin Rozer (CH) exhibited will of Samuell Clarke (CH), proved by Thomas Harris & John Cornish on 30 November 1676. John Dowglass (g) was sworn on 30 December last.

8A:474 Maj. Benjamin Rozer (high sheriff, CH) exhibited oath of Peter Carr (CH) executor of Elisabeth Lilly (CH), sworn 30 December last. Will of said Elisabeth was proved by Joseph Bullet on 30 December 1676. The other witness Anthony Bridges is living in VA.

Maj. Benjamin Rozer (high sheriff, CH) exhibited will
8A:475 of Richard Smoote (CH), proved by Will. Browne & Walter Davis on 31 October 1676. Also exhibited was oath of

William Banton, Jr. & Robert Roelants, appraisers sworn 2 November last.

Inventory of
8A:476 Giles Cole (CH) was exhibited.

Inventory of Owen Jones (CH) was exhibited.

Michaell Rochford (g) for the orphans of Capt. George Goldsmith (BA) petitioned that said Goldsmith made a will, whereby Mary (petitioners' mother) was sole executrix. Said Mary married Capt. Samuell Boston & she died before completion of the estate. Said Boston took administration of her estate as well as said Goldsmith.
8A:477 His surety was Nathaniell Stiles (now dec'd). Said Boston is since dec'd, before completion of the estate. His will constituted Dr. John Stanesby & John Mills as executors. Said Boston's estate is inconsiderable of itself & not able to pay his debts. Said executor Mills has neither personal or real estate to satisfy the portions to the petitioners of their father's estate. Said orphans are under age.
8A:478 Ruling: Commissioners of BA County to take security of James Mills executor of said Boston, for the portions of the said orphans.

Elisabeth Bellows widow of Francis Bellows (CE) exhibited that administration on his estate was originally granted to one Elisabeth West, due to mis-information that the widow had remarried.
8A:479 Said Elisabeth Bellows to have new LoA. Michaell Rochford (g) to administer oath.

27 February. Thomas Polton (CH) petitioned that Philip Cary (CH) made a will, bequeathing to Susanna Dunn. Before the will was proved, said Susanna died, with a will, bequeathing the legacy from said Cary to the petitioner & Samuell Barret,
8A:480 & as executors. Before her will was

proved, said Barret died, with a will, citing the petitioner as executor. Zachary Wade (g) to prove all 3 wills. Said Polton was granted administration on all estates. Appraisers: Roger Dickison, William Smith. Said Wade to administer oath.

8A:481 John Pollard (DO) was granted administration on estate of Thomas Newman (DO), who died at Pollard's house, single, unmarried, & childless, as principle creditor. Sureties: Thomas Pattison, Richard Swetnam. Appraisers: John Offley, Thomas Pattison. William Stephens (g) to administer oath.

Zachary Wade (g, CH) exhibited will of William Wilkinson (CH), proved by
8A:482 Edward Maddock & John Mun on 20 February 1676/7. Also exhibited was oath of Capt. Henry Aspinall executor sworn same day. Also exhibited was oath of Edward Maddock & John Mun, appraisers sworn same day.

28 February. Richard Charlton (CV) executor of John Murke
8A:483 (CV) exhibited his will. Tobias Norton (g) to prove said will. Said Charlton was granted administration. Appraisers: James Nutwell, Robert Dove. Said Norton to administer oath.

1 March. Elias Beech & his wife Sarah (one of daughters of William Cole (SM, dec'd) & administratrix of Richard Cole (eldest son of said William)) vs. Alexander Younger & his wife Sarah relict & executrix of said William Cole (St. Jerom's, SM).
8A:484 Said Alexander did not appear on 9 January nor proved an account, but has shipped a considerable portion of the goods & chattel. SM County Court
8A:485 remanded to action.

Elisabeth Bullen (TA) daughter & executrix of Robert Bullen (TA) exhibited his will. George Cowley (g) to prove said will. Said Elisabeth was granted administration.

Court Session: 1676/7

8A:486 Appraisers: Henry Alexander, Samuell Abbot. Said Cowley to administer oath.

John Stone (g, CH) exhibited will of Edmund Taylor, proved by Josias Lee & Peter Rawls on 22 February 1676/7. Also exhibited was oath of George Langham & Richard Chapman. appraisers sworn same day.
8A:487 Also exhibited was oath of Charles Cullis executor sworn same day.

2 March. John Yeo (CV) executor of James Varloe (CV) exhibited inventory.

Elisabeth Brispo (BA) petitioned that
8A:488 her husband Anthony Brispo made a verbal will, in presence of Christopher Bridgewater & Benjamin Tucker, leaving all to petitioner. Said petitioner is a poor, helpless woman. Her husband was born in Flanders under the King of Spain & naturalized "the Assembly before last". The petitioner is not able to travel to Office, due to the winter. Maj. George Wells (BA) to prove said will.
8A:489 Appraisers: William Osborne, William Hollis. Said Wells to administer oath.

3 March. Sarah Evans (CV) relict & executrix of Guy White exhibited inventory.

Thomas Gaunt (CV) administrator of Patrick Craford (CV) was granted continuance.

8A:490 John Darwell (SM) administrator of William Ratcliff (SM) exhibited inventory.

6 March. Thomas Aldwell (CV) administrator of his brother John Aldwell (CV) exhibited inventory.

7 March. Sarah Beach wife of Elias Beach (SM) administratrix of her brother Richard Cole was granted continuance,
8A:491 since there are goods in the hands of his mother Sarah Younger.

9 March. Edward Pack & John Feild (CV) executors of Martha Hill (widow of Henry Hill, CV) exhibited her will. Roger Brooke (g) to prove said will. Said Pack & Feild were granted administration.

8A:492 Dorothy Homan (SM) widow & executrix of Herbert Homan (SM) exhibited his will, proved by Peter Carwarden (witness). The other witness is Thomas Henton, who is absent abroad.
8A:493 Said Dorothy was granted administration. Appraisers: Capt. John Cambell, Daniell Smith. William Hatton (g) to administer oath.

10 March. Will of William Towlson (g, CE) was exhibited. Joseph Hopkins (g, CE)
8A:494 to prove said will. Ebenezar Blackiston & Anne Towlson (widow) executors were granted administration. Appraisers: Edward Skydmore, John Dickson. Said Hopkins to administer oath.

Will of
8A:495 Peter Mounce (CE) was exhibited. Augustine Herman (g) to prove said will. George Oldfield (overseer) was granted administration, during minority of Andrew Peterson (son of dec'd). Said Herman to administer oath.

8A:496 Mary Taylor (CV) relict & administratrix of Jasper Allen (CV) exhibited accounts. Notice
8A:497 given to creditors. Signed: William Stone.

Anne Skinner (CV) relict & administratrix of James Trueman (CV) exhibited accounts.
8A:498 Notice given to creditors.
8A:499 Mr. Thomas Trueman is one of overseers of estate of orphans per will of said Trueman, who thought he made a will, but is dec'd as intestate naming no executor.

Capt. Henry Aspinall (CH) one of executors of William Wilkinson (CH)

exhibited inventory.

8A:500 Edward Inglish (merchant) administrator of William Hewet exhibited that appraisers John Dickson & Robert Neves, were to be sworn by William Towlson (g, CE). Said Towlson is since dec'd. Joseph Hopkins (CE) to administer oath to said appraisers.

Edward Inglish (merchant) administrator
of Roger Thorpe
8A:501 (merchant, London) exhibited that
William Towlson (g, CE) was to
administer oath. Joseph Hopkins to
administer in his stead.

Richard Edelen (g, SM) exhibited verbal
will of Thomas Matthews, Jr. (SM). Also
exhibited oath of Robert Greene
8A:502 & James Bowring, appraisers sworn 29
January 1676.

Inventory of Thomas Shills (SO) was exhibited.

Inventory of Richard Ackworth (SO) was exhibited.

Capt. Richard Hill (AA) exhibited will
of William Crouche, proved by Robert
Burle (g).
8A:503 Also exhibited oath of James (son of
said William) executor sworn 25 March
1676. Also exhibited oath of Dr. Henry
Lewis & William Hawkins, appraisers
sworn same day.

12 March. Elisabeth Bayley (also
8A:504 Elisabeth Bailey, orphan of Godfrey
Bailey (dec'd), CE) petitioned that said
Godfrey made a will, constituting the
petitioner's sister Rosamond Bailey as
sole executrix & Mr. John Vanheck,
Joseph Hopkins, & Thomas Salmon as
overseers. Said Vanheck & Salmon were
granted administration, with sureties
Nathaniell Stiles & John Gilbert. Said
administrators are since dec'd, & have
not provided accounting. Said Rosamond
is also dec'd. Petitioner is of full
age.

8A:505 Said Elisabeth was granted administration on estate of her father Godfrey & her sister Rosamond. Joseph Hopkins (g, CE) to administer oath.

8A:506 Anne Clarke (SM) widow & executrix of Edward Clarke (SM) exhibited his will, proved by Peter Peake & William Didoll.
8A:507 Said Anne was granted administration. Appraisers: Henry Spincke, Peter Mills. Capt. John Jourdain to administer oath.

14 March. William Sheircliffe (SM) was granted administration on estate of his brother John Sheircliffe (SM).
8A:508 Surety: Henry Spincke. Appraisers: Robert Foord, Thomas Salmon. Capt. John Jourdain to administer oath.

William Sheircliffe (SM) was granted administration on estate of his mother Anne Sheircliffe (SM). Said William is her only child alive.
8A:509 Surety: Henry Spincke. Appraisers: Robert Foord, Thomas Salmon. Capt. John Jourdain to administer oath.

Will of Disborough Bennet (g, KE) was exhibited. Joseph Wickes (g) to prove said will. Mary widow & executrix was granted administration.
8A:510 William & Henry Coursey (gentlemen, TA) have each entered a caveat against said estate. Appraisers: Isaack Winchester, Thomas Osborne. Said Weekes to administer oath.

8A:511 16 March. Samuell Tovey (KE) was granted administration on estate of Vincent Atcheson (KE), as principle creditor. The widow Elisabeth renounced administration on 6 March 1676.
8A:512 Said Tovy to act for benefit of widow & orphan. Appraisers: Thomas Osborne, William Bateman. Henry Hosier (g) to administer oath.

8A:513 20 March. William Saunders (mariner, City of Bristol) executor of Margarett Rawbone (AA) exhibited her will. Col. William Burgess to prove said will. Said Margarett is widow of James

Rawbone. Said Saunders was granted administration on her estate.

John Llewellyn (g, SM) exhibited commission to Thomas Gerard (g) & self
8A:514 to prove will of John Shepheard (mariner, NE) & to take bond of William Adams father to Elisabeth Adams (under age, Topsham, ENG) executrix of said will. Said will was proved on 15th instant. Also exhibited was oath of said Adams, sworn same day. Said will was exhibited, proved by Elisabeth Tennison & Mary Tennison.
8A:515 Appraisers Capt. Thomas Shawe & Richard Angell were appointed; Capt. William Singleton & Thomas Angell were sworn as appraisers on 15th instant. William Adams (mariner, Topsham, ENG) administrator of
8A:516 John Shepheard (mariner, NE) exhibited inventory.

21 March. Henry Henley (CH) exhibited will of Richard Harrison (CH). Col. John Douglas to prove said will. Said Henry was granted administration on behalf of the orphans.
8A:517 Appraisers: Humphrey Warren, Robert Roelants. Said Douglas to administer oath.

22 March. Anne Fisher (SM) relict & administratrix of William Burgesse (SM) exhibited accounts. Discharge was granted.

James Frisby (g, CE)
8A:518 exhibited oath of MM Joseph Chew & Richard Edmons, appraisers of Peter Johnson (CE), sworn 3 February. Also exhibited was oath of Katharine Morris administratrix sworn 6 March.

23 March. George Lingan (CV) one of executors of Thomas Cox (CV) exhibited receipt by Henry Cole (CV) attorney for relict (now in ENG).
8A:519 Date: 14 February 1676/7. Witnesses: Edward Swan, Nicholas Terrett. Discharge was granted.

24 March. Elisabeth Hopkinson (TA) widow of Jonathon Hopkinson (TA) exhibited his will, written by William Finny.
8A:520 Matthew Ward (g) to prove said will.

Maj. George Wells (BA) administrator of John Turpinne (BA) was granted continuance.

8A:521 Capt. Richard Hill (AA) exhibited the will of William Luffman, proved. Also exhibited was oath of Mary Luffman (widow) administratrix sworn on 20 July last. Capt. Richard Hill (AA) exhibited oath of appraiser William Hopkins (AA) sworn on 10 August 1676. Robert Tiler, the other appraiser,
8A:522 was gone out of the Province. Said Hill petitioned for another appraiser: Matthew Howard. Said Tiler returned & with said Hopkins proceeded with the appraisement. Mary Luffman (AA) exhibited inventory.

John Broome (CV) exhibited that Robert Taverner (merchant) is dec'd
8A:523 & his brother Thomas Taverner (citizen, merchant, taylor, London) had LoA on 1 February 1675 per the Court at Canterbury. Said Broome is attorney for said Thomas. Administration had already been granted to Samuell Bourne (Cliffes, CV).
8A:524 Bridget Foulke exhibited a suit against estate of said Robert at Canterbury, before Sir Leoline Jenkins Knight. Said Robert made a will before leaving on voyage to VA or MD on 18 October 1675, constituting Mrs. Foulkes (whom he should have married) as executrix.
8A:525 Said Thomas got LoA by falsely indicating that Robert had died intestate.
8A:526 Date: 25 August 1676. Signed: Ralph Suchby (notary), Ste. Hill (notary). Witnesses: Thomas Bourne, Robert Hodges. [Paragraph in Latin.]
8A:527 ...
8A:528 Signed: Marcus Cottle. PoA from said Thomas Taverner to said John Brome (merchant).

Court Session: 1676/7

8A:529 Mentions: ship Baltimore, John Dunch master.

8A:530 Date: 15 February 1675. Witnesses: Samuell Williams, Tho. Rudyerd, Fra. Hickman, Thomas Mayo, Richard Mirritt, Robert Hooper. Sir Joseph Sheldon Lord Mayor of London,

8A:531 alderman or senator certified that said Thomas is sole administrator of estate of said Robert (bachelor).

8A:532 Date: 19 February 1675. Signed: William Lightfoot. Goods & chattel of said Robert to remain in hands of said Samuell until said suit is settled.

Court Session: 1703/4

8B:1 Inventory of David Deane. Date: 20 January 1703/4. Appraisers: John King, Robert Salter. Amount: £30.10.9.

8B:2 Inventory of Nathaniell Hawks (TA). Appraisers: Robert Harrison, Lofland McDaniell. Amount: £22.6.6.

Inventory of John Stanyard (TA). Appraisers: Jasper Cralk (?), James Sanford. Amount: £12.9.9.

8B:3 Inventory of Thomas Sevill (TA). Appraisers: Nicholas Kelly, John Morgan.

8B:4 Amount: £54.18.9.

3rd additional accounts of William Carlisle (SO). Administrator: Mr. Alexander Carlisle.

8B:5 Payments to: Mr. Peter Dent, Mr. John Borman, James Wallace, Maj. Cornish. Date: 5 May 1704. Amount of accounts: £30.16.3. Signed: William Dent.

8B:6 Additional accounts of Hugh Jones (CV). Executor: Rev. Mr. Cockshutt. Legatees: Christ Church paid to Capt. Richard Smith, Sr., Col. John Bigger. Payments to: Esq. Brooks, William Parker, Col. Walter Smith. Date: 8 May 1704. Amount of accounts: £68.7.10. Signed: William Parker (CV).

8B:7 Accounts of John Broomfield. Administrators/Executors: Louery

Court Session: 1703/4

Millward, Edward Crane. Payments to: Edward Ayres, Edward Charlton & Co., George Goldsmith, Benjamin Hamlin, Ebenezar Blackston, William Peirce. Date: 1 April 1703. Amount of accounts: #3966. Signed: M. V. Derheyden (CE).

Inventory of John Kendall.
8B:8 Appraisers: William Foreman, Jacob Peacock. Amount: £8.19.0.

Accounts of Charles Joy (SM). Administrator: Henry Jarboe. Amount of inventory: £7.13.6. Received from: Jos. Powell, William Thompson. Payments to: Mr. Young, Peregrine Browne, William Stone,
8B:9 Dr. Barth, John Nutwell, William Herd, Mr. Wright, Esq. Brookes, James Keetch. Date: 17 March 1704. Amount of accounts: #5407. Signed: James Keetch (SM).

Inventory of John Jaxon (TA). Date: 18 June 1703.
8B:10 ...
8B:11 Appraisers: Richard Jones, Walter Smithwald. Amount: £66.10.4.

8B:12 Inventory of Thomas Whitton. Appraisers: Benoni Clarke, Henry Gilldour. Date: 18 January 1703/4.
8B:13 Signed: Benony Clark, Henry Gildord. Amount: £31.10.0.

Court Session: 1677

9A:1 26 March. Dr. John Stanesby (BA) exhibited will of Capt. Samuell Boston (BA) proved.

27 March. Cornelius Howard (AA) was granted administration on estate of John Grange (BA).

George Parker (g, CV) exhibited PoA from Ralph Forth (citizen, alderman, London), with LoA by Rt. Rev. Archbishop of Canterbury
9A:2 regarding estate of Roger Thorpe (London) committed to said Forth. On 2 November 1676, before Anthony Wright

(notary, London), said Ralph Forth (citizen, leatherseller, London) appeared as a creditor of Roger Thorpe (merchant, London)

9A:3 & as administrator of said Thorpe & gave to Mr. George Parker (g) a PoA to recover from Mr. Edward English (merchant).

9A:4 ...

9A:5 Witnesses: Leon. Webber, John Boddy, J. Bovie. [Passage in Latin.]

9A:6 ...

9A:7 Signed: Marcus Cottle.

9A:8 Letter from: Sir Thomas Davis Knight, Lord Mayor & alderman or senator of London. James Andrew (merchant), age 30) & Samuell Hall, age 27, appeared & deposed that the letters were written by Roger Thorpe

9A:9 & attested by Anthony Wright. Date: 3 November 1676. Signed: (N) Wagstaffe.

9A:10 Said Parker requested the goods belonging to said Thorpe for accounting of said Forth. Edward Inglish (merchant, CE) was summoned to account to said Parker.

9A:11 Christopher Rowsby (g, CV) on behalf of Jarvase Ballard exhibited that William Caswell (mariner, Boston, NE) died on board the ship Thomas & Edward of London, Capt. John Browne commander, after its arrival in Petuxent, having goods now in possession of Mr. Jarvase Ballard for widow & children of said Caswell.

9A:12 Said Rousby is indebted to Theodore Plices his father. Said Ballard was granted administration on estate of said Caswell, for the widow & children in NE.

9A:13 John Hance (CV) administrator of James Marram (CV) exhibited inventory.

John Hance (Clifts, CV) executor of Francis Leigh (CV) exhibited inventory.

James Rigby (AA) executor of William Drewry (AA) exhibited inventory.

<u>28 March</u>. William Rawls (KE) exhibited nuncupative will of Thomas Deane

9A:14 (KE). Said Rawls was granted administration. Appraisers: Michaell Miller, John Jackson. Thomas Marsh (high sheriff, KE) to administer oath.

9A:15 William Lawrence (g, KE) exhibited depositions for proof of will of Arthur Wright (KE), by witnesses Michaell Miller & Thomas Wright. Katharine Browne executrix was granted administration. Appraisers: Michaell Miller, Patrick Gordon. Thomas Marsh (high sheriff, KE) to administer oath.

9A:16 Katharine Browne relict & executrix of Arthur Wright (KE) who was administrator of Richard Peerce (KE) exhibited inventory of said Peerce.

31 March. Nehemiah Birckhead (AA) exhibited that Col. Samuell Chew, who was to swear John Sollers & Nathan Smith as appraisers of estate of his father Christopher Birckhead (AA), is dec'd. Maj. Samuell Lane to administer in his stead.

9A:17 2 April. Anne Fisher (SM) relict & administratrix of William Burgesse (SM) exhibited her payment to Joseph Edloe (CV) executor of William Keene (CV). No assets remain to pay further debts of said Burgesse. Papers to remain in Office for
9A:18 defense of orphan (under age) of said Burgesse. Discharge was granted.

Margarett Ward (SM) widow & administratrix of Andrew Ward (SM) exhibited inventory.

Susannah Smith (SM) widow & executrix of John Smith (SM) exhibited his will. Thomas Gerrard (g) to prove said will.
9A:19 Said Susanna was granted administration. Appraisers: Maj. William Boarman, Lt. James Bowling. Said Gerrard to administer oath.

3 April. Ward Zachary (g, CH)
9A:20 exhibited wills of Philip Cary, Susanna Dunn, & Samuell Barrett (CH), proved.

Also exhibited was oath of Thomas Polton sworn 9 March 1676/7. Also exhibited was oath of William Smith & Roger Dickison, appraisers sworn same day.
9A:21 Said Polton exhibited inventory for Samuell Boston, Susanna Dun, & Philip Cary.

George Cowley (g, TA) exhibited will of Robert Bullen (TA), proved. Also exhibited was oath of Elisabeth Bullen executrix sworn 17 March 1676/7.
9A:22 Also exhibited was oath of Henry Alexander & Sam. Abbot, appraisers sworn same day. Elisabeth Bullen (TA) daughter & executrix of Robert Bullen (TA) exhibited inventory.

Samuell Hatton for William Wintersell (TA) was granted administration on estate of Alexander Pollard (TA), who was a lodger at said Wintersell's house & died there, single, unmarried, childless, & no relation in the Province.
9A:23 Appraisers: Thomas Alexander, said Samuell Hatton. George Cowley (g) to administer oath.

Elisabeth Gorsuch (TA) widow of Richard Gorsuch (TA)
9A:24 was granted administration on his estate. Appraisers: Thomas Alexander, Richard Gurling. George Cowley (g) to administer oath.

9A:25 On 2 April instant, Thomas Hargness (CH) exhibited will of Walter Russell (CH), witnessed by John Cassock & Charles Russell. Said Hargness testified that there was another will for said Russell, but he does not know what happened to it nor its date. John Cassock was summoned, but would not appear. Charles Russell appeared & was interrogated:
9A:26 ...
9A:27 Said Russell thinks that Capt. James Neale has the will. Said Russell believes that said Hargness would not prove said will in the lifetime of William Russell because: when William Russell went to Southward, he conveyed

his lands to Walter Russell purposely to defraud Capt. James Neale & other creditors & said Walter gave said William a bond, which Capt. Josias Fendall has.

9A:28 Mentions: that said William is the brother of said Walter,

9A:29 wife of Thomas Hargness, Capt. Allen.

9A:30 ...

- John Fen deposed that Charles Russell is the brother of said William Russell.
- Anne Russell deposed, mentioning:

9A:31 ...

her husband Charles Russell.

- Elisabeth Hargness deposed, mentioning: the wife of Charles Russell, Capt. Josias Fendall, her brother Walter Russell,

9A:32 ...

her brother William, Capt. James Neale.

- John Cassock

9A:33 ...

deposed, mentioning: Charles Russell.

<u>4 April</u>. Ruling:

9A:34 the will of Walter Russell was fraudulently written, and therefore null and void.

Henry Trippe (g, DO) exhibited

9A:35 oath of William Stephens (g) & John Offley, appraisers of William Worgin (DO) sworn 23 February last. John Brooke (g, DO) administrator of said Worgin exhibited inventory.

William Stephens (g, DO) exhibited oath of

9A:36 John Offley & Thomas Pattison, appraisers of Thomas Newman (DO) sworn 27 March last. John Pollard (DO) administrator of said Newman exhibited inventory.

Capt. William Adams (Topsham, ENG) administrator of John Shepheard (Boston, NE) exhibited accounts.

9A:37 Discharge was granted.

Maj. Thomas Truman (CV) executor of his brother Nathaniell Truman (CV) was granted administration on his estate.
9A:38 Appraisers: Thomas Greenfield, Richard Massam. Tobias Norton (g) to administer oath.

5 April. John Davis (TA) administrator of William Taylor (TA) exhibited accounts.
9A:39 Residue: orphans.

9A:40 Sibill Groome (CV) widow & executrix of William Groome (g, CV) exhibited his will
9A:41 & was granted administration on his estate. Appraisers: Lewis Jones, Arthur Storer. Roger Brooke (g) to administer oath.

6 April. Cornelius Howard (AA) was granted administration on estate of John Grange (BA), who died single, unmarried, childless, & with no relation in the Province, as principle creditor.
9A:42 Appraisers: Francis Watkins, (N). Richard Ball (g, BA) to administer oath.

9 April. Susanna Floyd & Alice Grave (CV) joint executrices of Cartwright Demetrius (CV) exhibited inventory.

9A:43 Sarah Warren (KE) widow of Thomas Warren, Jr. (KE) was granted administration on his estate. Appraisers: William Bateman, John Wedge. Samuell Tovy (g) to administer oath.

9A:44 William Ferguison (AA) administrator of Thomas Phelps (AA) unadministered by said Ferguison's wife Elinor (now dec'd) late relict & administratrix of said Phelps exhibited his bond formerly passed to Lancelot Todd who married the only daughter of said Phelps. Date: 16 March 1676. Witness: Richard Hill. Discharge was granted to said Ferguison.

9A:45 10 April. Thomas Bowdle (CV) administrator of John Martin (merchant, Barbadoes) unadministered by Jasper Allen (CV) exhibited inventory for estate of said Martin.

Peter Stokes (DO) administrator of George Bolton (DO) exhibited inventory.

9A:46 12 April. Capt. William Adams (Topsham, ENG) administrator of John Shepheard (Boston, NE) exhibited a letter from executor of Andrew Shepherd (brother of said John), dated 26 June 1676 Boston. Andrew & his wife both fell sick. He died, and she died within 2-3 days afterwards.
9A:47 Mentions: Mr. Hawford. Signed: John Indecott, John Scuttow.

9A:48 Thomas Starling (g, Clifts, CV) administrator of Benjamin Brasseur (CV) exhibited accounts.

Thomas Starling & Robert Heigh (CV) executors of James Humes (CV) exhibited his will.
9A:49 Appraisers: John Cobreath, Marke Clare. Capt. Samuell Bourne (g) to administer oath.

13 April. Anne Assetter (SM) widow of William Assetter (SM) was granted administration on his estate.
9A:50 Appraisers: Peter Mills, Thomas Bassett. Capt. John Jourdain to administer oath.

16 April. Thomas Marsh (high sheriff, KE) exhibited oath of Michaell Miller & Patrick Gordon, appraisers of Arthur Wright (KE) sworn 5 April. Also exhibited was oath of Michaell Miller & John Jackson, appraisers of Thomas Deane (KE) sworn 5 April.

9A:51 17 April. Samuell Taylor & Lt. Ninian Beale (CV) 2 of overseers of Alexander Magruder (CV) exhibited his will. The widow is also lately dec'd. She was named executrix with orphans (under age 17). Said Taylor & Beale were granted administration, on behalf of said orphans during their minority.
9A:52 Appraisers: Richard Massam, Peter Archer. Maj. Henry Jowles to administer oath.

18 April. Abigail Wright (DO) widow of Arthur Wright (DO)
9A:53 exhibited his will. Said Abigail was granted administration. Stephen Gary (g) to take bond. Appraisers: Anthony Dawson, John Rawlins.
9A:54 John Brooke (g) to administer oath.

Capt. Richard Hill for Sarah Todd (AA) widow of Thomas Todd (AA) was granted administration on his estate.
9A:55 Appraisers: Robert Proctor, Edward Dorsey. Said Hill to administer oath.

Richard Fenwick (CV) administrator of his brother Cuthbert Fenwick was granted continuance.

19 April. Humphrey Warren (g, CH) was granted administration on estate of Thomas Howell (CH), who died leaving 3 orphans (under age).
9A:56 Surety: Maj. Benjamin Rozer. Appraisers: Col. John Douglas, Capt. Robert Henley. Said Rozer to administer oath.

Maj. Benjamin Rozer (high sheriff, CH) exhibited will of Job Cornor (CH) proved.
9A:57 Anne Cornor widow was granted administration. Appraisers: John Boswell, Michaell Minock. Said Rozer to administer oath.

Mary Credwell (CH) widow & executrix of George Credwell (CH) exhibited his will.
9A:58 Maj. Benjamin Rozer to prove said will. Said Mary was granted administration. Appraisers: Humphrey Warren, John Fanning (gentlemen). Said Rozer to administer oath.

Elisabeth Corker (CH) widow & executrix of Thomas Corker (CH) exhibited his will. Maj. Benjamin Rozer to prove said will.
9A:59 Said Elisabeth was granted administration. Appraisers: George Godfrey, Robert Middleton. Said Rozer to administer oath.

James Smallwood (CH) was granted administration on estate of his brother John Evans (CH).
9A:60 Appraisers: Michael Minock, Thomas. Said Rozer to administer oath.

20 April. Sheriff (TA) to summon Benony Bishop, John Morris, & Robert Colson (material witnesses to will of John Beard (TA), by his widow concealed) & testify on said will.

Nicholas Hacket (TA) was granted administration on estate of
9A:61 John Richards (DO), who died with neither wife nor child nor any other relation but one sister in DO who refused administration, as principle creditor. Surety: John Rawlins. Appraisers: Richard Holland, John Richardson. Bartholomew Reynolds (g, DO) to administer oath.

9A:62 Col. Vincent Lowe (high sheriff, TA) one of overseers of estate of Thomas Hawkins (KE) exhibited his will. Thomas Marsh (high sheriff, KE) to prove said will. Said Lowe was granted administration on behalf of widow & orphans. Appraisers: William Lawrence, Philip Conniers. Said Marsh to administer oath.

9A:63 Anne Chew (AA) widow & executrix of Col. Samuell Chew, Esq. (AA) exhibited his will. Lt. Col. Thomas Taillor to prove.

George Parker (g) for Dorothy Whittle (Cliffts, CV) widow of George Whittle (CV) was granted administration on his estate.
9A:64 Appraisers: John Hance, William Kent. William Parker (g) to administer oath.

Lt. Col. Thomas Taillor (AA) exhibited will of John Cumber (AA) proved.
9A:65 Judith Cumber widow was granted administration. Appraisers: Henry Stocket, Robert Francklin (gentlemen). Col. William Burgess to administer oath.

Court Session: 1677

Maj. George Wells (BA) exhibited verbal will of Anthony Brispo (BA).
9A:66 Elisabeth Brispo widow was granted administration.

Thomas Overton (BA) executor of his brother Bernard Utie (BA) exhibited accounts. Discharge was granted.

Maj. George Wells (BA) exhibited oath of William Hollis & William Osborne, appraisers of Anthony Brispo (BA) sworn 3 April.
9A:67 Elisabeth Brispo (BA) widow & executrix of Anthony Brispo exhibited inventory.

Elisabeth Palmer (BA) widow of William Palmer (BA) was granted administration on his estate.
9A:68 Appraisers: William Hollis, Michaell Gibson. George Utie (g) to administer oath.

21 April. Jervase Ballard (merchant, Boston, NE) was granted administration on estate of William Caswell (merchant, late of Boston). Surety: Mr. Christopher Rousby.
9A:69 Said Ballard was granted administration for widow & orphans of said Caswell, living in Boston. Appraisers: Joseph Edloe, John Evans. John Griggs (g, CV) to administer oath.

Anne Avery (DO) widow & executrix of John Avery (DO) exhibited his will, proved by Thomas Pattison.
9A:70 Said Anne was granted administration. Appraisers: Thomas Pattison, William Robson.

Per Charles James (CE), the personal estate of Francis Barnes (CE) was seized & escheated
9A:71 to His Lordship. Administration had been granted to John Cox as principle creditor. Said administration is revoked.

Edward Man (merchant) for widow Earle (TA) widow of Thomas Earle (TA) exhibited that said widow is unwilling to administer on the estate. Capt. George Cowley to prove will said will.

9A:72 Administration was granted to her father on behalf of her & her children. Appraisers: Thomas Martin, Thomas Alexander. Said Cowley to administer oath.

9A:73 Thomas Potter (SM) executor of George Marshall (SM) exhibited accounts. Discharge was granted.

Anthony Mayl (g, TA) exhibited oath of Edward Man, administrator of Thomas Reade (TA), sworn 16 January 1676/7. Also exhibited was oath of Henry Parker &
9A:74 George Hurlock, appraisers sworn same day.

Henry Adams (g, CH) exhibited oath of Archibald Wahop, administrator of Edward Fox (CH), sworn 20 March.
9A:75 Also exhibited was oath of Philip Hoskins & Hugh Thomas, appraisers sworn same day.

Zachary Wade (g, CH) exhibited oath of John Wheeler & Thomas Shuttleworth, appraisers of Nicholas Proddy (CH) sworn 11 April 1677.

Zachary Wade (g, CH) exhibited oath of John Wright, executor of Thomas Gailey sworn 30 March 1677.
9A:76 Also exhibited was oath of William Smith & Abraham Sapcoate, appraisers sworn same day. The other appraiser is dec'd, & Sapcoate was substituted.

Maj. Benjamin Rozer (high sheriff, CH) exhibited oath of William Wells, administrator of David Maddox.

9A:77 Maj. Benjamin Rozer (high sheriff, CH) exhibited oaths of Richard Carpenter & Silvanus Gilpin, witnesses to nuncupative will of Nicholas Proddy, sworn 2 April 1677.

Court Session: 1677

Maj. Benjamin Rozer (high sheriff, CH) exhibited
9A:78 oath of John Cable, administrator of Luke Greene sworn 16 March 1676. Also exhibited was oath of John Ward & Thomas Shuttleworth, appraisers sworn 10 March 1676.

Maj. Benjamin Rozer (high sheriff, CH) exhibited
9A:79 oath of John Wood administrator of Philip Browne sworn 16 March 1676. Surety: Edward Williams. Also exhibited was oath of George Langham & Garret Sinnot, appraisers sworn 17 March 1676.

23 April. George Parker attorney for Ralph Forth administrator of Roger Thorpe vs. Edward Inglish.
9A:80 Administration per Rt. Rev. Gilbert Archbishop of Canterbury & attested by Thomas Davis Knight, Lord Mayor of London & Anthony Wright (notary). Said Parker exhibited that said Inglish was granted administration on estate of said Thorpe in this Province, since said Inglish was administrator of John Allen as principle creditor of said Thorpe. However, said Allen was a debtor to said Thorpe.
9A:81 Ruling: Lt. Col. Thomas Taillor summon both said Inglish & Parker to review their powers from said Forth, Timothy Harmor, et. al. &
9A:82 to review accounts & report back.

Edward Inglish (merchant) administrator of Roger Thorpe petitioned to give bond per direction to William Toulson (g, dec'd) & then to Joseph Hopkins (g, CE).
9A:83 Sureties: Capt. Jonathon Sibrey, James Ringold (g).

24 April. Thomas Todd (merchant, Glocester Co., VA), now living in this Province, exhibited will of his father Thomas Todd (BA). Capt. Thomas Long (high sheriff, BA) to
9A:84 prove said will. Said Thomas Todd, Jr. was granted administration. Appraisers: Richard Ball (g), Dr. John Stanesby. Said Long to administer oath.

Court Session: 1677

Giles Blizard for Mary Clemens (TA) widow & executrix of John Clemens (merchant, TA) exhibited that William Cannons (merchant,
9A:85 TA) has a wife in ENG, but no attorney for her. Said Cannons was indebted to her husband. Said Mary was granted administration on estate of said Cannons, for the widow & any orphans in ENG.
9A:86 Appraisers: George Robins, Thomas Alexander. Edward Man (g) to administer oath.

Joseph Hopkins (g, CE) exhibited will of William Toulson (g, CE), proved. Also exhibited was oath of
9A:87 Ebenezar Blackiston & Anne Toulson, executors of said estate sworn 24 March 1676/7. Also exhibited was oath of Edward Skidmore & John Dixon, appraisers sworn same day.

Joseph Hopkins (g, CE) exhibited oath of Capt. Jonathon Sibrey (high sheriff, CE), administrator of Joseph Seers (CE),
9A:88 sworn 29 March 1677.

Capt. Richard Hill (g, AA) exhibited oath of appraisers of estate of Stephen White (AA): Ralph Hawkins, sworn 19 March last, & Ralph Duncastle sworn 1 April last. Also exhibited was oath of Anne White widow & executrix of said Stephen
9A:89 sworn 19 March last.

Capt. Richard Hill (g, AA) exhibited oath of John Hammond, administrator of Richard Russell, sworn 5 April 1677. Security: Edward Dorsey. Also exhibited was oath of
9A:90 Samuell Howard & Abraham Child, appraisers sworn 5th instant.

Matthew Ward (g, TA) exhibited will of Jonathon Hopkinson (inholder, TA), proved by William Finney (clerk who wrote said will).

Dr. Henry Lewis (g, AA) exhibited
9A:91 oath of Robert Proctor & Robert

Clarkeson, appraisers of David Griffith (AA) sworn 11 April instant.

Augustine Hirrman (g, CE) exhibited will of James Magruder (CE), proved.

Augustine Herman (g, CE) exhibited oath of Hugh Fouche & John Browning, appraisers of James Magruger (CE) sworn 8 February last. Also exhibited was
9A:92 oath of Hugh Magruger (son of said James, CE) executor.

Zachary Wade (g, CH) exhibited will of Thomas Gailey (CH), proved.

Capt. Richard Hill (g, AA) exhibited will of Stephen White (AA), proved.

Tobias Norton (g, CV) exhibited will of
9A:93 John Ramsey, Sr. (CV), proved.

Matthew Ward (g, TA) exhibited will of Jonathon Hopkinson (inholder, TA) written by William Phinney (only witness) with said Phinney's deposition.

Archibald Wahop (CH) administrator of Edward Fox exhibited inventory.

9A:94 John Addison (CH) executor of Nicholas Proddy (CH) exhibited inventory.

John Wright (CH) executor of Thomas Gailey (CH) exhibited inventory.

John Browne (SM) administrator of John Thomas (SM) exhibited inventory.

9A:95 John Cable (CH) administrator of Luke Greene (CH) exhibited inventory.

John Wood (CH) administrator of Phillip Browne (CH) exhibited inventory.

Henry Truelock (CV) administrator of Robert Turner (CV) exhibited inventory.

Anne White (AA) widow & executrix of Stephen White (AA) exhibited inventory.

Court Session: 1677

9A:96 John Hammond (AA) administrator of Richard Russell (AA) exhibited inventory.

John Cousins (CV) administrator of John Ramsey, Sr. (CV) exhibited inventory.

Capt. Richard Hill (AA) administrator of David Griffith (AA) exhibited inventory.

9A:97 Hugh Magruger, Jr. (CE) executor of his father James Magruger (CE) exhibited inventory.

Elisabeth Benson (CV) widow & executrix of John Benson (CV) exhibited inventory.

25 April. John Edmundson for Katharine Mountague (DO) exhibited that Dr. Robert Winsmore was to administer oath to her as administratrix of her husband Henry Mountague (TA).
9A:98 John Brooke (g, DO) now to administer oath.

Susanna Streete (CV) widow & executrix of Francis Streete (CV) exhibited his will. Maj. Henry Jowles to prove said will. Said Susanna was granted administration.
9A:99 Appraisers: Richard Massam, James Williams. Said Jowles to administer oath.

Capt. Thomas Long for Richard Bale (g, BA) administrator of Robert Wilson (BA) was granted continuance.
9A:100 John Waterton (g, BA) exhibited oath of Katharine Shadwell widow & administratrix of John Shadwell (BA). Also exhibited was oath of Thomas Jones & James Collier, appraisers sworn 30 November. Said Katharine
9A:101 exhibited inventory.

26 April. Col. Baker Brooke, Esq. for Elisabeth Sherridine (CV) widow & executrix of Thomas Sherridine (CV) exhibited his will. Said Brooke to prove said will. Said Elisabeth was granted administration.

Court Session: 1677

John Wilmoth (BA) executor of
9A:102 John Melem (BA) exhibited his will. Capt. Thomas Long (high sheriff, BA) to prove said will. Said Wilmoth was granted administration. Appraisers: Nicholas Ruxstone, Nicholas Corbin. Said Long to administer oath.

9A:103 Maj. Henry Jowles (CV) administrator of Andrew Higgs (chirurgeon, CV) exhibited inventory.

George Robins (TA) administrator of Peter Underwood (DO) exhibited inventory.

Thomas Clipsham (CH) administrator of Roger Bowder (CH) exhibited inventory.

Mary Tilghman (TA) widow & executrix of Dr. Richard Tilghman (TA) exhibited inventory.

9A:104 James Mills (BA) administrator of Robert Mattocks (BA) exhibited inventory.

James Mills (BA) executor of Capt. Samuell Boston exhibited inventory.

Maj. George Wells (BA) administrator of John Turpin (BA) exhibited inventory.

9A:105 William Rawls (KE) executor of verbal will of Thomas Deane (KE) exhibited inventory.

Mary Eaton (KE) widow & executrix of Jeremiah Eaton (KE) exhibited inventory.

Joane Workman (KE) relict & executrix of Robert Dun (KE) exhibited inventory.

Richard Nash (CE) executor of Joseph Herendon exhibited his will.
9A:106 Augustine Herrman (g) to prove said will. Said Nash was granted administration. Appraisers: John Cocks, Bartholomew Henderson.

Col. Baker Brooke, Esq. (CV) exhibited
9A:107 oath of Thomas Tennant & David Davis, appraisers of Cuthbert Fenwick (CV)

sworn 13 December 1676.

27 April. William Coursey (g, TA) exhibited oath of James Coursey, administrator of John Scott (TA),
9A:108 sworn 7 November last. Also exhibited oath of Arthur Emery & Robert Ellis, appraisers sworn same day. James Coursey (g, TA) exhibited inventory.

9A:109 William Coursey (g, TA) exhibited oath of Arthur Emery administrator of John Wright (TA), sworn on 7 November last. Katharine relict & executrix died soon after dec'd.
9A:110 Also exhibited oath of Thrustram Thomas & Robert Ellis, appraisers sworn same day.

28 April. Lt. Col. Thomas Taillor, Esq. (AA) attorney for John Keynes (g, Marleborough, Wilts, ENG) executor of Joseph Burges (grocer, Marleborough, Wilts, ENG) late of AA (merchant & planter)
9A:111 exhibited his accounting to said Keynes. Discharge was granted.

Col. Thomas Taillor for Andrew Roberts (AA) executor of Charles Lawrence (AA) exhibited accounts.
9A:112 Discharge was granted.

John Winne (chirurgeon, SM) exhibited will of John Ribton (merchant, Whitehaven, Cumberland, ENG), proved by George Gray. Said Winne exhibited that widow & daughters named in will now live in ENG, & that said Winne is principle creditor.
9A:113 Said Winne was granted administration. Appraisers: Henry Phippes (g), John Evans. William Hatton (g) to administer oath.

ultimate April. Elinor Brooke (CV) widow & executrix of Col. Thomas Brooke (CV) was granted continuance.

9A:114 Edward Man (merchant, TA) administrator of Thomas Reade (TA) was granted continuance.

Per Matthew Ward (g), sheriff (CE) is to summon Thomas Todd & Charles James (CE) sureties for Arthur Carleton administrator of his brother Thomas Carleton
9A:115 (CE) to show cause why the bond should not be assigned to said Ward.

Matthew Ward (g) for Elisabeth Beard (TA) widow of John Beard (TA) exhibited his will. Said
9A:116 Ward to prove said will. Appraisers: William Finney, Robert Noble. Said Ward to administer oath.

Matthew Ward (g) for Elisabeth Hopkinson (TA) widow & executrix of Jonathon Hopkinson (inn holder, TA) exhibited that it is material what William Phinney (only witness) can depose.
9A:117 Said Ward to interrogate said Phinney
9A:118 & to stop embezzlement of the estate. Appraisers: William Phinney, Philip Steevenson. Said Ward to administer oath.

Robert Smith for Bridget Powell (TA) widow & executrix of William Powell (TA) exhibited his will. Matthew Ward (g) to prove said will.
9A:119 Said Bridget was granted administration. Appraisers: Richard Jones, John Chafe. Said Ward to administer oath.

1 May. Dorothy Homan (SM) widow & executrix of Herbert Homan (SM) exhibited inventory.

9A:120 Edward Inglish (merchant, CE) exhibited PoA from constituents, attested by Thomas Davis Knight, Lord Mayor of London, & alderman or senator: on 7 December 1676, before Anthony Wright (notary, London) Timothy Harmer (merchant, London) came &
9A:121 constituted a PoA to Edward Inglish (merchant, MD) to recover from estate of William Hewet as well as goods received by John Turpin administrator of said Hewet. Said Hewet was bound with Josiah Tidd (mariner, London).
9A:122 ...

9A:123 Signed: Tim. Harmer. Witness: John Randall. [Paragraph
9A:124 in Latin.] Condition of agreement. Signed: William Hewitt, Josiah Tidd. Witnesses: John Flavell, John Hearne.

Bill to:
9A:125 Timothy Harmer. Date: 21 October 1671. Signed: William Hewit. Witnesses: Fran. Harmer, Thomas Jenkins.

9A:126 On 18 September 1676, MM William Pococke & Timothy Harmer (merchants, London) came before Anthony Wright (notary) & constituted a PoA to Edward Inglish (merchant, MD) to administer the estate of Roger Thorpe (merchant, MD).
9A:127 ...
9A:128 Signed: William Pocoke, Tim. Harmer. Witnesses: John Body, J. Bovie.

Sir Thomas Davies Knight, Lord Mayor & alderman or
9A:129 senator of London certified the following depositions:

- John Hearne (g, London), age 30, attested to bond by William Hewit & Josiah Tidd, with conditions to pay

9A:130 ...

  Timothy Harmer (citizen, merchant, taylor, London).
- William Pococke (merchant, London), age 47, attested to sale to Roger Thorpe (merchant, London).

Said Lord Mayor certified Anthony Wright (notary).
9A:131 Date: 8 December 1676. Signed: (N) Wagstaffe.

On 9 October 1676,
9A:132 Mr. John Phillips (fishmonger, London) came before Anthony Wright (notary) for self & his mother Mrs. Sarah Phillips & constituted a PoA to Edward Inglish (merchant, CE) to recover from John Newton (merchant, Farby Creek, MD) goods & chattel delivered here by the constituent to Roger Thorpe (merchant, London).
9A:133 ...
9A:134 Witnesses: Leon. Webber, John Body, J. Bovie. Sent by Mr. Roger Thorpe on 24

November 1675 in commission of my mother Sarah Phillips & partner John Phillips upon return of goods from MD:
9A:135 list of goods. Amount: £7.6.0.

On 9 October 1676,
9A:136 Mr. Thomas Bibbey (weaver, Newington Butts, Surrey) came before Anthony Wright (notary) & constituted a PoA to Mr. Edward Inglish (merchant, CE) to recover from John Newton (merchant, Farby Creek, MD) goods & chattel delivered here by said constituent to Roger Thorpe (merchant, London).
9A:137 ...
9A:138 Witnesses: John Body, Leon. Webber, J. Bovie. From London dated 24 November 1675, an invoice of goods on the ship Golden Lyon Leonard Webber commander consigned to Roger Thorpe at head of Bay in MD in VA: list
9A:139 of goods.
9A:140 Amount: £32.1.4.

4 May. William Parker (g, Cliffts, CV) exhibited that George Whittle (CV) died intestate & that administration was granted to Dorothy Whittle widow.
9A:141 Said Dorothy died before administering said estate. Said George left 4 orphans (under age) & said Parker married the aunt of said orphans, & said Parker is also principle creditor. Said Parker was granted administration, on behalf of orphans.
9A:142 Appraisers: William Parker (Hunting Creek), John Hance (Cliffts). Col. Samuell Bourne to administer oath.

5 May. Joseph Pile (g, SM) exhibited oath of Thomas Simpson & Thomas Stonestreete, appraisers of Andrew Ward (SM) sworn 27 March 1677.

9A:143 7 May. John Addison (SM) executor of Nicholas Proddy (CH) was granted administration on his estate.

8 May. Anthony Tall (g, DO) administrator of William Hambridge (DO)
9A:144 exhibited accounts. Discharge was granted.

Court Session: 1677

9 May. Francis Spencer for his neighbor Joane Jenkins (CV) widow of William Jenkins (CV) was granted administration on his estate.

9A:145 Appraisers: said Spencer, John Johnson. Maj. Samuell Lane (g, AA) to administer oath.

11 May. Col. William Burgess (g, AA) exhibited the will of Margaret Rawbone proved. Capt. Richard Hill (g, AA) exhibited

9A:146 letter of William Saunders executor: William Saunders (boatswain of the ship Charles) executor of widow Rawbone, will proved by Col. Burgesse, petitions to take possession of the widow's estate: a plantation. Presented at the request of said

9A:147 Sanders. Date: 4 May 1677. Said William Sanders was granted administration.

Edward Cowdrey for Anne Pritchet (CV) widow & executrix of William Pritchet (CV)

9A:148 exhibited his will & her petition. Said Anne is unacquainted with the affairs of the world & unable to travel, have "a great many small children" & nobody to look after them in her absence.

9A:149 Roger Brooke (g) to prove said will. Anne Pritchet widow was granted administration. Appraisers: Thomas Robinson, John Winnell. Said Brooke to administer oath.

Edward Cowdrey (CV) was granted administration on estate of John Greer (CV), who left 4 motherless orphans (under age) & no relations in the Province. His estate is very inconsiderate.

9A:150 Said Cowdrey was granted administration, as principle creditor. Appraisers: Nicholas Butterum, Samuell Goozey. Roger Brooke (g) to administer oath.

9A:151 14 May. Thomas Innes (SM) administrator of Thomas Loquer (SM) exhibited accounts. Discharge was granted.

Court Session: 1677

15 May. Roger Brooke (g, CV) one of executors of Edward Keene (CV) exhibited accounts.
9A:152 Continuance was granted.

Roger Brooke (g, CV) exhibited will of Martha Hill (widow of Henry Hill, CV) proved.
9A:153 Edward Pack & John Field (CV) executors of Martha Hill (CV) exhibited inventory.

William Barton, Jr. (CH) exhibited inventory of Richard Smoote (CV) by appraisers John Cage & George Credwell. Letter from Judge to Commissioners of CH: I understand that Mr. Barton, Jr. has intermeddled with goods & chattels of
9A:154 estate of Richard Smoote though he is not administrator. I accepted the inventory but won't accept accounts unless he is the administrator. The orphans are in your care. Signed: Philip Calvert.

16 May. Marke Cordea (SM) was granted administration on estate of Samuell Brockhurst (SM), who died leaving 4 orphans under age, as principle creditor.
9A:155 Surety: Walter Hall (g). Appraisers: said Hall, John Askin.

17 May. Samuell Bourne (g, Clifts, CV) exhibited will of James Hume (CV), proved, by John Sunderland (CV) who lately married the widow. Said Sunderland exhibited that Thomas Stirling & Robert Heigh (executors named in the will) refused to administer the estate & his wife Sarah the relict
9A:156 will not administer the estate. Said Sunderland was granted administration on behalf of said Sarah & the orphans. Ruling: said James had died intestate.
9A:157 Said Bourne to take bond & renunciations. Capt. Samuell Bourne (Clifts, CV) exhibited oath of John Cobreath & Marke Clare, appraisers sworn 18 April last.
9A:158 John Sunderland (Clifts, CV) administrator of James Hume (CV)

exhibited inventory.

Henry Henley (CH) administrator of Richard Harrison exhibited inventory.

19 May. John Welsh (high sheriff, AA) exhibited summons to Thomas Francis to account for goods & chattel of John Shawe (AA) & for goods of Sarah relict of said John & late wife of said Thomas.

Stephen Murtey (SM) administrator of John Bailey (SM) exhibited inventory
9A:159 & was granted continuance.

Henry Darnall (high sheriff, CV) exhibited summons to Mary Griggs relict & executrix of Richard Keene (CV).

21 May. Thomas Bucknall (AA) who married Mary relict & administratrix of Edward Wheelocke (AA) exhibited accounts. Capt. Richard Hill (AA) to obtain oath of said Mary
9A:160 & to give notice to creditors.

Rebecca Addison relict & executrix of Thomas Dent (SM) executor of Henry Hull (g, SM) exhibited accounts for said Hull. Discharge was granted.

28 May. Summons was issued to Thomas Todd (BA) & Charles James (CE) sureties for Arthur Carleton (CE) administrator of Thomas Carleton (CE)
9A:161 to appear & show cause by bond should not be assigned to the creditors of said Thomas.

30 May. Commissions to Richard Ball (g, BA) returned:

- to prove will of Lewis Bryen (BA).
- to exhibit said will & inventory.
- to take bond of Jonas Bowing father of Elisabeth executrix in the will & one of the overseers.
- to take bond of Nicholas Corbin the other overseer.
- Sureties: Richard Bale & John Harding.

Richard Ball was at that time dec'd.

Court Session: 1677

9A:162 Thomas Todd (Mop. Jacke Bay, VA) exhibited that Thomas Long (high sheriff, BA) was to prove will of his father Capt. Thomas Todd (BA). One of the witnesses is dec'd, & the other has left the Province for an unknown destination. Said Todd petitioned to be permitted to prove will as he was able, in order to preserve the estate which was

9A:163 in danger of being wasted & destroyed by relict of dec'd who is since married to a wasteful spendthrift. A letter from the father to son mentions: that father is aboard the ship Virginia Factor, commander Capt. James Connaway, bound for ENG & desires to see his son or to hear from his son by letter to Mr. Barnaby Dunch; that your mother, brothers, & sisters are well;

9A:164 Mr. John Robinson. Date: 10 April 1676.

- Miles Gibon (BA), age 29, deposed that about a year ago, Mrs. Anne Todd then wife of Thomas Todd, Sr. show the deponent the dec'd's will & asked the deponent to read it to her. After her husband's death, she left her habitation in the custody of her eldest daughter, as well as said will. Said daughter kept it until her marriage to said deponent, who delivered it to Thomas Todd, Jr.

9A:165 Said Thomas Todd (Mop. Jacke Bay, VA) executor was granted administration. Richard Ball (Petapsco), one of the original appraisers, is since dec'd. New appraisers: Nathaniell Hinchman, John Harding.

9A:166 Capt. Thomas Long to administer oath.

<u>ultimate May</u>. Mary Griggs relict & executrix of Richard Keene (CV) appeared & deposed:

- since her marriage to John Griggs, she has not been privy to any payments to any creditors.
- her eldest son by said Keene has received his portion.
- her husband is now gone to ENG.

Said Mary was granted continuance.

2 June. Mary widow of James Nicholson (SO) was granted administration on his estate. She cannot travel to the Office, without danger to her life.
9A:167 Appraisers: John Bosman, John Laws. Charles Ballard (g) to administer oath.

6 June. Hannah Hawkins widow of Thomas Hawkins (Popleys Island, KE) exhibited the petition that Thomas Marsh (high sheriff, KE) prove the will. However, the commission was given to Col. Vincent Lowe. It is requested that said Marsh prove the will.
9A:168 Said Hannah was granted administration. Mentions: her daughter Elisabeth (infant, under age), her son born since death of dec'd.

Nathaniell Teagle (TA) exhibited that Robert Woolverton (TA) became sick on 22 March 1675/6 & made his will, constituting said Teagle as sole executor. Said Wollverton died 6 days later. Witnesses to said will are not able to travel to the Office.
9A:169 Capt. (now Maj.) George Cowley to prove said will. Appraisers: Robert Knap, Clement Sayles. Said Teagle was granted administration. Said Cowley to administer oath.

8 June. Henry Bonner (g, CH) exhibited that:

- John Emmerson (merchant, CH) was indebted to Walter Story.
- Said Emmerson assigned to said Story a debt of Anthony Bridges.
- Since the death of said Story, Elisabeth Bonner relict of said Story was granted administration on his estate.

9A:170 Said Henry was granted administration on estate of John Emmerson, as greatest creditor. Maj. Benjamin Rozer to take bond.

15 June. Edward Turner (CV) executor of William Singleton (CV) exhibited accounts.
9A:171 Notice sent to creditors.

9A:172 Maj. Benjamin Rozer for Thomas Clipsham (CH) exhibited that John Cage (CH) was granted administration on estate of Charles Gregory (chirurgeon, SM), for benefit of widow. Said Cage is since dec'd. Said Clipsham is greatest creditor to said Gregory.
9A:173 Said Clipsham was granted administration on estate of said Gregory, for benefit of widow. Appraisers: Humphrey Warren, John Fanning (gentlemen). Maj. Benjamin Rozer (CH) to administer oath.

Maj. Benjamin Rozer for executrix of
9A:174 John Cage (CH) exhibited his will. Said executrix is unable to travel to the Office. Said executrix was granted administration. Appraisers: Robert Henley, Robert Roelants. Said Rozer to administer oath.

16 June. Edward Pinder (DO)
9A:175 on behalf of widow & orphans of John Hudson, Sr. (DO), petitioned that said Hudson made a will, constituting David Cuffyn & Edward Fisher (Nantecoake) executors, & leaving a widow & 3 small children (begotten of her). Said widow is since dec'd. The estate & the children are in ruinated condition; neither the executors nor John Hudson (son of dec'd) are taking care to maintain such. Said petitioner & said widow contracted a marriage,
9A:176 but it was never solemnized. The executors proved the will, but will not administer the estate. The dec'd's son intends to administer the estate, but makes no haste for the good of the children. It is wildly known that said son is a young wild & dissolute person & is incapable of managing his own considerable estate left by his father. He also showed ill to his young & tender brothers.
9A:177 Sheriff (DO) to summon David Cuffyn & Edward Fisher executors of John Hudson, Sr. (DO) to either accept or renounce the executorship of said estate.

9A:178 19 June. George Parker for Elisabeth Paget (CV) widow & executrix of Thomas

Paget (CV) exhibited his will. Robert Heighe (g) to prove said will. Said Elisabeth was granted administration. Appraisers: William Kent, Marke Clare. Said Heighe to administer oath.

9A:179 Maj. George Cowley (TA) executor of John Slaughter (TA) petitioned for Col. Vincent Lowe (high sheriff, TA) to prove the will. Said Cowley was granted administration on said estate. Appraisers: Edward Stephens, Edward Winles. Said Lowe to administer oath.

9A:180 Col. Vincent Lowe for Mary Broadacre, wife of Thomas Broadacre (TA), relict of James Oliver (TA) petitioned for said Lowe to prove said Oliver's will. Appraisers: Edward Elliot, Hugh Sherwood. Said Lowe to administer oath.

9A:181 20 June. Walter Davis (CH) exhibited that Richard Smoote (CH) is dec'd, citing Robert Roelants & William Barton, Jr. as overseers. They had the will recorded & the goods & chattels secured, but nothing else. Said Davis is greatest creditor, & Richard Smoote (eldest son of dec'd) is of age to have chosen said Davis as his guardian. Said Davis was granted administration, on behalf of the orphans. Capt. Humphrey Warren to administer oath.

9A:182 Matthew Ward (g, TA) exhibited for the second time the will of Jonathon Hopkinson (inn holder, TA), as well as the oath of William Finney (who wrote the will) & the letter of Thomas the nephew of the dec'd. Said will was ruled valid.

9A:183 Elisabeth widow & executrix was granted administration. Said Warde to administer oath.

Thomas Todd (Mop. Jacke Bay, VA) son & executor of Capt. Thomas Todd (BA) requested a copy of the will & LoA for transmission to the legatees in ENG.

9A:184 Roger Diggins (SM) sole surviving executor of William Bourk (SM) was granted continuance. Clement Haly who married widow of said Bourke has the management of the estate.

21 June. Joseph Weeks (g, KE) was commissioned to prove will of Disborough Bennet
9A:185 & to swear Mary relict & executrix of said Bennet. Caveats were entered by William & Henry Coursey (gentlemen, TA). Said Mary assumed the estate was insolvent & not capable of satisfying their debts. Lewis Blangey who married said Mary reached an agreement with said William & Henry, who are not home to certify. Said Weekes to be security for said Blangey.

9A:186 Joseph Chew for Anne Gibbs now wife of John Gibbs (CE) exhibited that her husband Edward Best (KE) is dec'd. Said Anne was granted administration on said estate. Appraisers: John James, Giles Porter. Capt. Joseph Hopkins to administer oath.

Thomas Preston (BA)
9A:187 executor of Thomas Arminger (BA) exhibited accounts. Residue: orphan of said Arminger.
9A:188 Discharge was granted.

Abigail Wright (DO) widow of Arthur Wright (DO) exhibited that John Brooke & William Stephens (gentlemen, DO) had agreed to be her securities, but now refuse.
9A:189 Stephen Gary to administer oath to said Abigail.

Thomas Pattison (g, DO) administrator of William Killman (DO) exhibited accounts.

22 June. John Rawllings (DO) was granted administration on estate of William Rubert (DO), who died single, unmarried, childless, & has no relation in this Province,
9A:190 as chief creditor. Surety: Thomas Pattison. Appraisers: Henry Turner, Anthony Dawson. Henry Bradley (g) to administer oath.

Augustine Hirrman (g) for George Oldfield (CE) administrator of Peter Mounce (CE) petitioned for new appraisers: William Brocas, John Hyland. Said Hirrman to administer oath.

9A:191 Henry Stocket for John White (CE) executor of William Tison (taylor, KE) exhibited his will. Joseph Hopkins (CE) to prove said will. Appraisers: Isaac Harnesse, Ebenezar Blackistone. Said Hopkins to administer oath.

James Coursey for Robert Ellis (TA) executor of John Underwood (Wye River, TA) exhibited his will. William Coursey (g) to prove said will.
9A:192 Said Ellis was granted administration. Appraisers: Thrustram Thomas, Nicholas Broadway. Said Coursey to administer oath.

<u>23 June</u>. Hanah Edwards (CV) relict & executrix of John Pott (CV) exhibited accounts.
9A:193 Estate is overpaid. Discharge was granted.

Commissioners of CE Co. Court exhibited accounts of John Owen (CE). Thomas Matthews (CE) executor is since dec'd. Capt. Jonathon Sibrey requested discharge for widow of said Matthews.
9A:194 Discharge was granted.

Capt. Jonathon Sibrey for widow Matthews (CE) exhibited that her husband Thomas Matthews (CE) is dec'd. Said widow was granted administration on said estate.
9A:195 Appraisers: George Oldfield, William Salsbury. Joseph Hopkins (g) to administer oath.

Dr. Henry Lewis for widow Norman (AA) executrix of George Norman (AA) exhibited his will. Said Lewis to prove said will. Said widow was granted administration. Appraisers: Matthew Howard, James Smith. Said Lewis to administer oath.

9A:196 George Parker procurator for Cornelius Howard (AA) administrator of John Sisson (AA) exhibited that William Yieldhall (AA) who married one of the daughters of said Sisson has refused to render an account of those items in his hands. Sheriff of AA is to summon said Yieldhall to show cause why he should not provide said accounting.

25 June. George Robins (TA) administrator of Peter Underwood (DO) exhibited accounts. Estate is overpaid.
9A:197 Discharge was granted.

David Cuffyn (DO) one of executors of John Hudson, Sr. (DO) for self & other executor Edward Fisher exhibited that per Edward Pindar (DO) the executors were summoned to show cause why the will was not yet proved. The executors could not get the witnesses together.
9A:198 Said Cuffyn also exhibited that neither he nor Edward Fisher will take the oath of executors, citing that it is a practice against their Religion, & therefore renounce the executorship. Henry Bradley (g) to prove said will.

9A:199 Col. George Wells (BA) administrator of John Turpin (BA) was granted continuance.

Elisabeth Bailey (CE) administratrix of her father Godfrey Bailey (CE) unadministered by John Vanheck & Thomas Salmon & administratrix of her sister Rozamund Bailey (daughter of said Godfrey, CE) was granted continuance.

9A:200 Henry Stocket (AA) & James Stavely (CE) administrators of Nathaniell Stiles (CE) exhibited inventory. Said Stocket & Stavely petitioned for copies of the documents to be sent to William Scrimshire (ENG) executor of said will.

9A:201 Col. William Calvert, Esq. (Principle Secretary of Province) for Francis Lucas (SM) widow & executrix of William Lucas (g, SM) was granted discharge.

Maj. Thomas Long (high sheriff, BA) exhibited that administration was granted to Richard Bale (g, BA, dec'd) administrator of Robert Wilson (BA). Said Bale had disposed of some part of the estate before taking the oath & then dying.

9A:202 George Parker (Cliffes, CV) exhibited the commission to Lt. Col. Thomas Taylor (AA) on 23 April last per agreement between said Parker & Edward Inglish (merchant, CE) administrator of Roger Thorne (merchant, London) to frame the inventory for said Thorpe. Inglish was represented by his procurators Robert Carvile & Robert Ridgely, arguing
9A:203 that as attorney for Ralph Forth (merchant, London) administrator of said Thorpe, he was principle creditor to said Thorpe. Said Inglish as administrator of John Allen (merchant) was indebted to estate of said Thorpe. Judge ordered delay of 1 month.

Capt. Richard Hill (AA) exhibited
9A:204 oath of Sarah Todd (AA) widow & administratrix of Thomas Todd (AA), sworn 7 May last. Also exhibited was oath of: Robert Proctor & Edward Dorsey, appraisers sworn 10 May.

Thomas Gerard (g, SM) exhibited
9A:205 oath of Susanna Smith (SM) widow & executrix of John Smith (SM), sworn 28 April. Also exhibited was oath of Maj. William Boarman & Lt. James Bowling, appraisers sworn 28 April.

9A:206 Robert Doyne (g, CH) exhibited oath of John Stone (g), Samuell Eaton, appraisers of John Blackfan (merchant, CH) sworn 12 March.

Maj. George Cowley (TA) exhibited oath of Samuell Hatton & William Combes (instead of Thomas Alexander who was seized by sickness), appraisers of Alexander Pullard (TA)
9A:207 sworn 30 April.

Maj. George Cowley (TA) exhibited oath of John Paddeson (TA) brother & executor of John Blower (TA). Appraisers: Thomas Martin, Henry Alexander.

9A:208 Richard Edelen (g, SM) executor of Samuell Cressey (CH)
9A:209 was granted continuance.

Dr. Henry Lewis (g, AA) exhibited oath of Matthew Howard & William Hopkins, appraisers of Abraham Dawson (AA) sworn 7 April. Also exhibited was oath of Anne Dawson (AA)
9A:210 widow & executrix, sworn 29 March.

Dr. Henry Lewis (g, AA) exhibited oath of Elisabeth Bennet (AA) widow & executrix of verbal will of Richard Bennet (AA), sworn on 2 April.

Henry Adams (g, CH) exhibited oath of Thomas Helger appraiser with
9A:211 Randolph Brandt of the estate of James Chancellor (CH), sworn on 4 April.

Henry Adams (g, CH) exhibited oath of Thomas Helger appraiser with Randolph Brandt of the estate of Stephen Champ (CH), sworn on 4 April.

Maj. Henry Jowles (CV)
9A:212 exhibited oath of Susanna Streete (CV) widow & executrix of Francis Streete (CV), sworn on 16 June. Also exhibited was oath of Richard Massam & James Williams, appraisers sworn same day. Richard Clarke was appointed in lieu of said Massam, who is dangerously sick.

9A:213 Capt. Samuell Bourne (g, CV) exhibited oath of William Parker & John Hance, appraisers of George Whittle (CV) sworn 8 May.

9A:214 Col. John Dowglas (CH) exhibited will of Richard Harrison (CH), proved. Administrator Henry Henley was sworn on 15 June.

Matthew Ward (g, TA) exhibited oath of appraisers of Jonathon Hopkinson (inn holder, TA): William Finney sworn 9 May & Philip Steevenson sworn 7 May.

9A:215 Matthew Ward (g, TA) exhibited will of William Powell (TA), proved. Bridget Powell widow & executrix was sworn on 2 June. Appraisers Richard Jones & John Chafe
9A:216 were sworn on 12 June.

Tobias Norton (g, CV) exhibited oath of Thomas Greenefield & Richard Marsham, appraisers of Nathaniell Truman (CV) sworn 10 April.

Capt. Gerard Slye (high sheriff, SM) exhibited summons to Richard Edelen executor of Samuell Cressey (CH).

9A:217 Maj. Thomas Long (high sheriff, BA) exhibited summons to Thomas Todd (BA) one of sureties of Arthur Carleton (CE) administrator of his brother Thomas Carleton (CE), since said Arthur has not exhibited accounts. Said Todd is dec'd in Old ENG.

9A:218 Capt. Samuell Bourne (Cliffts, CV) exhibited oath of William Parker (g, CV) administrator of George Whittle (CV), sworn on 8 May.

Maj. Thomas Long (high sheriff, BA) exhibited summons to Thomas Preston (BA) executor of Thomas Arminger (BA)
9A:219 to exhibit accounts.

Capt. Gerard Slye (high sheriff, SM) exhibited summons to Roger Diggins (SM) sole surviving executor of William Bourke (SM), to exhibit accounts.

9A:220 Col. William Burgesse (AA) exhibited oath to Diana Hollaway (AA) widow of Oliver Hollaway (AA), sworn on 12 June.
9A:221 Appraisers Robert Francklin (g) & Walter Carr were sworn on same day.

William Stephens (g, DO) exhibited will of Dr. Robert Winsmore (DO), proved. Katharine Winsmore widow & executrix was sworn on 8 February. Appraisers Henry

Tripp & John Brooke (gentlemen)
9A:222 were sworn same day.

Capt. Samuell Bourne (Cliffts, CV), exhibited bond of John Sunderland (CV) administrator of James Hume (CV), with sureties Thomas Stirling & Robert Heighe. Also exhibited was renunciation of said Stirling & Heighe as executors. Date: 17 May.
9A:223 Said Thomas Starling & Robert Heighe renounced on 2 June. Witnesses: Samuell Bourne, William Travers.

9A:224 Capt. Jonathon Sibrey (high sheriff, CE) exhibited summons to Edward Inglish (merchant, CE) administrator of Roger Thorpe (merchant, London) to exhibit accounts to George Parker (Cliffts, CV) attorney for Ralph Forth (merchant, London) administrator of said Thorpe in ENG.

9A:225 Capt. Jonathon Sibrey (high sheriff, CE) exhibited commission to swear Elisabeth Bellows (CE) widow of Francis Bellows. She could not find security. Michaell Rochford (g) directed to take bond.

John Cox (CE) exhibited administration on estate of Francis Barnes (CE) dated 25 June 1675. Said Cox had not taken oath
9A:226 nor given bond. Charles James was directed to secure said Barnes' goods & chattels. LoA to said Cox were revoked.

26 June. Thomas Gerard (g, SM) exhibited will of John Smith (SM), proved.

Robert Doyne (g, CH) exhibited will of John Blackfan (merchant, CH), proved.

Maj. George Cowley (TA) exhibited will
9A:227 of John Blower (TA), proved.

Dr. Henry Lewis (g, AA) exhibited will of Abraham Dawson (AA), proved.

Maj. Henry Jowles (CV) exhibited will of Francis Streete (CV), proved.

Augustine Hirrman (g, CE) exhibited will of Peter Mounce (CE), proved.

9A:228 Lt. Col. Thomas Taylor (AA) exhibited will of Col. Samuell Chew (AA), proved.

Col. John Douglas (CH) exhibited will of Richard Harrison (CH), proved.

Matthew Warde (g, TA) exhibited will of William Powell (TA), proved.

William Stephens (g, DO) exhibited will of Dr. Robert Winsmore (DO), proved.

9A:229 Edward Inglish (merchant, CE) administrator of Roger Thorpe (merchant, London) exhibited 2 inventories.

Susanna Streete (CV) widow & executrix of Francis Streete (CV) exhibited inventory.

Samuell Tovy (g, KE) administrator of Vincent Atchison (KE) exhibited inventory.

9A:230 Said inventory cites when Henry Hosier (g) swore the appraisers.

Thomas Pattison (g, DO) administrator of William Killman (DO) exhibited accounts.

27 June. Sarah Beach (SM) wife of Elias Beach (SM) administratrix of her brother Robert Cole (SM) exhibited inventory.

9A:231 Katharine Winsmore (DO) widow & executrix of Dr. Robert Winsmore (DO) exhibited inventory.

Sibill Groome (CV) widow & executrix of William Groome (g, CV) exhibited inventory.

Thomas Truman (g, CV) executor of his brother Nathaniell Truman (CV) exhibited inventory.

Court Session: 1677

9A:232 Matthew Ward (g, TA) exhibited inventory of Jonathon Hopkinson (inn holder, TA).

Bridget Powell (TA) widow & executrix of William Powell (TA) exhibited inventory.

Jervase Ballard (mariner, Boston, NE) administrator of William Caswell (merchant, Boston) exhibited inventory.

9A:233 William Lee (CH) administrator of James Chancellor (CH) unadministered by Judeth relict of said James & late wife of said William exhibited inventory.

Anne Toulson (CE) & Ebenezar Blackiston (CE) executors of William Toulson (g, CE) exhibited inventory.

Robert & Francis Goodrick (CH) executors of their father George Goodrick (CH) exhibited inventory.

9A:234 Memorandum: On 22 May last, Thomas Francis (AA) administrator of John Shaw (AA) unadministered by Sarah Francis late wife of said Thomas & relict of said John exhibited accounts for both estates.

28 June. Anne Dawson (AA) widow & executrix of Abraham Dawson (AA) exhibited inventory.

William Sheircliffe (SM) administrator of his brother John Sheircliffe
9A:235 exhibited inventory.

William Sheircliffe (SM) administrator of his mother Anne Sheircliffe (SM) exhibited inventory.

Memorandum: on 19th instant, Mary Reevely (SM) relict & administratrix of William Hampstead (SM) exhibited accounts.

29 June. John Paddison (TA) executor of John Blower (TA)
9A:236 exhibited inventory.

William Wintersell (TA) administrator of Alexander Pullard (TA) exhibited inventory.

John Cornish (CH) administrator of Stephen Champ (CH) exhibited inventory.

Sarah Todd (AA) widow & administratrix of Thomas Todd (AA) exhibited inventory.

9A:237 5 July. Roger Brooke (g, CV) one of executors of Capt. Edward Keene (CV) exhibited accounts.

6 July. Anne Assetter (SM) widow & administratrix of William Assetter (SM) exhibited inventory.

11 July. Capt. Gerard Slye (high sheriff, SM) petitioned for a copy of will of his father Robert Slye (g,
9A:238 SM) for legatees that are in ENG.

12 July. Richard Edelen (g, SM) executor of Samuell Cressey (attorney, CH) exhibited accounts.
9A:239 Continuance was granted.

13 July. Maj. Samuell Lane (AA) exhibited bond of Joane Jenkins (CV) widow & administratrix of William Jenkins (CV).
9A:240 Said Joane was sworn on 16 May last. Appraisers Francis Spencer & John Johnson were sworn on same day.

Maj. Samuell Lane (AA) exhibited bond of Thomas Docton (AA) administrator of William Paget (AA). Said Thomas was sworn on 29 July 1676.
9A:241 Appraisers Thomas Knightson & Patrick Hall were sworn same day.

Thomas Bankes (CV) administrator of George Beckwith (CV) exhibited that Richard Meakings has received goods of said estate from Elisabeth orphan of said George.
9A:242 Sheriff of DO to summon said Richard. Per John Miles (CV) who married Mary one of orphans of said George, Thomas Bankes (CV) administrator of George Beckwith

(CV) exhibited accounts.
9A:243 Continuance was granted.

16 July. Col. John Dowglas (CH) executor of Sarah Clarke (CH)
9A:244 was granted administration on her estate. Appraisers: Ralph Shaw, William Hensey. Maj. Benjamin Rozer to administer oath.

Maj. Rozer for Mary Credwell (CH) widow & executrix of George Credwell (alias George Grodtwell) exhibited that said George was administrator of her brother-in-law Richard Fouke
9A:245 (CH). Said Mary was granted administration on his estate.
9A:246 Appraisers: Humphrey Warren, John Fanning (gentlemen). Maj. Benjamin Rozer to administer oath.

William Moffet for Susanna Barbery (CV) widow & executrix of Thomas Barbery (CV) exhibited his will. Maj. Henry Jowles to prove said will. Appraisers: Daniell Golstone, Samuell Goozey.
9A:247 Said Jowles to administer oath.

Capt. George Cowley (TA) exhibited oath of Thomas Alexander & Richard Gurling, appraisers of Richard Gorsuch (TA)
9A:248 sworn 28 June last. Also exhibited was the bond by the widow & administratrix, with sureties Samuell Hatton & Richard Keene. Elisabeth Gorsuch (TA) widow & administratrix of said Richard exhibited inventory.

9A:249 17 July. William Parker (g, Cliffts, CV) administrator of George Whittle (CV) exhibited inventory.

18 July. Capt. Humphrey Warren (CH) exhibited bond of Walter Davies administrator of Richard Smoote, Sr. (CH), with sureties John Hatch & Robert Inglsby.
9A:250 Capt. Humphrey Warren (CH) administrator of Capt. Thomas Howell (CH) exhibited inventory.

20 July. Thomas Gaunt (CV) administrator of Patrick Craford (CV) exhibited inventory.

23 July. Henry Bradle exhibited
9A:251 will of John Hodson (DO), proved. David Cuffyn & Edward Fisher executors renounced executorship, 14 July 1677.
9A:252 ...
9A:253 Signed: David Cuffin, Edward Fisher. Witnesses: Barthol. Ennalls, Tho. Daniell. Administration was granted to John Hodson, Sr. (DO) son by a former wife, on behalf of Thomas Hodson, John Hodson, Jr., & Joseph Hodson his brothers by a second venter. Said John Hodson, Sr. was a stranger in these parts.
9A:254 Appraisers: William Dorsey, Thomas Harper. William Stevens (g, DO) to administer oath.

25 July. Elisabeth Magruder (CV) widow & executrix of Alexander Magruder (CV) exhibited that because of a falsehood, that she was dec'd, LoA were granted to Samuell Taylor & Ninean Beale &
9A:255 Maj. Henry Jowles to prove said will, by John Johnson & James Soulivant. Said Elisabeth was granted administration.
9A:256 Appraisers: Richard Massam, Peter Archer. Said Jowles to administer oath.

Henry Howard for Alice Skydmore (AA) exhibited that Edward Skydmore had made a will, constituting said Alice as executrix.
9A:257 Said Alice Skidmore widow & relict of Edward Skydmore (AA) has renounced administration. Said Edward died May last. Per the will, said Alice would have received 1/5th. [By renouncing, she gets 1/3rd.]
9A:258 The children are under age. Date: 24 July 1677. Witness. Hen. Lewis. Capt. Joseph Hopkins to summon Ebenezar Blackiston & John Louder (witnesses) to prove will & to preserve the rights of the younger sons of said Edward (who ought not to be prejudiced by the renunciation of their mother). In case Henry Howard & the rest of the overseers

refuse
9A:259 administration, administration will be granted to said Elisabeth [sic].

27 July. Col. William Ball (Rorotoman, Rapahanack River, VA) was granted administration on estate of his son Richard Ball (Petapsco, BA), who died leaving a daughter, on behalf of said orphan.
9A:260 Maj. Thomas Long or Dr. John Stanesby to administer oath.

9A:261 Thomas Taillor (high sheriff, DO) exhibited summons to Anne O'Bryan widow of Denis O'Bryan (DO), to explain why Henry Harris as principle creditor should not be granted administration, since said Anne is unable to find security.

Anne Avery (DO) widow & executrix
9A:262 of John Avery (DO) exhibited inventory.

Susanna Smith (SM) widow & executrix of John Smith (SM) exhibited inventory.

28 July. Anne Edwards (SM) relict & administratrix of Daniell Murphey (SM) exhibited accounts.
9A:263 Discharge was granted.

ultimate July. Sarah Barnes (Cliffts, CV) relict & executrix of Nicholas Carre (CV) exhibited his will, proved before Capt. Samuell Bourne.
9A:264 Said Sarah was granted administration. Appraisers: Tobias Miles, John Kent. Said Bourne to administer oath.

Henry Barnes & Francis Malden (Cliffes, CV) executors of Owen Griffith (chyrurgeon, CV) exhibited inventory.

9A:265 2 August. Richard Charleton (CV) executor of John Murke (CV) exhibited inventory.

4 August. Anne Clarke (SM) widow & executrix of Edward Clarke (SM) exhibited inventory. Continuance was granted.

9A:266 Richard Fenwick (CV) administrator of his brother Cuthbert Fenwick (CV) was granted continuance.

6 August. The will of Nicholas Holmes (TA) was proved before Richard Gorsuch (g, now dec'd). Samuell Abbot one of the executors exhibited renunciation of John Dickison (another executor). Date: 30 October 1676.
9A:267 Signed: John Dickeensen. Said Samuell as sole remaining executor was granted administration. Samuell Abbot (TA)
9A:268 exhibited inventory.

Samuell Abbot (TA) administrator of Edward Vearing (TA) exhibited accounts.
9A:269 Residue is
9A:270 to be secured for the orphans.

Maj. George Cowley (TA) exhibited will of Thomas Earle (TA), proved. The widow Earle exhibited inventory.

8 August. Hannah Hawkins (Popley's Island, KE) widow & executrix of Thomas Hawkins (KE) exhibited inventory.

14 August. Robert Carvile (recorder, SMC) exhibited that Dominicke Bodkin (merchant,
9A:271 Galloway, Ireland) died "in the parts beyond the seas some years since." In 1674, said Dominicke became indebted to said Carvile. Said Carvile is executor of Elisabeth Moy executrix of Richard Moy (inn holder, SM) & said Dominicke was indebted to said Moy. Said Carvile was granted administration on estate of Dominick Bodkin.
9A:272 Bondsmen: Geritt Vansweringen (alderman, SMC), Richard Sweatnam (inn holder, St. John's).

17 August. John Yeo (clerk, CV) executor of James Varloe (CV) exhibited accounts. Discharge was granted.

9A:273 29 August. Maj. Samuell Lane for William Mere (AA) was granted administration on estate of Francis Hill (AA), who died single, unmarried, childless, & has no relations, as principle creditor. Appraisers: Richard Bedwart, George Lingan. Said Lane to administer oath.

9A:274 Maj. Samuell Lane for Nathan Smith (AA) was granted administration on estate of Thomas Howard (AA), who died single, unmarried, childless & having no relation in the Province, as principle creditor. Appraisers: Thomas Morgan, Henry Bennet. Said Lane to administer oath.

9A:275 Robert Heighe (Cliffts, CV) exhibited oath of Elisabeth Paget widow & executrix of Thomas Paget (CV), sworn on 16 July last. Also exhibited was the will proved, and oath of William Kent & Marke Clare, appraisers
9A:276 sworn 14 July last. Elisabeth Paget exhibited inventory.

Sheriff of AA exhibited summons to William Yieldhall to exhibit accounts to Cornelius Howard administrator of John Sisson.

9A:277 Sheriff of AA exhibited summons to Alice Skydmore widow of Edward Skydmore (AA) to exhibit will of said Edward, & to either accept or renounce administration.

John Hance (Cliffts, CV) administrator of James Marram (CV) exhibited accounts.

John Hance (Cliffts, CV) who married Sarah relict & executrix of Sampson Waring (g, CV)
9A:278 exhibited accounts. Administration was granted to said Sarah 7 years ago. Discharge was granted.

Robert Carvile (recorder for SMC) exhibited that administration on estate of Dominicke Bodkin (merchant, Galloway, IRE) was granted to him
9A:279 as principle creditor. Since then, Maj. Benjamin Rozer (CH) has received PoA from executors of will of said dec'd, now living in ENG, to administer on

their behalf.

ultimate August. Mary Clemens (TA) widow & executrix of John Clemens (merchant, TA) had administration on estate of William Cannons (TA) as principle creditor,
9A:280 & relinquished administration on said estate.

3 September. Richard Meekins (DO) was granted administration on estate of George Bacon (DO), who died at Meekin's house, single, unmarried, childless & having no relation in this Province, as principle creditor.
9A:281 Appraisers: Joseph Stannaway, John Merriday. Henry Hooper (g) to administer oath.

5 September. Richard Edelen for Thomas Alcock (CH) & Edward Rookwood (CH) exhibited will of David Towell (CH). Zachary Wade (G) to prove said will.
9A:282 Said Alcock & Rookwood were granted administration. Appraisers: John Munn, Roger Dickeson. Said Wade to administer oath.

10 September. Sarah Warren (KE) widow & administratrix of Thomas Warren, Jr. exhibited inventory.
9A:283 Samuell Tovy (g, KE) exhibited oath of Sarah Warren widow & administratrix of Thomas Warren, Jr.

12 September. Nathaniell Teagle (TA) executor of Robert Woolterton (TA) exhibited that Maj. George Cowley (TA) was to prove said will. New warrants are needed.
9A:284 Appraisers: Thomas Alexander, Nicholas Hacket. William Crosse (g) to administer oath.

Col. Vincent Lowe, Esq. (high sheriff, TA) exhibited will of John Slaughter (TA), proved. Also exhibited was oath of Edward Wincles & Edward Stephens, appraisers
9A:285 sworn 22 August. Also exhibited was oath of Maj. George Cowley executor.

Said Cowley executor of John Slater (TA) exhibited inventory.

Sarah Evans (CV) relict & executrix of Guy White (CV) exhibited additional inventory.

9A:286 13 September. Edward Isaack attorney for his sister Rebecca Brooke (CV) widow & administratrix of John Brooke (CV) exhibited accounts. Several creditors live in ENG. Continuance was granted.

9A:287 Thomas Marsh (high sheriff, KE) exhibited will of Thomas Hawkins (Poplar Island, KE), proved. Also exhibited was oath of William Lawrence & Philip Conniers, appraisers sworn 4 July. Also exhibited was oath of Hannah widow & executrix, sworn same day.

14 September. Morgan Jones (St. Jerome's, SM) executor of John Harrington (SM) exhibited inventory
9A:288 & accounts.

Maj. George Cowley (TA) executor of John Slater (TA) was granted administration on his estate.

9A:289 15 September. Henry Harris (DO) exhibited that Denis O'Bryan (DO) died intestate & his widow has refused administration. Thomas Gilbert testified to the widow's refusal last August. Said Harris was granted administration as principle creditor, on behalf of Anne widow of dec'd.
9A:290 Sureties: Thomas Pattison, said Gilbert. Appraisers: said Pattison, John Steward. John Brooke (g) to administer oath.

Maj. Thomas Long (BA) exhibited bond of Col. William Ball (Rapahanack River, VA) father & administrator of Richard Ball (g). Sureties: Miles Gibson, John Boring.
9A:291 Said Ball was sworn 31 July. Also exhibited was oath of Nicholas Ruxstone & William Shelburne, appraisers sworn same day.

Maj. Thomas Long (high sheriff, BA) exhibited warrant to swear John Wilmoth executor of John Melems (BA),
9A:292 with will & certified that said Melems [sic] would not take oath, because his Religion denies use of swearing. Charles Gorsuch deposed on behalf of said Wilmoth that a part of the estate of said Melems that was given to said Wilmoth was omitted. There are witnesses who can declare such.
9A:293 Said Long to take depositions.

18 September. Richard Beck (BA) administrator of his brother Lewis Beck (BA) exhibited accounts.

John Stone (g, CH) exhibited the will of Richard Midgely
9A:294 (CH), proved. Also exhibited was oath of John Wright & Edward Price, appraisers sworn 22 December 1676. John Hanson (CH) & Elisabeth Midgely (CH) exhibited inventory.

Charles Cullis (CH) executor of Edmund Taylor (CH) exhibited inventory.

9A:295 19 September. Nicholas Gazaway (AA) exhibited letter regarding orphans of John Shaw (AA). Mentions: he & Richard Tydings were appraisers of estate of said Shaw. Signed: Nicholas Gassaway. Date: 15 September 1677.

Col. William Burgesse for John Stimson (AA) exhibited letter dated 14th instant
9A:296 regarding summons to his now wife Rachell Stimson late Rachell Clarke relict & executrix of Neale Clarke (AA). He & his family have been very sick & unable to travel to Office.
9A:297 Continuance was granted.

Richard Beard, Jr. (AA) executor of Daniell Taylor (AA) exhibited summons to exhibit accounts. Other executor Peter Barnard has renounced administration.
9A:298 Continuance was granted.

Robert Richardson (SO) administrator of John Teage (SO) exhibited inventory.

Col. William Calvert, Esq. (SM) & Thomas Keiting (SM) administrators of
9A:299 Bryan O'Daley (SM) exhibited inventory.

20 September. Nehemiah Birckhead (AA) executor of his father Christopher Birckhead (AA) exhibited inventory.

Anne Clarke (SM) widow & executrix of Edward Clarke (SM) exhibited a list of credits.

Joane Jenkins (CV) widow & administratrix of William Jenkins (CV) exhibited inventory.

9A:300 John Stone (g, CH) executor of his mother Verlinda Stone (CH) petitioned for new appraisers. New appraisers: John Hanson, Symon Steevens.

21 September. Edward Gunnell (merchant, BA) was granted administration on estate of Joseph Sears (merchant, CE), who died leaving a wife in ENG, as factor for Edward Bleake & Co. (merchants, London).
9A:301 Appraisers (CE): John James, John Gibbs. Joseph Hopkins (CE) to administer oath.

Anne Jane Overton (BA) widow of Thomas Overton (BA) was granted administration on his estate.
9A:302 Appraisers: Dr. John Stanesby, William Hollis. George Uty (g) to administer oath.

Martha Morris (CV) widow of Thomas Morris (CV) exhibited that said Thomas had made a will. Said Martha renounced administration & petitioned for administration without probate of the will. Said Martha was granted administration as such.
9A:303 Appraisers: Joseph Baker, William Williams. Capt. Samuell Bourne to administer oath.

Thomas Bland for John Gray (AA) executor of Thomas Jones (Petapsco, BA) exhibited that said Jones' will was proved by Robert Burle (g, AA, dec'd). Said Gray was never sworn.

9A:304 Inventory was filed. Appraisers: Robert Tiles, William Jones. Dr. Henry Lewis (g, AA) to administer oath.

Augustine Herrman (g, CE) exhibited will of Joseph Herenden (CE), proved.

9A:305 Dr. Henry Lewis (g, AA) exhibited will of George Norman (AA), proved. Also exhibited was oath of Johannah Norman widow & executrix, sworn on 7th instant. Also exhibited was oath of appraisers: Matthew Howard sworn 27 August, James Smith sworn 30 August. Said Johannah (AA)
9A:306 exhibited inventory.

22 September. John Edmundson for Thomas Loggins (TA) exhibited that said Loggins was granted administration on estate of Richard Walters (TA) on 2 October 1676 & Richard Gorsuch (g) was to administer oath. Said Gorsuch is since dec'd, & bond has expired. Said Loggins was granted administration.
9A:307 Appraisers: John Whittington, Samuell Farmer. Philip Steevenson (g) to administer oath.

Abigail Wright (DO) widow & administratrix of Arthur Wright exhibited inventory.

25 September. James Frizby (g, CE) exhibited that Thomas Reade (TA) made a will, bequeathing land to said Frisby. The executor has fled the Province & was one of Bacon's followers of VA & took the will with him. Richard Woollman (g, TA) to
9A:308 summon James Doude & Joseph Billitrey (witnesses) & take depositions.

Thomas Walker for Elisabeth Hutson (SO) widow of Nicholas Hutson (SO) was granted administration on his estate.
9A:309 Appraisers: Edward Wale, John Vigrios. William Steevens (Pocomoake) to administer oath.

Henry Boston (SO) administrator of Henry Boston, Sr. (SO) exhibited inventory.

Col. George Wells (BA) executor of James Ogdon (AA)
9A:310 was granted continuance.

26 September. Ralph Dawson (TA) executor of Humphrey Archer (TA) exhibited accounts.

9A:311 William Coursey (g, TA) exhibited will of John Underwood, proved by John Glandining & Richard Mirax (witnesses). Also exhibited was oath of Robert Ellis executor sworn on 13 July last. Also exhibited was oath of Thrustram Thomas & Nicholas Broadway, appraisers sworn same day. Said Ellis (TA) exhibited inventory.

John White (CE) executor of William Tyson (KE) exhibited inventory.

9A:312 1 October. Richard Nash (CE) executor of Joseph Herenden (CE) exhibited inventory.

2 October. Capt. Richard Hill for Elisabeth North (AA) widow of Thomas Toyson (AA) was granted administration on his estate. Appraisers: Jacob Harness, Jacob Lusby. Said Hill to administer oath.

9A:313 4 October. Maj. Benjamin Rozer exhibited that Dominick Bodkin fitzJames (merchant, Galloway, IRE) had traded in the Province in 1674 & left debts & papers with Benjamin Solley (now dec'd). Said Bodkin fitzJames made will at Dunkirke, constituting Peter Kirwan, Francis Blake, & James Bodkin as executors. Said will has been proved in London in December 1674. [Paragraph in Latin.
9A:314 Signed: Tho. Rooke (notary). Attested by Johannes Mayer (notary), Jo. Roberts (notary).] Said Peter, Francis, & James constituted Richard Foote (merchant, London) PoA to recover goods & chattel.
9A:315 Mentions: Anthony Checkley, (merchant, Boston, NE), Benjamin Solley (MD). Date: 8 July 1675.
9A:316 Signed: Peeter Kirwan, Francis Blake,

James Bodkin. Witnesses: Ralph Grant, Jr., Jarvis Brocket. Signed: Nic. Hayward (notary). Lydia Solley widow of said Benjamin Solley & her attorney Benjamin Rozer substituted for said Benjamin Solley. Letter to Mr. Benjamin Rozer.

9A:317 Mentions: she (Lydia) came over to North of ENG & she left Mr. Bodkin papers with Mr. Clement Hill (high sheriff, SM). Signed: Rich. Foote. Said Benjamin Rozer was granted administration on estate of Dominick Bodkin on behalf of executors.

Maj. Benjamin Rozer (CH) administrator of Edmund Lindsey (CH) exhibited inventory

9A:318 & accounts.

Maj. Benjamin Rozer (CH) administrator of Robert Prowse exhibited accounts.

Maj. Benjamin Rozer (CH) administrator of Joseph Pearce (Dartmouth, ENG) exhibited accounts.

Maj. Benjamin Rozer (CH)

9A:319 exhibited oath of Mary Credwell administratrix of Richard Fowke (CH), sworn on 1 September 1677. Bondsmen (CH): Francis Wyne, William Ward.

Maj. Benjamin Rozer (CH) exhibited proof of will of Thomas Corker (CH), by Thomas Coates & Thomas Darcy sworn 12 May 1677. Also exhibited was oath of Elisabeth Corker widow & executrix sworn same day.

9A:320 Also exhibited was oath of George Godfrey & Robert Middleton, appraisers sworn same day.

Maj. Benjamin Rozer (CH) exhibited will of John Cage (CH), proved by John Fanning & Henry Reynolds sworn 9 July 1677. Also exhibited was oath of Susanna Cage widow & executrix sworn same day. Also exhibited was oath of Robert Henley & Robert Roelants,

9A:321 appraisers sworn same day.

Maj. Benjamin Rozer (CH) exhibited oath of Thomas Clipsham administrator of Charles Gregory (SM), sworn on 4 August 1677. Bondsmen: John Fanning, Francis Wyne.

Diana Fitting (AA) widow & administratrix of Robert Fitting (AA) exhibited inventory.

9A:322 Diana Holloway (AA) widow & administratrix of Oliver Holloway (AA) exhibited inventory.

Mary Clemens (TA) widow & administratrix of John Clemens (TA) exhibited accounts.

Robert Francklin (AA) executor of William Collier (AA) exhibited accounts.

John Watkins (AA) executor of John Groce (AA) exhibited accounts.

Henry Stocket (AA) & James Stavely (CE) administrators of Nathaniell Stiles (CE)
9A:323 exhibited list of credits.

Roger Diggins (SM) sole surviving executor of William Bourke (SM) exhibited accounts.

Peter Watts (SM) executor of Robert Cager (SM) exhibited accounts.

William Hatton (g, SM) exhibited oath of appraisers of John Ribton (SM): Henry Phippes & John Evans
9A:324 sworn on 1 May last.

William Hatton (g, SM) exhibited oath of appraisers of Herbert Homan (SM): Capt. John Cammell & Daniell Smith sworn on 16 March last.

John Brooke (DO) exhibited oath of appraisers of Arthur Wright (DO): Capt. Anthony Dawson & John Rawlings sworn on 6 June last.

George Oldfield (CE) administrator of Peter Mounce (CE) exhibited inventory.

Court Session: 1677

9A:325 Edward Man (g, TA) exhibited will of Thomas Duncombe (TA), proved. Mary Rowe mother & executrix was sworn on 14 April last. Said Rowe exhibited inventory.

Mary Blackfan (CH) relict & executrix of Thomas Stone (CH) exhibited inventory.

Thomas King (CH) administrator of
9A:326 Samuell Sherrill (CH) exhibited inventory.

Capt. John Coode (SM) administrator of Thomas Ceely (SM) exhibited accounts, attested by Nehemiah Blackiston (CE).

Mary Blackfan (CH) widow & executrix of John Blackfan (CH) exhibited inventory of Richard Owen (CH).

5 October. John & Matthew Erickson (KE) administrators of Edward Jones (KE) exhibited accounts.

9A:327 Stephen Murty (inn holder, SM) was granted administration on estate of Patrick Lewis (SM). Said Lewis is indebted to John Balley (said Murty is administrator). Said Lewis has no assets other than due for service against Indians in 1676. Said Lewis died single & has no blood in the Province.
9A:328 Security: Thomas Clipsham (CH).

Thomas Clipsham (CH) administrator of Roger Bowder (CH) exhibited accounts.

Thomas Bland procurator for Mary Roper (AA) widow of Thomas Roper (AA) exhibited his will. Said Mary was granted administration. Appraisers: Robert Francklin, Thomas Bland. Col. William Burgess to administer oath.

9A:329 James Rumzey who married Anne relict & executrix of John Bigger (CV) was granted continuance. Said Anne is very sick.

Mary Roe (TA) widow & administratrix of Edward Roe was summoned for accounts of

Robert Hale (TA). Said Edward was administrator. Said Mary was informed by Samuell Hatton that Mr. Roe, with the consent of the widow of said Hale, had LoA. Said widow remarried &
9A:330 fled the Province. Said Hatton to take Mary's oath.

Edward Man (g, TA) administrator of Robert Harwood (TA) was granted continuance. Mentions: debts at Delaware. Said Man as administrator of Thomas Reade (TA) was granted continuance.

9A:331 6 October. Lancellot Todd (AA) exhibited that George Langley (AA) died intestate, & administration was granted to Richard Featherstone who fled the Province before the estate was fully administered. Said Langley left orphans (under age) still living. Said Todd is greatest creditor. Said Todd was granted administration, on behalf of the orphans. Appraisers: Samuell Howard, Abraham Child. Capt. Richard Hill to administer oath.

Thomas Smethwick (AA) who married Magdalen relict of Edmund Townehill
9A:332 was granted continuance to deliver the child's portion to guardian of Edmund (son of dec'd).

Dr. Henry Lewis (g) & John Ricks (AA) executors of William Slade (AA) executor of Quinton Parker (BA) was granted discharge. Mentions: orphans of said Quinton.

8 October. Randolph Hinson (SM) administrator of Thomas Hatton (SM) was granted continuance.

9 October. Miles Gibson (BA) executor of John Newton (BA)
9A:333 petitioned for discharge. Denied.

Miles Gibson (BA) administrator of Abraham Clarke (BA) unadministered by his widow Sarah Clarke
9A:334 was granted continuance.

Philip Lynes (CH) administrator of Robert Clarke (CH) was granted continuance. Mentions: debt of Robert Thompson, estate of Thomas Hunt.

9A:335 Thomas Allanson (CH) executor of Edward Roberts (CH) exhibited his will. Zachary Wade (g) to prove said will. Said Allanson was granted administration. Appraisers: William Boyden, Thomas Alcock. Said Wade to administer oath.

Robert Benjar (BA) who married Katharine relict & administratrix of John Shadwell (BA) petitioned for John Waterton (g) to take oath of said Katharine. She cannot travel to the Office, because of great sickness.

9A:336 Robert Benjar (BA) executor of Margaret Therrell (BA) exhibited her will. John Waterton (g) to prove said will. Said Benjar was granted administration. Appraisers: John Arden, John Boaring. Said Waterton to administer oath.

John Arden (BA) executor of David Williams exhibited his will. Maj. Thomas Long to prove said will. Said Arden was granted administration. Appraisers: John Boaring, John Leakings. Said Long to administer oath.

9A:337 John Boaring (BA) who married Margaret widow & administratrix of Roger Sidwell (BA) exhibited that said Margaret is dec'd. Said Boaring was granted administration on estate of said Sidwell.
9A:338 Appraisers: John Arden, John Leakings. Maj. Thomas Long to administer oath.

James Phillips (BA) on behalf of self & William Hollis administrators of estate of Thomas Wingfield (BA) exhibited accounts. John Waterton (g) to summons administrators & take proof of accounts.

Gilbert Turbervile (St. Innagos Hundred, SM) administrator of Francis Graile
9A:339 (SM) exhibited accounts.

Thomas Casey (CH) executor of nuncupative will of Patrick Farlum (CH) exhibited accounts.

Edward Mumford (BA) executor of William Poultney (BA) exhibited accounts & inventory.

9A:340 Katharine Wright (KE) widow & executrix of Arthur Wright (KE) exhibited inventory.

Joseph Edley (SM) administrator of his brother John Edley (SM) exhibited accounts.

Elinor Brooke (CV) widow & executrix of Col. Thomas Brooke (CV) exhibited inventory.

Richard Simms (BA) administrator of Roger Hill (BA) exhibited accounts.

9A:341 Arthur Taylor (BA) executor of nuncupative will of his father John Taylor (BA) exhibited accounts.

John Bird (BA) administrator of Joseph Pierce (BA) exhibited accounts.

Randolph Hinson (SM) administrator of Thomas Hatton (SM) exhibited inventory.

Henry Hawkins (CH) executor of Giles Cole (CH) exhibited accounts.

9A:342 Vincent Mansell (SM) administrator of Richard Foster (SM) exhibited accounts.

On 6 October, Stephen Burle (AA) executor of his father Robert Burle (AA) exhibited accounts.

On 6 October, Dr. Henry Lewis (AA) administrator of Thomas Turner (AA) exhibited accounts.

On 6 October, Dr. Henry Lewis (AA) administrator of
9A:343 Nathaniell & Thomazin Stinchcombe (AA) unadministered by Thomas Turner (AA) exhibited accounts for said

Stinchcombes.

Richard Owen (DO) who married Jane relict & executrix of John Raven (DO) exhibited accounts. Said Jane is visited with great sickness.

William Dossey (DO) administrator of John Wigfield (DO) exhibited accounts.

9A:344 Col. William Ball administrator of his son Richard Ball (BA) exhibited accounts.

On 4 October, Richard Proctor (AA), on behalf of self & John Gather executors of Joseph Morley (AA), petitioned that no goods or chattels have been found,
9A:345 except for real estate. Administration is dismissed.

On 2 October, Col. Vincent Lowe, Esq. (high sheriff, TA) exhibited will of Nicholas Lorkey (TA), proved.

10 October. William Steevens (g, DO) exhibited oath to
9A:346 John Hodson, Sr. (DO) administrator of his father John Hodson (DO). Sureties: Bartholomew Ennolls, Henry Bradle. Said Hodson exhibited inventory.

John Rawlings (DO) administrator of William Rubert (DO) exhibited inventory.

Nicholas Shaw (CE) who married Martha widow & executrix of Thomas Middlefield (CE) exhibited accounts. Said Martha lies very sick.

9A:347 Nicholas Shaw (CE) administrator of his brother William Shaw (TA), unadministered by Joyce Shaw (TA) widow of said William, was granted continuance.

Joseph Hopkins (g, CE) exhibited:
- oath of Martha Matthews administratrix of Thomas Matthews (CE), sworn on 22 August 1677.
- oath of appraisers of said Matthews: George Oldfield & William Salsbury

sworn same day.

9A:348 Said Martha exhibited inventory.

Joseph Hopkins (g, CE) exhibited:

- oath of Anne Gibbs administratrix of Edward Best (KE), sworn 22 August 1677.
- oath of appraisers of said Best: John James & Giles Porter sworn same day.
- said Anne exhibited inventory.

Richard Miller who married Guelthian relict of Richard Graves (TA) exhibited that administration was granted to her but she never gave a bond.

9A:349 Said Richard & Guelthian were jointly granted administration. Appraisers: Capt. George Cooley, Henry Alexander. Col. Vincent Lowe to administer oath.

9A:350 Richard Collins (TA) & his wife Sarah relict of William Hambleton (TA) were jointly granted administration on his estate. Appraisers: John Newman, Hugh Sherwood. Col. Vincent Lowe to administer oath.

9A:351 Robert Carvile (SM) executor of Elisabeth Moy (SM) executrix of Richard Moy (SM) was granted continuance for both estates.

13 October. Jane Bread (CH) relict & executrix of Dr. Thomas Matthews (CH) exhibited accounts.

Capt. Richard Hill (AA) administrator of Philip Dawson (AA), Edward Gardner (AA), & Dorothy Bruton (AA) was granted continuance on all three estates,

9A:352 since he is very sick.

George Young (CV) administrator of his brother William Young (CV) exhibited accounts. Discharge was granted.

Francis Hopewell (CV) administrator of his brother-in-law John Booth (SM) exhibited accounts. Continuance was granted, in order to present accounts in proper form.

Court Session: 1677

9A:353 William Yorke (BA) administrator of Capt. John Collier (BA) unadministered by Lodowick Williams was granted discharge.

Randolph Hanson (SM) administrator of Thomas Hatton (SM) exhibited accounts. Said Hanson exhibited that Robert Hatton (SM) was a sojourner at the house of said Hatton, & died
9A:354 intestate soon after the interment of said Thomas. Said Randolph was granted administration on estate of said Robert.

Richard Chillman (SM) administrator of John Hall (SM) exhibited accounts.

9A:355 Mary Bucknall (AA) relict & administratrix of Edward Wheellock (AA) exhibited accounts. Discharge was granted.

Richard Guinne (AA) administrator of Thomas Guinne (AA) exhibited accounts.

On 9 October, Arthur Carleton (CE) administrator of Thomas Carleton (CE) exhibited accounts.

On 11 October, Charles Cullis (CH)
9A:356 executor of Edmund Taylor (CH) exhibited accounts.

Lydia Turbervile (St. Innago's Hundred, SM) relict & administratrix of Thomas Peerce (SM) exhibited accounts.

William Rozewell (g, SM) administrator of Francis Mountfort (SM) exhibited inventory.

William Rozewell (g, St. Clement's Bay, SM) administrator of Nicholas Richardson
9A:357 (SM) exhibited inventory & accounts.

On 12 October, Frances relict & executrix of Henry Hyde (g, St. George's Hundred, SM) exhibited accounts.

William Wells (CH) administrator of David Maddox (CH) exhibited inventory.

William Watts (SM) administrator of Thomas Cager (SM) exhibited accounts.

9A:358 Thomas Coke (SM) executor of his brother John Coke (SM) exhibited accounts.

Henry Phippes (merchant, West St. Mary's, SM) who married Elisabeth executrix of Patrick Forrest (SM) exhibited accounts.

Thomas Gerard (g, SM) administrator of Marmaduke Snow (SM) exhibited accounts.

9A:359 15 October. Mary Ward (TA) widow & executrix of Matthew Warde (g, TA) exhibited his will. Col. Henry Coursey to prove said will. Said Mary was granted administration. Appraisers: Thomas Hinson, Richard Jones. Said Coursey to administer oath.

9A:360 Mary Finch (KE) widow & executrix of Francis Finch (KE) exhibited his will. Maj. James Ringgold to prove said will. Said Mary (executrix) was granted administration. Appraisers: Henry Hosier, Samuell Tovy (gentlemen). Said Ringgold to administer oath.

9A:361 Richard Guinne & his wife Susanna (AA) relict & executrix of William Neale (AA) exhibited accounts. Said Susanna had great sickness. Capt. Richard Hill to take oath.

Sheriff (CH) to summon Philip Lynes (CH) to show why he detains the papers of Mary Ware of her account on estate of her late husband Thomas Pope (CH).

9A:362 William Deane (CH) one of executors of John Greene (CH) exhibited that William Stannard the other executor has departed the Province & gone to live in VA. Said estate was dismissed.

16 October. Thomas Carvile (SM) executor of Robert Hunt (SM) exhibited inventory, credits, & accounts. Discharge was granted.

9A:363 Thomas Keiting (SM) one of administrators of Bryen O'Daley (SM) exhibited accounts. Col. William Calvert, Esq. (Principle Secretary) is the other administrator.

Robert & Francis Goodrick (CH) executors of their father George Goodrick (CH) exhibited accounts.

Joseph Edloe (CV) executor of William Kaine (SM) exhibited additional accounts.

9A:364 Elisabeth Spracklin (St. George's Hundred, SM) relict & executrix of John Mackye (SM) exhibited accounts.

Elisabeth Spracklin (late Elisabeth Mackye, SM) executrix of Elisabeth Rawlings (SM) exhibited accounts.

Samuell Tovy (g, KE) executor of Richard Fillingham (KE) exhibited his will. Maj. James Ringgold to prove said will. Said Tovy was granted administration. Appraisers: William Bateman, Richard Lowder.
9A:365 Said Ringgold to administer oath.

Mary Moore (KE) relict & executrix of Stephen Whetstone (KE) exhibited accounts. Maj. James Ringgold to take oath, since she cannot travel to the Office.

9A:366 Cornelius Comagies (KE) exhibited that William Davies (KE) died intestate. Elisabeth Davies widow renounced administration on 27 September 1677. Witnesses: Thomas Fisher, John Perry.
9A:367 Said Comagies was granted administration on behalf of said Elisabeth. Appraisers: John David, Robert Neeves. Henry Hosier (g) to administer oath.

Martha Huddell (CE) widow & executrix of William Huddell (CE) exhibited his will. Joseph Hopkins (g) to prove said will. Said Martha was granted administration.
9A:368 Appraisers: Thomas Hawker, Richard Adams. Said Hopkins to administer oath.

17 October. Henry Warde (g, CE) administrator of Abraham Coffyn (CE) & of Richard Gore (CE) exhibited accounts. Discharge was granted for both. Said Warde attested that he was never granted administration on estate of Daniell Gover.

9A:369 Mary Deale (CE) widow of Thomas Deale (CE) was granted administration on his estate. Appraisers: William Salsbury, Nicholas Shaw. Joseph Hopkins (g) to administer oath.

Martha Browne (CH) widow & executrix of Gerard Browne (CH) exhibited his will. Henry Adams (g) to prove said will.
9A:370 Said Martha was granted administration. Appraisers: John Godson, William Boyden. Said Adams to administer oath.

18 October. Marmaduke Semme (SM) administrator of Abell James (SM) & of Samuell Dickeson (SM) was granted continuance.

Elisabeth Murwent (late Elisabeth Blunt) now relict of Richard Blunt, Jr. (KE) exhibited his will,
9A:371 which constituted her as executrix. The will was never proved. Estate was dismissed.

Bennet Morgan (CE) widow & administratrix of Robert Morgan (CE) was granted continuance, since she is by long & grievous sickness disabled.

GENERAL INDEX

Anderson
John 83, 110
Mary 83, 110
Robert 141
Andrew
James 165
John 150
Andrews
Christopher 25
John 150
Angell
Richard 136, 161
Thomas 161
Anketill
Francis 51, 58
Apelford
Tobias 10
Archer
Henry 100, 124
Humphrey 100, 117, 211
Peter 15, 79, 170, 202
Arden
John 89, 144, 216
Arding
John 121, 154
Arenson
Cornelius 17, 60, 108
Armiger
Thomas 59
Arminger
Thomas 98, 191, 196
Armston
Elisabeth 47
James 47
Armstrong
Edward 140
Arnold
Thomas 47, 48, 100, 154
Ascomb
Charles 85
Ashbury
Francis 121
Askin
John 185
Aspinall
Henry 2, 142, 156, 158
Mary 142
Asseter
William 30
Assetter
Anne 170, 200
William 170, 200
Atcheson
Elisabeth 160
Vincent 44, 160
Atchison
Vincent 198
Atkins
Jonathon 99
Atkinson
Thomas 145
Attwood
Goody 49
Richard 35
Avery
Anne 173, 203
John 173, 203
Ayres
Edward 164

Backer
John 88
Bacon
(N) 210
George 206
Baggbay
Margueritt 21
Bagsbay
Margueritt 21
Baiers Grove 37
Bailey
Elisabeth 159, 193
Godfrey 159, 193
John 186
Rosamond 159
Rozamund 193
Bailley
George 50
Katherine 50
Baine
Christopher 44
Baker
Elisabeth 49
John 28, 32, 33, 37, 42, 46, 49, 53, 55
Joseph 98, 209
Mary 30
Patience 30
Roger 97, 98, 126
Thomas 38, 94, 114
William 30, 32, 37

Bale
Richard 88, 129, 131, 178, 186, 194
Thomas 122, 123, 125
Ball
Richard 94, 143, 144, 145, 169, 175, 186, 187, 203, 207, 218
William 203, 207, 218
Ballard
Charles 188
Jarvase 165
Jervase 173, 199
Balley
John 214
Bancks
Thomas 61, 110, 117, 118, 122, 135
Bankes
Thomas 200
Bankhurst
James 15
Banton
William 155
Barbery
Susanna 201
Thomas 201
Barbier
Coniers 37
Luke 6
Barbor
Coniers 16
Barckhurst
James 71
Barckhust
James 88
Barker
John 108
Barkus
John 31
Barnard
Peter 208
Barnell
Francis 86, 106
Barnes
Francis 2, 12, 67, 149, 173, 197
Henry 93, 116, 120, 203
John 20, 30
Sara 93
Sarah 93, 116, 203
Thomas 132, 149
Barnett
Peter 116
William 120, 121, 130
Barns
Francis 132
Barret
Samuell 155
Barrett
John 144
Samuell 166
Barth
Dr. 164
Bartlett
Catherine 65
George 78, 107
Katherine 78
Bartley
George 30
Katherine 30
Barton
Mr. 185
William 102, 185, 190
Bassett
Thomas 170
Bateman
William 160, 169, 222
Baty
Ferdinando 101
Baxter
Hanna 75, 106
Thomas 75, 106
Bayle
Thomas 34, 35
Bayley
(N) 98
Edward 63
Elisabeth 159
John 132, 134
Richard 98
Baylie
Edward 63
Richard 61
Bayly
Richard 151
Bayne
Christopher 22, 23
Beach

Elias 157, 198
Sarah 157, 198
Beakely 10
Beaks
Elisabeth 31
Richard 31
Beale
Joane 3, 5, 6, 10
John 3, 5, 6, 10, 50, 89
Ninean 202
Ninian 111, 170
Rebecca 50, 89
Beall's Chance 37
Beall
Ninian 57
Beard
Elisabeth 181
John 172, 181
Richard 103, 116, 208
Robert 141
Beauchamp
Edm. 24
Beck
John 58
Lewis 20, 73, 114, 208
Richard 20, 73, 114, 208
William 85
Beckwith
Elisabeth 200
Frances 61, 66, 67, 104, 109, 117, 122
George 40, 61, 66, 67, 101, 104, 108, 109, 110, 117, 118, 122, 135, 200
Henry 43
Mary 135, 200
Bedwart
Richard 205
Beech
Elias 156
Sarah 123, 156
Beeche
Elias 22, 32, 53, 122, 124, 125, 126, 132
Sarah 124, 126, 132
Bell
Ringam 97
Bellows
Elisabeth 155, 197
Francis 133, 155, 197
Benjar
Katharine 216
Robert 216
Bennet
Disborough 149, 160, 191
Elisabeth 149, 195
Henry 205
Mary 160, 191
Richard 149, 150, 195
Bennett
Andrew 93
Benjamin 93
Desboro 82, 118, 132
Elisabeth 126
Henry 91, 130
Mary 76
Peter 124
Richard 126
Thomas 76
William 110
Benson
Elisabeth 140, 151, 178
John 140, 151, 178
Berry
Shelton 135
William 61, 98
Best
Edward 191, 219
Beven
Charles 92
Bevin
Charles 70
Bewsy
Paul 140, 151
Bibbey
Thomas 183
Bigger
Anne 37, 38, 65, 66, 214
James 37
John 37, 65, 163, 214
Walter 37
Billingsly
Elisabeth 110

Thomas 110
Billitrey
Joseph 210
Bincks
Thomas 97, 98, 126
Bing
Robert 77
Robertt 77
Birckhead
Christopher 86, 94, 166, 209
Nehemiah 86, 94, 166, 209
Bird
Charles 7
John 62, 90, 217
Margueritt 7
Bishop
Benony 14, 172
Henry 24, 93
William 45, 46, 74, 86, 87, 104, 109, 134, 135
Bisse
William 63, 84, 133
Blackfan
John 109, 153, 194, 197, 214
Mary 101, 116, 153, 214
Blackhall
Ralph 15, 22, 31, 68, 71, 135
Blackiston
Ebenezar 158, 176, 199, 202
Nehemiah 214
Blackistone
Ebenezar 192
Blackston
Ebenezar 164
Blackstone
Ebenezar 11
Blake
Francis 211
Bland
Da. 84
Damaris 85, 86, 88, 101, 111
Thomas 9, 75, 83, 84, 86, 88, 101, 111, 209, 214
Blangey
Lewis 7, 24, 101, 191
Mary 191
Bleake
Edward 209
Blinckhorne
Robert 87
Robertt 71, 108, 132
Blizard
Giles 87, 176
Bloise
Thomas 130
Blomfield
John 6, 50, 103, 141
Bloome
Robert 54
Blower
John 148, 195, 197, 199
Blunt
Elisabeth 223
Richard 10, 45, 69, 81, 223
Boaring
John 154, 216
Margaret 216
Boarman
William 166, 194
Boddy
John 165
Bodkin
Dominick 204, 211, 212
Dominicke 204, 205
James 211, 212
Mr. 212
Body
John 97, 182, 183
Bolton
George 138, 141, 170
Bonner
Elisabeth 188
Henry 87, 188
Booth
Isack 58
John 2, 6, 219
Judith 2
Boothe
widow 58
Boreman
Capt. 34
William 9, 32, 35,

41, 42, 48, 79, 111
Boren
John 89, 144
Boring
John 207
Borman
John 163
Borne
Sam. 115
Bosman
John 188
Boston
Henry 117, 129, 210
Mary 6
Samuell 6, 36, 93, 143, 147, 155, 164, 167, 179
Boswell
John 171
Boteler
C. 61
Charles 44, 61, 75, 136, 148
Boughton
Richard 84
Bould
John 21
Bourcke
William 90
Bourk
William 190
Bourke
William 35, 41, 196, 213
Bourne
Samuell 43, 69, 75, 78, 105, 108, 110, 121, 162, 170, 183, 185, 195, 196, 197, 203, 209
Thomas 162
Bovie
J. 165, 182, 183
Bowder
Roger 179, 214
Bowdle
Thomas 136, 169
Bowen
John 151
Bowing
Elisabeth 143, 186
Jonas 143, 186
Bowles
John 16, 45, 76, 92, 130
Bowlin
James 34
Bowling
James 166, 194
Bowring
James 159
Bowton
William 36
Boyd
James 9, 20
Boyden
William 216, 223
Bradely
Thomas 112
Bradle
Henry 151, 202, 218
Bradley
Henry 191, 193
Brandt
Rando. 141, 142
Randolph 127, 142, 195
Brannack
Edmund 55, 72
Brannock
Edmund 18
Brasseur
Benjamin 52, 57, 90, 92, 170
Martha 57
Bread
Jane 219
Breake Neck 47
Breden
Anne 63
Brennock
Edmund 138, 141
Brent
Rand. 76
Bretton
William 100
Brewer
John 100
Brewerton
William 41
Bricks
John 10
Bridges
Anthony 154, 188
Mary 4
Richard 4

Bridgewater
Christopher 157
Brien
Thomas 82
Briges
Mary 14
Richard 14
Robert 14
Thomas 14
Brispo
Anthony 157, 173
Elisabeth 157, 173
Broadacre
Mary 190
Thomas 190
Broadway
Nicholas 192, 211
Brocas
William 82, 192
Brocket
Jarvis 212
Brockett
Briant 134
Brockhurst
Samuell 185
Brome
John 162
Brommall
Richard 115
Brooke
Baker 22, 23, 44, 134, 136, 154, 178, 179
Col. 134
Elinor 136, 180, 217
John 22, 29, 44, 61, 135, 138, 149, 151, 168, 171, 178, 191, 197, 207, 213
Rebecca 22, 44, 207
Rog. 115
Roger 23, 44, 60, 61, 66, 71, 87, 89, 96, 133, 136, 148, 158, 169, 184, 185, 200
Tho. 115
Thomas 95, 111, 119, 136, 180, 217
Brookes
Esq. 164
Francis 115, 140
John 44, 72, 131
Roger 7, 16, 17
Brooks
Esq. 163
Broome
John 162
Broomfield
John 163
Broughton
Ri. 148
Browne
(N) 86
Gerard 223
John 85, 141, 165, 177
Katharine 166
Martha 223
Mary 136
Peregrine 164
Philip 129, 175
Phillip 177
Robertt 110
Thomas 136
Will. 154
Browning
John 56, 82, 89, 112, 127, 177
Bruer
Elisabeth 19, 20
John 19, 20, 100
Bruff
Joseph 65
Thomas 134
Brumale
Richard 114
Brummale
Joyce 79, 114
Richard 79
Bruton
Anne 11
Dorothy 11, 19, 88, 219
Elisabeth 11
John 11
Mary 11, 88
Bryen
Lewis 143, 186
Bucknall
Mary 53, 68, 186, 220
Thomas 53, 186
Bull

Thomas 21
Bullen
Elisabeth 156, 167
Robert 156, 167
Bullet
Joseph 154
Bullock
John 67
Burges
Capt. 86
Joseph 180
Burgess
William 19, 129, 160, 172, 184, 214
Burgesse
Anne 55, 66
Capt. 85, 86
Col. 184
Emia 5, 14
John 5, 14, 87, 114
William 5, 19, 20, 29, 35, 55, 66, 68, 74, 88, 101, 103, 104, 116, 127, 148, 161, 166, 196, 208
Burgett
Richard 83
Burle
Mr. 24
Richard 150
Robert 84, 89, 107, 148, 151, 152, 159, 209, 217
Robertt 7, 17, 24, 25, 26, 52, 53, 61, 62, 67, 68, 82, 88, 94
Stephen 61, 94, 151, 217
Burridge
John 80
Burt
(N) 36
Mary 36
Burwell
Will. 143
Bussey
Hesekiah 60
Bussy
Paul 54
Butler
Thomas 141, 142, 151, 152
Butterum
Nicholas 184
Buttler
Charles 22, 23
George 91
Thomas 127, 137
Bysie
William 11

Cable
John 140, 143, 175, 177
Cage
John 102, 110, 130, 139, 185, 189, 212
Susanna 212
Cager
Robert 213
Robertt 39, 40, 91
Thomas 81, 107, 110, 221
Calvert
Charles 51
Philip 138, 185
William 18, 28, 29, 55, 80, 97, 120, 193, 209, 222
Cambell
John 41, 158
Cammell
John 58, 77, 213
Campher
Mary 71
Thomas 71
Canaday
James 38
Canady
James 66
William 81, 89, 109
Cane
William 40, 41, 77, 79, 97
Caneday
James 37
Cannons
William 176, 206
Cantwell
Edmund 87, 112
Carew
Henry 28, 44, 49, 50, 132

Carey
Thomas 100
Carleton
Arthur 181, 186, 196, 220
Thomas 181, 186, 196, 220
Carlile
Thomas 54, 139
Carlisle
Alexander 163
Thomas 109, 135, 139
William 163
Carpenser
William 113
Carpenter
(N) 85, 86
Edy 33, 91
Richard 174
Robertt 25
William 150
Carr
Peter 154
Walter 152, 196
Carre
John 69, 113, 115
Nicholas 203
Peter 129
Peternella 69
Walter 50, 99
Carter
Henry 153
Cartwright
Demetrius 16, 17, 136, 140
Carvile
Mr. 122
Robert 32, 49, 98, 112, 141, 194, 204, 205, 219
Robertt 28, 37, 49, 111, 120
Thomas 37, 63, 72, 75, 77, 221
Carvill
Mr. 98
Thomas 22
Carwarden
Peter 158
Carwardine
Peter 2
Carwardyn
Peter 77
Cary
Philip 155, 166, 167
Casey
Thomas 82, 106, 217
Cassock
John 167, 168
Cassocke
John 140
Caswell
William 165, 173, 199
Causin
Ignatius 48, 64
Caussin
Ignatius 111
Cecill
John 76, 141
Ceely
Peter 99
Thomas 99, 117, 214
Chadborne
William 17, 26
Chafe
John 181, 196
Chamberlin
William 87
Champ
Stephen 127, 141, 142, 195, 200
Chancellor
James 195, 199
Judeth 199
Chancelor
James 86, 127, 142
Chancelour
James 142
Chandler
Thomas 2, 25, 35, 69
William 42, 100, 116
Chapman
Richard 142, 157
Charlesworth
George 32, 34, 55
Charleton
Richard 203
Charlton
Edward 164
Richard 156
Chase
John 74
Checkley

Anthony 211
Cherod
Hugh 71
Cheseldyn
Kenelm 16, 45, 46, 97, 100, 103, 121
Mr. 65
Chesson
John 73
Chetham
John 124
Chevrill
John 39, 50, 65, 78, 107
Robertt 39
Chew
Anne 172
Joseph 133, 161, 191
Samuel 72
Samuell 2, 9, 10, 25, 32, 35, 52, 70, 73, 84, 86, 91, 92, 100, 124, 151, 166, 172, 198
Chewe
Samuell 43, 57, 63, 140
Chilcot
James 2, 92
Chilcott
James 70
Child
Abraham 113, 147, 176, 215
Childe
Abraham 74, 91
Chillman
Richard 220
Chilman
Mr. 125
Richard 32, 33, 37, 58, 123
Chivrall
Ellinor 46
John 46
Christenson
Elisabeth 103
Wenlock 99, 103
Christopher
Mary 26
Clagett
Thomas 26, 97
Claie
Marke 73
Clare
Marke 73, 170, 185, 190, 205
Clark
Benony 164
Clarke
Abraham 64, 121, 154, 215
Anne 160, 203, 209
Benoni 164
Edward 160, 203, 209
John 110
Jonathon 39, 40
Marke 33, 43
Neale 88, 104, 208
Rachael 88
Rachell 208
Richard 195
Robert 73, 119, 216
Robertt 3, 66
Samuell 154
Sarah 3, 64, 121, 201, 215
Thomas 3, 6, 13
Clarkeson
Robert 147, 177
Clarkson
Robertt 11
Claw
Sarah 22, 48, 53
widow 34
William 4, 9, 22, 48
Clay
Henry 100
Clayland
James 104
Mary 104
Clegett
Thomas 98, 119, 126
Clemens
John 176, 206, 213
Mary 176, 206, 213
Clements
John 16, 25, 87, 102, 103
Mary 87, 102, 103
Clerk
Rachell 115
Clerke

Samuell 77
Cooley
George 219
Coomes
Elisabeth 3
Cooper
John 81, 95
Margrett 74, 107
Nicholas 100
Samuell 21, 114
Thomas 74, 107
Walter 73
Copman
Anthony 100
Coppedge
Edward 56
Coppidge
Edward 93
Corbin
Nicholas 143, 179, 186
Cordea
Marck 134
Marke 185
Corker
Elisabeth 34, 171, 212
Thomas 34, 66, 171, 212
Corner
Anne 129
Jobe 129
Cornish
John 127, 141, 142, 154, 200
Maj. 163
Cornor
Anne 171
Job 171
Cosford
Thomas 48, 100
Costin
Henry 131
Cottle
Marcus 146, 162, 165
Cottman
Benjamin 62
Cotton
Edward 9
Coulston
John 24
Coursey
Henry 31, 46, 113, 119, 160, 191, 221
James 103, 180, 192
William 30, 31, 62, 71, 103, 104, 132, 160, 180, 191, 192, 211
Courtenay
Thomas 32
Courtney
Thomas 4, 55, 97, 123, 125
Courts
John 21
Cousens
John 141
Cousins
John 178
Covan
John 24
Covill
James 144
Coward
Stephen 16
Cowdrey
Edward 184
Cowdry
Coward 115
Cowley
George 87, 103, 120, 128, 148, 156, 167, 174, 188, 190, 194, 195, 197, 201, 204, 206, 207
Cox
Jeremiah 124
John 1, 66, 89, 173, 197
Thomas 136, 145, 161
Coxe
John 1, 12, 13, 53, 67
Thomas 81, 83, 133
Crackson
Thomas 101
Craford
Patrick 132, 157, 202
Cralk
Jasper 163
Crane
Edward 164

John 83, 101, 106, 115, 121, 140, 143, 169
Jonathon 92, 93
Mary 5, 9
Robert 130
Thomas 165, 175, 181
Walter 154, 190
William 34, 45, 122, 125
Dawe
Nath. 59
Nathaniell 59
Dawson
Abraham 148, 195, 197, 199
Anne 195, 199
Anthony 171, 191, 213
Philip 11, 30, 219
Ralph 71, 117, 211
Daylie Desire 22
de la Roche
Charles 33, 35, 36, 48
Elisabeth 33, 35, 36, 48
Peter 36
de Masso
Peter demasse 145
de Witt
Peter 146
Deale
Mary 223
Thomas 223
Deane
David 163
Thomas 165, 170, 179
William 93, 116, 221
Deaver
Richard 92
Deavor
Richard 70, 92, 131
Deery
John 112, 120
Demetrius
Cartwright 169
Demontadire
Anthony 145
Dent
Peter 163
Rebecca 27, 78, 80, 105
Tho. 40
Thomas 18, 27, 33, 38, 39, 40, 41, 46, 49, 50, 54, 57, 58, 74, 78, 80, 105, 186
William 163
Denten
James 23
Denton
James 8, 59, 60, 62
Devenport
Humphry 14
Devet
Peter 146
Devett
Peter 145
Dickeensen
John 204
Dickenson
Roger 145
Dickeson
Roger 206
Samuell 89, 107, 139, 223
Dickison
John 204
Roger 137, 156, 167
Dickson
Elisabeth 33
John 127, 129, 146, 147, 152, 158, 159
Robertt 33
Didoll
William 160
Diggins
Roger 190, 196, 213
Digins
Roger 35, 41, 90
Dilerrit 14
Dillon
William 80
Ditchfield
John 58
Dixon
John 11, 60, 176
Robertt 91
Docton
Thomas 93, 96, 98, 99, 137, 200
Dod

Sarah 157, 207
Evett
Nath. 86
Evetts
Nathaniell 88
Ewen
Anne 46, 47
Richard 112
William 46, 47
Exon
Henry 47, 48, 55, 100

Fanning
John 21, 74, 94, 110, 114, 139, 171, 189, 201, 212, 213
Farloe
Patrick 106
Farlum
Patrick 82, 100, 217
Farmer
Samuell 113, 210
Farquison
William 1
Farquisson
William 62
Farrar
Joanna 31
Robertt 31
Farrer
Joanna 18
Joannah 17
Robertt 17, 18
Farrow
Richard 79
Featherstone
Richard 215
Feild
John 158
Fen
John 141, 168
Fendall
Josias 168
Fenwick
Cutbert 13
Cutberth 119, 134
Cuthb. 115
Cuthbert 6, 141, 171, 179, 204
Cuttbert 102
John 134
Richard 119, 134, 141, 171, 204
Robertt 134
Ferguison
Elinor 169
William 169
Ferguson
William 11
Ferrell
Margueritt 64
Richard 64
Fetherston
Richard 147, 148
Fetherstone
Richard 32, 50, 51, 52
Field
Enoch 134
John 185
Fielding
Edward 29
File
James 7, 24
Fillingham
Richard 222
Finch
Francis 221
Mary 221
Finney
William 176, 181, 190, 196
Finny
William 162
Fish
Edmund 12
Fisher
Anne 161, 166
Edmund 12
Edward 46, 65, 189, 193, 202
Henry 7
Nathaniell 40
Robertt 7
Thomas 222
Fitting
Diana 99, 213
Robert 99, 152, 213
Fitzgeorge
William Parker 128
Fitziarrett
Mary 58
fitzJames
Dominick Bodkin 211

Martha 10
Mary 7, 155
Philip 10
Samuell 10
Sarah 10
Golstone
Daniell 201
Goodaker
Richard 58
Goodrick
Francis 116, 199, 222
George 116, 199, 222
Robert 116, 199, 222
Robertt 64
Goodricke
George 64
Goodridge
Timothy 14, 71
Goodwin
Robertt 8
Goozey
Samuell 184, 201
Gordon
Patrick 166, 170
Gore
Richard 13, 223
Gorsuch
Charles 208
Elisabeth 167, 201
Ri. 103
Richard 1, 5, 10, 12, 25, 68, 87, 88, 96, 102, 103, 108, 113, 115, 120, 167, 201, 204, 210
Gossage
Charles 26
Gouge
John 134
Gould
Richard 14
Gover
Daniell 66, 223
Grace
Anne 63, 95
John 63, 95
Graham
Robertt 41, 109
Grahame
Robertt 40
Graile
Francis 64, 80, 105, 216
Grammar
John 136
Grammer
John 98
Grange
John 164, 169
Grant
Ralph 212
Grave
Alice 169
Graves
Alice 140
Richard 128, 219
widow 128
Gray
George 180
Jane 25, 120, 135
John 5, 17, 26, 209
Sarah 25
Zacharia 25, 26
Green's Plantation 4
Green
John 63
Greene
John 116, 221
Luke 140, 143, 175, 177
Robert 159
Robertt 48
William 17
Greenefield
Thomas 196
Greenfield
Thomas 72, 169
Greer
John 184
Gregory
Charles 102, 110, 130, 139, 189, 213
Margrett 102, 110
Griffin
(N) 126
Elisabeth 49
Lewis 81
Richard 49
Tho. 49
Thomas 22, 28, 32, 33, 34, 42, 46, 49, 57, 120, 122, 123, 125,

126
Griffith
David 147, 177, 178
Elisabeth 14
Owen 120, 130, 203
Richard 28
Thomas 49
Griggs
John 118, 119, 140, 173, 187
Mary 186, 187
Grimes
Joyce 150
William 150
Groce
Frances 65
John 65, 108, 112, 213
Roger 65
William 65
Grodtwell
George 201
Groome
Sibill 169, 198
William 38, 83, 94, 110, 139, 169, 198
Grose
Anne 51, 111
Elisabeth 51
Frances 51, 111
John 51, 62, 78, 85, 90, 111, 115
Roger 51, 111
William 51, 111
Grosse
Francis 65
John 65
Roger 65
William 65
Gruns
Joyce 87
William 87
Guibert
Joachim 22, 35
Joshua 41
Guibertt
Joachim 69
Joshua 41
Guilbert
Jochim 6
Guilbertt
John 56
Guin
Richard 61
Thomas 61
Guines
Robert 139
Guinn
Richard 151
Thomas 151
Guinne
Richard 220, 221
Susanna 221
Thomas 220
Guither
(N) 126
Nicholas 120, 123, 126
William 120, 123, 125, 126
Gunnell
Edward 119, 209
George 119
Gurling
Richard 167, 201

Hacker
Richard 10, 88
Thomas 53, 66
Hacket
Nicholas 172, 206
Hackney
Joseph 37
Haile
Oliver 144
Hailes
John 17, 37, 38
Mary 37, 38
Hale
Robert 215
Robertt 9
Hales
Anna 64
Anne 78
John 17, 48
Spencer 51, 64, 79
Halfehead
John 142
Halfhead
Jane 64
John 38, 41, 77
Hall
Barbary 82
Charles 24, 130
Edward 143
Ellen 9

Henry 27
John 33, 37, 46, 58, 67, 109, 111, 220
Josias 151
Margrett 95, 96
Patrick 99, 200
Richard 81, 83
Samuell 165
Walter 4, 17, 22, 28, 32, 35, 36, 46, 50, 53, 80, 95, 185

Halles
John 3, 5, 6, 13, 40, 47

Halls
Charles 117
John 61, 66, 117, 118, 119, 122, 140

Haltett
Lancelott 85, 86

Haly
Clement 6, 81, 191

Haman
Jane 11

Hambidge
William 55, 90

Hambleton
Elisabeth 138
Sarah 128
William 25, 128, 219

Hambridge
William 72, 183

Hamelton
John 114
William 4

Hamilton
John 73

Hamleton
Betty 138

Hamlin
Benjamin 164

Hammon
John 113

Hammond
John 74, 147, 176, 178

Hamond
John 91

Hampstead
William 199

Hamsted
Mary 97
William 97

Hamstid
Mary 105
William 96, 105

Hanaway
Joseph 81

Hance
John 13, 43, 89, 110, 111, 120, 121, 128, 130, 137, 165, 172, 183, 195, 205
Sarah 205

Hancock
Benjamin 14, 23
Sarah 14, 23

Handson
Barbary 39
Elisabeth 39
Randolph 39
Richard 39
Thomas 39
Timothy 39

Hanman
William 138

Hannington
William 3, 5

Hanson
Barbary 39
Elisabeth 39
John 128, 208, 209
Rand. 39, 80
Randolph 58, 220

Hapcote
William 20

Harden
John 143

Harders
Henry 73

Hardidge
William 29

Harding
John 144, 186, 187
Joseph 83

Hardy
Henry 87

Harges
Elisabeth 141

Hargness
Elisabeth 168
Thomas 167, 168

Hargnesse

Thomas 140
Harman
Augustine 10, 13
Harmer
Elisabeth 8
Fran. 146, 182
Francis 146, 147
Mary 8
Sarah 8
Tim. 182
Timo. 146
Timothy 146, 147, 181, 182
Harmor
Timothy 145, 175
Harness
Jacob 211
Harnesse
Isaac 192
Harney
Richard 127
Harper
Thomas 202
William 7, 39, 58, 59, 74, 78
Harrington
John 23, 79, 207
Harris
Henry 203, 207
Thomas 92, 154
William 1
Harrison
Richard 161, 186, 195, 198
Robert 163
Symon 2
Hart
Richard 29
Hartwell
Samuell 29
Thomas 29
Harwood
Andrew 44
John 12
Peter 1, 12
Philip 23, 44, 89
Robert 103, 215
Robertt 1, 12, 13, 120
Samuell 12
Hasfurt
George 24
Haslewood
Henry 7, 8, 23, 36, 62, 79, 84, 118, 133, 134
Haswell
Christopher 29
Hatch
John 201
Hatton
Anne 58
Elisabeth 27, 39, 49
John 100
Richard 58, 74, 106
Robert 220
Robertt 46
Samuell 5, 10, 22, 167, 194, 201, 215
Thomas 18, 28, 33, 39, 42, 46, 49, 80, 215, 217, 220
William 18, 27, 28, 38, 39, 40, 49, 58, 59, 65, 74, 77, 78, 81, 89, 106, 107, 109, 139, 158, 180, 213
Haverd
William 93
Haward
William 57
Hawford
Mr. 170
Hawker
Thomas 222
Hawkins
Elisabeth 16, 188
Hannah 188, 204, 207
Henry 5, 16, 73, 217
John 4, 15, 16, 50, 68, 96
Mary 50, 68, 96
Ralph 7, 43, 53, 67, 68, 82, 84, 94, 111, 126, 130, 145, 150, 152, 176
Thomas 16, 172, 188, 204, 207
William 7, 43, 52, 53, 67, 68, 84,

94, 126, 150, 152, 159
Hawks
Nathaniell 163
Hayward
Nic. 212
Heabound
Charles 73
Head
Elisabeth 55, 56, 66, 93
William 55, 56, 66, 110, 118
Hearne
John 182
Heath
Richard 33
Heathcote
Nath. 88
Nathaniell 1, 84, 86, 107
Heather
William 121, 143
Hedge
Daniell 32
Tho. 97
Heigh
Robert 57, 92, 170, 185
Robertt 110, 121
Heighe
Robert 190, 197, 205
Helgar
Thomas 141, 142
Helger
Thomas 195
Heliard
Daniell 1
Jane 1
Helmes
John 73
Helms
John 77
Penelope 73, 77
Hemsley
William 93, 104, 131
Hemstid
William 2
Henderson
Bartholomew 179
Hendricks
John 108
Henfrey
Thomas 131
Henley
Henry 161, 186, 195
Robert 171, 189, 212
Henricks
John 88, 115
Henry Leies 46
Hensey
William 201
Henson
Elisabeth 58
Randolph 58
Henton
Thomas 158
Hepbourne's Choice 41
Hepworth
John 46, 65
Herbert
Thomas 136
Herberth
William 7
Herd
William 164
Herenden
Joseph 210, 211
Herendon
Joseph 179
Herman
Augustine 45, 66, 69, 81, 82, 87, 112, 113, 127, 158, 177
Herne
John 146
Herrman
Augustine 179, 210
Hershbury
Francis 143
Hert
Arthur 97
Hewet
William 145, 146, 147, 159, 181
Hewett
John 39, 77, 134
William 8, 77, 115
Hewit
William 182
Hewitt
William 182
Hewton
Joyce 71, 91, 92

Math. 92
Mathew 71, 91
Heyden
Francis 137, 151, 152
Thomazin 151, 152
Tomlin 137
Hickman
Fra. 163
Higgs
Andrew 32, 75, 110, 148, 179
Hill
Clement 49, 212
Francill 46
Francis 39, 40, 65, 204
Henry 158, 185
James 101
John 59
Margrett 81, 104
Martha 158, 185
Mathew 114
Richard 10, 11, 19, 25, 29, 30, 32, 33, 43, 52, 67, 68, 74, 82, 83, 84, 87, 88, 91, 94, 95, 101, 111, 113, 130, 132, 145, 147, 148, 149, 150, 151, 152, 159, 162, 169, 171, 176, 177, 178, 184, 186, 194, 211, 215, 219, 221
Roger 47, 73, 217
Ste. 162
William 81, 95, 117, 118, 119
Hilliard
Daniell 5
Joane 5
Hillis
William 62
Hilmes
John 34
Hinchman
Nathaniell 187
Hinson
John 5, 30, 31, 68, 71, 94
Randolph 215, 217
Thomas 22, 30, 45, 46, 68, 71, 86, 88, 91, 134, 135, 221
Hinton
Thomas 77
Hirrman
Augustine 177, 192, 198
Hobson
Dominick 31
Hocker
Thomas 77
Hodges
Robert 162
Hodson
(N) 147
John 202, 218
Joseph 202
Thomas 202
Hoges
Symon 93, 96
Holbrooke
John 29
Holebrook
Thomas 130
Holebrooke
Thomas 118
Holford
John 124
Holland
Francis 100
James 103
Richard 172
Hollaway
Diana 148, 196
Oliver 148, 196
Holleger
Philip 92
Hollins
John 59, 87, 136, 140
Hollinsworth
Charles 14, 87
Hollis
Henry 140
William 8, 23, 60, 157, 173, 209, 216
Holloway
Diana 213
Oliver 213
Holmen

James 33
Holmes
Nicholas 204
Homan
Dorothy 158, 181
Herbert 158, 181, 213
Homes
Nicholas 102
Homewood
Sarah 11
Hood
Robert 80
Hooker
Thomas 50, 146
Hooper
Henry 81, 106, 206
Robert 163
Hope
Isabella 126
Hopewell
Francis 2, 6, 219
Hugh 48
Hopkins
Jonathon 45
Joseph 17, 26, 27, 32, 43, 59, 60, 82, 104, 108, 109, 119, 158, 159, 160, 175, 176, 191, 192, 202, 209, 218, 219, 222, 223
William 12, 24, 26, 52, 67, 68, 84, 88, 127, 148, 150, 162, 195
Hopkinson
Elisabeth 162, 181, 190
Jonathon 162, 176, 177, 181, 190, 195, 199
Horlock
George 113
Horne
Mrs. 49
Horsey
Stephen 130
Horsy
Stephen 117
Hosier
Henry 15, 16, 18, 45, 82, 90, 130, 160, 198, 221, 222
Hoskins
Philip 122, 174
House
William 66
How
Philis 94, 106
Thomas 94, 106
Howard
Cornelius 74, 85, 86, 91, 101, 113, 128, 150, 151, 164, 169, 193, 205
Henry 27, 145, 202
Mathew 101
Matthew 147, 148, 162, 192, 195, 210
Samuell 32, 147, 176, 215
Thomas 205
William 45
Howell
Elisabeth 26
John 11, 26, 27, 43, 68, 69
Mrs. 8
Nathaniell 11, 17, 26, 27
Thomas 1, 8, 11, 26, 27, 43, 68, 129, 171, 201
Howerton
John 70, 91, 92, 131
Howman
Herberth 2
Huddell
Martha 222
William 222
Hudson
Elisabeth 45
John 29, 152, 189, 193
Richard 45
Sarah 29, 152
Hull
Edward 4
Henry 27, 58, 105, 186
Humphry 27
Hulse

69, 73, 172, 190, 205
Keynes
John 180
Keytin
Thomas 29
Keyting
Thomas 28, 29
Keyton
Nell 29
Kieeff
Constantine 32
Kieff
Arthurtin 29
Killey
John 148
Killman
William 191, 198
Kilman
William 153
King
John 163
Thomas 21, 42, 66, 72, 73, 114, 214
William 97, 98, 120, 121, 122, 126, 136
Kingsland
Anthony 57
Kinsey
Jonas 115, 140
Kirby
Walter 75
Kirckly
Thomas 83
Kirwan
Peeter 211
Peter 211
Knap
Robert 188
Knighton
Mr. 98
Thomas 98, 99
Knightson
Thomas 200

Lacey
Rachell 63, 69, 72, 131
Thomas 63, 69, 72, 131
Lad
Richard 13, 32, 108
Ladd
Rich. 115
Richard 23, 33, 38, 43, 47, 59, 61, 66, 67, 75, 76, 79, 89, 91, 98, 109, 119, 133, 140
Lambert
Mr. 85
Lambertt
Mr. 86
Lane
Samuell 5, 9, 83, 95, 99, 151, 166, 184, 200, 204, 205
Langam
George 81, 129
Langham
George 142, 157, 175
Langley
George 147, 148, 215
Langlie
George 32
Langly
George 50, 51, 52
Langwoorth
William 42
Langworth
William 124, 148
Larey
William 16
Large
Robertt 37, 55
Larkin
John 82
Lawrence
Charles 101, 124, 153, 180
John 7, 154
William 80, 81, 99, 104, 149, 153, 166, 172, 207
Laws
John 188
Lawson
Thomas 94, 139
Leach
Edward 99
Leadbeater
Samuell 139

Leake
Richard 2, 23, 118
Leakings
John 131, 216
Margrett 131
Lederland
Robertt 21
Lee
Florence 84, 118
James 127
John 84, 118
Josias 157
Judeth 199
Judith 86, 127
William 75, 76, 86, 127, 141, 142, 199
Lefebure
J. 36
Leigh
Francis 128, 137, 165
Sarah 99
William 99
Lemare
John 16
Lesby
Jacob 7
Lewis
Hen. 202
Henry 24, 26, 52, 82, 88, 95, 113, 126, 127, 130, 131, 132, 147, 148, 149, 150, 159, 176, 192, 195, 197, 210, 215, 217
James 18, 36, 37
Patrick 214
Libry
Will 58
Lightfoot
William 163
Lilly
Elisabeth 129, 154
Linche
Thomas 56
Lindsey
Edmund 70, 212
Robertt 79
Lingam
George 83, 133
Lingan
George 136, 145, 161, 205
Lingon
George 93
Linsey
Edmund 16
Lisbie
Jacob 24
Llewellin
John 151
Llewellyn
John 161
Lloyd
Phi. 103
Philemon 5, 16, 25, 42, 45, 60, 62, 68, 113, 115, 120, 131, 140
Richard 41, 54, 58, 59, 74, 78
Lluellin
John 137
Lluellyn
John 136
Lockwood
Robert 95
Lodge
Margueritt 1, 12
Loggins
Elisabeth 88, 115
Thomas 113, 210
Loghlin
Anthony 28, 29
Lomax
Thomas 25
Long
Capt. 63
Thomas 8, 63, 64, 121, 129, 154, 175, 178, 179, 187, 194, 196, 203, 207, 208, 216
William 64
Longwoorth
William 15
Longworth
William 30
Loquer
John 33
Thomas 37, 53, 96, 184
Lorckie
Mary 71

Hugh 127
James 127
Magy's Jointure 41
Mahram
John 127
Maile
Anthony 87, 103, 113, 120, 133
Maister
Thomas 54
Makary
Daniell 112
Malden
Francis 120, 130, 203
Malding
Francis 33
Male
Anthony 103
Malickson
Samuell 37
Man
Edward 6, 68, 103, 113, 139, 140, 173, 174, 176, 180, 214, 215
Lawrence 56
Nathaniell 56
Manne
Edward 68, 103, 113
Manning
John 59
Mannor of Little Eltonhead 51
Mansell
Vincent 217
Mansfield
Edward 63
Sara 63
Vincent 63, 72, 105
Maram
James 130
Marcanallie
Walter 70
Markline
Robertt 31
Marram
James 165, 205
Marsh
Thomas 20, 88, 107, 119, 121, 143, 151, 166, 170, 172, 188, 207
Marshall
Adriaen 46
George 32, 46, 65, 66, 174
Marsham
Richard 61, 196
Marshegay
Bennet 117
Marshigaiy
Bennett 73
Marshigay
Bennett 42
Martin
(N) 4
James 26, 130
John 38, 72, 74, 76, 105, 136, 169
Robert 14
Robertt 4, 15
Thomas 102, 139, 148, 174, 195
William 128, 137
Marum
James 120
Mascall
James 130
Mason
Ann 138
Anne 138
Massam
Richard 169, 170, 178, 195, 202
Masso
Peter demasse de 145
Mather
Tho. 144
Mathews
Jane 55, 111
Martha 59
Morrice 36
Morris 72
Thomas 32, 48, 55, 59, 80, 88, 105, 108, 111, 114
Matthews
Martha 218
Thomas 159, 192, 218, 219
widow 192
Mattocks
Robert 179
Maxewell
Alexander 7

Mary 7
Mayer
Johannes 211
Mayl
Anthony 174
Mayle
Anthony 113, 137
Mayo
Thomas 163
McDaniell
Lofland 163
Meacock
Seabright 74
Meakings
Richard 200
Medley
Anne 102, 105
George 83, 105
John 83, 102, 105, 122
Meeck
Isabell 11
Meeke
Guy 87
Meekins
Richard 206
Meers
John 10
Mary 10
Melem
John 179
Melems
John 208
Mere
William 204
Merriday
John 206
Merrikin
Joshua 130
Merson
John 19
Margrett 19
Middlefield
Thomas 59, 109, 131, 218
Middleton
Robert 171, 212
Midgely
Elisabeth 128, 208
Richard 128, 208
Migley
Richard 109
Miles
Francis 97
John 200
Mary 135
Tobias 203
Mill
Tabitha 79, 106
William 79, 106
Miller
Guelthian 219
Michael 81, 99, 118, 132
Michaell 153, 166, 170
Richard 219
Mills
James 36, 62, 143, 155, 179
John 155
Mary 60
Peter 76, 102, 160, 170
Millward
Louery 164
Milner
John 17
Minock
Michael 172
Michaell 171
Mirax
Richard 211
Mirritt
Richard 163
Mitchell
Henry 59, 79
Moffet
William 201
Mollings
Margery 95
Monfrett
Edward 88, 131
Montague
Hugh 21
Katherine 21
Montefort
Francis 15, 30
Montegue
Catherine 113, 115
Henry 113, 115
Moonshott
John 5, 9
Moore
Jackeline 59, 89
James 59, 89, 103
Mary 222
Rebecca 80, 132

Richard 80, 104, 106
Sarah 59
Morain
Cornelius 5
Morecroft
John 55
Morgan's Clift 47
Morgan's Fresh 47
Morgan
Bennet 223
Bennett 89, 112, 116
Elisabeth 70, 92, 115
Frances 42, 112, 113, 119, 121, 132
Henry 42, 112, 113, 119, 120, 121
Janus 5, 10
Jarvis 124
Jervis 102
John 70, 92, 115, 163
Martha 82, 106
Robert 116, 223
Robertt 89, 112
Thomas 205
William 24, 82, 104, 106
Morley
Joseph 67, 218
Morrice
Thomas 9, 21, 42
Morris
Catherine 133
John 172
Katharine 161
Martha 209
Thomas 209
Morrise
Thomas 9
Moss
Elisabeth 149, 150
Richard 149, 150
Mosse
Elisabeth 67, 83, 126
Richard 67, 83, 126, 149, 152
Mounce
Peter 158, 192, 198, 213
Mount Misery 47
Mountague
Henry 178
Katharine 178
Mounten
John 3
Mountfort
Francis 220
Moy
Daniell 28, 49
Elisabeth 28, 49, 141, 204, 219
Mr. 98
Richard 28, 49, 97, 141, 204, 219
Muffett
John 54
Mumford
Edward 145, 217
Mun
John 156
Munn
John 142, 206
Munns
John 2
Murke
John 156, 203
Murphey
Anne 37
Daniell 37, 63, 203
Murphy
Anne 6, 63
Daniell 6, 108
James 4, 15
Murtey
Stephen 186
Murty
Stephen 132, 214
Murwent
Elisabeth 223
Mussell Shell 37

Nash
Anne 10, 81
Richard 10, 45, 56, 87, 179, 211
Nashes Rest 25
Neale
Anthony 68
Dr. 20
Henry 16
Jacob 20
James 167, 168

Susanna 43, 67
William 43, 67, 221
Neeves
Robert 222
Negroes
Charles 41
Fornie 41
Franck 27
Jack 99
Jane 41
Joley 99
Kate 41
Mary 27
Ned 99
Philip 41
Rose 41
Sarah 40
William 41
Neshamne
Benjamin 35
Neves
Robert 146, 159
Nevill
John 15
Newman
Abraham 51
Ellinor 51
John 83, 219
Thomas 156, 168
Newport
William 22, 35
Newton
John 18, 61, 182, 183, 215
Nicholson
James 188
Mary 188
Nicolls
Humphrey 69
Noake
Mary 86
William 86
Noble
Marmaduke 10
Robert 181
Norman
Edward 15
George 192, 210
Henry 110
Johannah 210
John 46, 47
widow 192
Norris
Thomas 74
North
Elisabeth 211
Norton
Tobias 15, 54, 57, 66, 81, 83, 97, 124, 133, 141, 156, 169, 177, 196
Norwood
Andrew 19, 20, 29, 30, 68, 152
Anne 9, 20
John 9, 20, 22
Notley
John 15, 19
Thomas 15, 19, 25, 28, 63, 72, 75, 97, 98, 100, 126
Nuby
John 134
Nuthall
John 95
Nutter
Christopher 62
Nutwell
James 156
John 164

O'Baile
Thomas 35
O'Brian
Therlagh 120, 151
O'Briant
Anne 128
Dennis 128
Turlogh 133
O'Bryan
Anne 203, 207
Denis 203, 207
O'Cane
John 34
O'Daley
Bryan 209
Bryen 222
O'Dally
Brien 29
O'Daly
Andree 28
Brine 28
Bryne 28
O'Kieff
Constantine 18, 28, 29

Quinton 7, 8, 130, 215
Thomas 69, 82
Timothy 29
William 13, 43, 69, 89, 92, 118, 120, 128, 130, 137, 163, 172, 183, 195, 196, 201
Parkinson
Luke 51
Parremore
John 93
Parrimore
Arnall 93
Parrott
Gabriell 74
Paschall
George 137
Pattison
Thomas 128, 153, 156, 168, 173, 191, 198, 207
Peacock
Jacob 164
Mr. 29
Peake
George 8
Mary 8
Peter 160
Pearce
Edward 64
John 64
Joseph 212
Thomas 64
Peasly
John 126, 149, 150
Pecks
John 19
Peerce
John 50
Richard 166
Thomas 220
Peerse
John 56
Peighim
Thomas 99
Peirce
William 164
Peirse
William 12
Penroy
Margaret 149, 154
Margrett 100, 121, 127
Perrish
Edward 19, 58
Perry
John 222
Robertt 15, 30, 104
Peterson
Andrew 158
Jacob 21, 65, 73, 116
Pew
Robert 92
Phelps
Elinor 169
Thomas 62, 169
Will. 87
Philips
James 84, 133
Phillips
James 23, 60, 62, 135, 143, 144, 216
John 182, 183
Sarah 182, 183
Thomas 10
Phinney
William 177, 181
Phippes
Elisabeth 221
Henry 180, 213, 221
Phips
Henry 65, 78
Piece
William 133
Pierce
John 100
Joseph 62, 90, 217
Richard 99
William 67, 74, 127
Pierse
Lidia 35
Thomas 35, 56
Pikrin
John 40
Pile
John 9, 42, 96
Joseph 42, 81, 96, 124, 144, 148, 183
Sarah 79, 96
Pille
John 79
Joseph 79

Pinck
Thomas 50, 56
Pindar
Edward 193
Pinder
Edward 189
Pine
Francis 98
widow 98
Pines
(N) 98
Pinie Point 41
Pitt
John 98
Pitts
John 97
Planner
William 24
Plices
Theodore 165
Plum
John 69
Mary 69
Pococke
William 182
Pocoke
William 182
Poier
Mary 41
Pollard
Alexander 167
John 156, 168
Pollart
John 18
Polton
Thomas 155, 167
Poole
John 56, 82, 112, 113
Ralph 123, 124
Sara 82
Sarah 113
Pooltney
William 62
Poore
John 128
Pope
Mary 94, 114
Thomas 94, 114, 221
Pore
Richard 66
Porter
(N) 85, 86
Giles 60, 108, 191, 219
Mathew 26
Peter 30, 150, 152
Sarah 30, 150
Pott
Hanna 7, 96, 111
John 7, 96, 111, 192
Potter
Thomas 18, 28, 32, 36, 46, 65, 66, 174
Poultney
William 88, 131, 217
Powell
Bridget 181, 196, 199
David 137
Howell 13, 91
John 17, 53, 66
Jos. 164
Thomas 17
Walter 50, 54, 108
William 82, 181, 196, 198, 199
Preene
John 93
Preston
Thomas 13, 43, 59, 69, 70, 91, 92, 98, 191, 196
Price
Edward 21, 101, 116, 128, 208
John 11
Mary 92, 104
Thomas 55
William 92, 104
Prince
Caesar 85, 90
Casar 52
Pritchet
Anne 184
William 184
Procter
Robertt 67
Proctor
Richard 218
Robert 147, 171, 176, 194
Proddy
Nicholas 78, 93, 116, 137, 140,

142, 145, 154, 174, 177, 183
Prody
Nich. 114
Prowse
Robert 212
Robertt 2
Pullard
Alexander 194, 200
Purnell
Thomas 24
Pyne
(N) 86

Quadman
Peter 56

Ramsey
John 141, 177, 178
Richard 8
Ramsley
Samuell 139
Randall
J. 146
John 146, 182
Ratcliff
Ben. 124
William 123, 157
Ratcliffe
William 148
Rateliff
Emanuell 54
Rathman
William 107
Raven
Jane 44, 90
John 44, 72, 90, 218
Rawbone
James 29, 68, 147, 161
Margaret 184
Margarett 160
widow 184
Rawlings
Elisabeth 222
John 213, 218
Rawlins
Anth. 11
Elisabeth 77, 90
John 171, 172
Nicholas 77
Richard 128
Rawllings
John 191
Rawls
Elisabeth 118
Peter 157
William 80, 165, 179
Raxbeg
Richard 44
Ray
Alexander 137
Joane 137
Rayley
Elisabeth 11
Read
Elisabeth 11
George 3
John 27
Thomas 113
Reade
Elisabeth 19
George 3
John 57
Margarett 95
Sarah 1
Thomas 174, 180, 210, 215
William 11, 19
Reathman
William 75
Reed
Sarah 12
Reede
Sarah 12
Reevely
Mary 199
Renalds
Thomas 58
Reycroft
John 13, 23, 47, 72
Reynold
Thomas 58
Reynolds
Bartholomew 172
Henry 212
John 4, 9, 14
Reynols
John 14
Rhoades
Abraham 39
Mrs. 49
Rhoads
Abraham 39

Ribton
John 180, 213
Rice
Nicholas 118, 130
Richard's Mannor 40
Richards
John 172
Richardson
George 14, 71
John 172
Nicholas 220
Robert 208
Robertt 24
Thomas 47, 53
Rick
John 7
Ricks
John 10, 24, 82, 130, 132, 215
Ridgely
Henry 88, 103, 116
Mr. 98
Robert 139, 194
Robertt 97, 98, 112, 134
Rieves
Edward 47
Rigby
James 111, 130, 165
Riggs
Francis 54
Right
Arthur 153
Katharine 153
Thomas 153
Rightty
Anna 64
Ringe
Richard 58
Ringgold
James 221, 222
Ringold
James 16, 55, 66, 69, 75, 91, 107, 175
Rissy
Richard 4
Ritcheson
Nicholas 117
Ritchison
Daniell 73
Rithson
Anastasie 42
Nicholas 42
Rix
John 52, 95, 113
Roacht
Hen. 29
Roberts
Andrew 180
Edward 216
Jo. 211
Richard 119, 140, 145
Robertts
Andrew 101, 124
John 6
Peter 6
Richard 119, 133
Robesson
George 44
Robins
George 24, 133, 176, 179, 193
Robert 76, 116, 117
Robinson
John 123, 124, 187
Mary 64
Thomas 184
Robisson
William 23
Robson
Thomas 44
William 173
Roche
Alexander 18
Charles de la 33, 35, 36, 48
Elisabeth de la 33, 35, 36, 48
Peter de la 36
Rochford
Michael 13, 39, 49, 135
Michaell 155, 197
Rodaway
John 30, 68, 94
Margueritt 30
Mary 30
Rodoway
John 71
Rodway
John 31, 88
Roe
Edward 9, 14, 16, 21, 25, 68, 87, 91, 102, 103, 214

Elisabeth 68
Mary 68, 102, 103, 214
Mr. 215
Roelants
Robert 155, 161, 189, 190, 212
Robertt 102, 103
Rooke
Tho. 211
Rookwood
Edward 206
Roper
Alice 5, 10, 102, 124
Mary 214
Thomas 214
William 20
Rosewell
William 6, 15, 25, 30, 37, 42, 63, 67, 79, 99, 104, 108, 117, 124, 148
Rousby
Christopher 173
Rowdell
Thomas 115
Rowder
Roger 94, 114
Rowe
Mary 139, 214
Rowlan
John 124
Rowland
John 133
Rowlin
James 48
Rowring
John 121
Rowsby
Barbara 112, 113, 119, 121
Chr. 56
Christopher 37, 40, 51, 61, 64, 66, 77, 78, 98, 100, 126, 165
John 54, 56, 112, 113, 119, 120, 121, 132
Rowse
Gravier 33
Royall
Elisabeth 86, 106
Royston
Mr. 98
Richard 1
Roystone
Richard 12, 13
Rozer
Benjamin 2, 9, 16, 21, 42, 57, 64, 66, 70, 72, 73, 76, 77, 82, 86, 92, 93, 94, 96, 100, 101, 102, 109, 114, 116, 117, 128, 129, 140, 143, 154, 171, 174, 175, 188, 189, 201, 205, 211, 212, 213
Maj. 201
Rozewell
William 220
Rubert
William 191, 218
Rudyerd
Tho. 163
Rumsey
James 66, 83, 110
Thomas 2, 67
Rumzey
Anne 214
James 214
Rusle
Robert 83
Russell
Anne 141, 168
Charles 140, 141, 167, 168
Edw. 132
John 69
Richard 147, 176, 178
Walter 140, 141, 167, 168
William 25, 35, 69, 124, 167, 168
Russy
Edward 60
Ruxston
Nicholas 143
Ruxstone
Nicholas 145, 179, 207

Ryatt
Eadoth 98
Ryder
Benjamin 120
Henry 34, 35
Rye
Anne 106, 107
John 106, 107

Salesbery
William 17
Salesbury
William 27, 32, 59, 60
Salmon
Peter 11, 129
Thomas 1, 11, 97, 129, 152, 159, 160, 193
Salsbury
William 108, 127, 129, 152, 192, 218, 223
Salter
Robert 163
Sampson
John 74, 91
Sanders
Richard 27
Robertt 26
William 184
Sanford
James 163
Sanson
John 128
Sant Verlindas 21
Sapcoate
Abraham 174
Sargeson
William 47, 48
Saunders
William 160, 184
Sauvage
Edward 153
Sayer
Frances 42, 112, 119, 121, 132
Peter 68, 104, 112, 119, 121, 132
Sayers
Frances 113
Peter 112, 113
Sayles
Clement 188
Scott
James 60
John 103, 180
Margrett 103
Scrimshire
William 193
Scuttow
John 170
Seale
Roger 28
Seares
Fran. 138
Sears
Joseph 17, 60, 105, 108, 119, 209
Sebastian
Stephen 95
Sedbury
William 16
Sedgewick
James 119
Sedgwick
James 139
Seers
Joseph 176
Sellers
John 25
Semme
Marmaduke 223
Semmes
Marmaduke 89
Semms
Marmaduke 139
Sethberry
William 17
Sethbery
John 94
William 60, 105, 108
Sevill
Thomas 163
Sewell
Elinor 154
Henry 87
John 154
Shadwell
Catherine 118
John 63, 118, 178, 216
Katharine 178
Shattenwhite
George 13
Shaw

John 86, 107, 109, 199, 208
Joyce 45, 218
Martha 109, 131, 218
Nicholas 60, 90, 218, 223
Ralph 70, 201
Sarah 86, 109, 199
William 45, 59, 60, 90, 218
Shawe
John 186
Thomas 136, 161
Sheacock
Roger 8
Sheircliffe
Anne 160, 199
John 160, 199
William 160, 199
Shelburne
William 207
Sheldon
Joseph 146, 163
Shelton
Israell 143
Shepheard
John 136, 161, 168, 170
Shepherd
Andrew 170
Sherridine
Elisabeth 178
Thomas 178
Sherrill
Samuell 114, 214
Sherwood
Hugh 190, 219
Shiles
Alice 130
Thomas 130
Shills
Thomas 118, 159
widow 118
Shrigley
John 70
Shuttleworth
Thomas 154, 174, 175
Sibrey
Frances 120
Jonathon 4, 5, 70, 92, 115, 119, 120, 154, 175, 176, 192, 197
Sidwell
Roger 216
Sidwells
Roger 144
Simes
Richard 47
William 47
Simmes
Marmaduke 57, 62
Richard 73
Simms
Richard 217
Simonds
James 27
Simpson
John 91
Thomas 79, 102, 132, 144, 183
Simson
William 10
Sineck
William 5
Singleton
Jacob 152
John 87, 104
William 16, 24, 75, 161, 188
Sinneck
William 9
Sinnot
Garret 175
Garrett 129
Sisson
John 193, 205
Skidmore
Alice 202
Edward 25, 80, 176
Skinner
A. 19
Andrew 45, 60
Anne 158
Elisabeth 43, 82
Thomas 43, 82
Skydmore
Alice 202, 205
Edward 158, 202, 205
Slade
William 7, 25, 52, 82, 95, 113, 130, 131, 215
Slater
John 207

Stoakely
Mary 37
Stoaker
John 12
Stockely
Mary 66
Stocket
Henry 172, 192, 193, 213
Stockett
Francis 23, 32, 117
Henry 22, 117, 127, 129
Thomas 117
Stockley
James 65
Stokes
Peter 138, 141, 170
Stone
Doyen 21
John 2, 21, 78, 109, 128, 142, 153, 157, 194, 208, 209
Margery 93, 114, 116
Mary 93
Math. 93
Mathew 2, 109, 114, 116
Thomas 101, 116, 214
Verlinda 2, 21, 109, 209
William 125, 158, 164
Stonestreete
Thomas 79, 144, 183
Storer
Arthur 169
Story
Walter 188
Strainer
William 64, 80
Stran
Abraham 53, 74
Streete
Francis 178, 195, 198
Susanna 178, 195, 198
Stringer
Benjamin 150
Sturdevant
William 93
Suchby
Ralph 162
Sudenam
Jeremiah 35
Sudevant
Anne 106
Jeremiah 106
Sullevant
Jeremiah 70
Sullivant
Anne 70, 92
Jeremiah 92
Patrick 15
Sumner
John 1, 12
Sunderland
John 185, 197
Sarah 185
Sutton
Philip 122, 138
Swan
Edward 161
Swanson
Edward 23, 84
Francis 38
Henerietta 84
Swanston's Lott 56
Swanston
Francis 56, 78
Isabell 56
Isabella 56, 78
Sweatnam
Richard 204
Swetnam
Richard 156
Swettnam
Richard 103
Swinfen
Francis 97

Taillor
Thomas 99, 101, 124, 172, 175, 180, 203
Tall
Anthony 55, 90, 183
Taney
Michael 60, 61
Tant
John 33, 40, 41
Tapticoe
Anne 26

Peter 26
Tarleton
Thomas 1
Tasker
Thomas 133
Taverner
Robert 162
Robertt 43, 105, 108
Thomas 162
Tayler
Robert 94
Robertt 16, 37
Thomas 16, 25
Taylor
Arthur 53, 59, 82, 217
Daniell 103, 116, 208
Edmund 100, 142, 157, 208, 220
Grace 138
John 59, 82, 138, 217
Joseph 24
Mary 158
Mr. 85, 86
Robert 133
Robertt 16, 75
Samuell 16, 170, 202
Tho. 148
Thomas 1, 12, 35, 50, 60, 62, 68, 78, 85, 86, 87, 88, 99, 101, 102, 111, 112, 124, 128, 131, 148, 152, 194, 198
William 83, 106, 107, 169
Teage
John 208
Teagle
Nathaniell 188, 206
Tege
Elisabeth 24
John 24
Tennant
Thomas 179
Tennison
Elisabeth 161
Mary 161
Terrett
Nicholas 161
The Gore 59
The Plaines 10
Theobald
Clement 34
Therrell
Margaret 216
Margueritt 64
Richard 64
Thomas
Benony 21
Elisabeth 54
Hugh 122, 174
John 141, 177
Maccom 108
Macom 50, 54, 89
Martha 10
Philip 10
Robert 44
Samuell 10
Sarah 10
Thrustram 104, 180, 192, 211
William 28, 55, 125
Thompson
Geore 98
George 38, 40, 41, 51, 98
James 15, 78, 96
Jane 78, 96
John 35, 50, 80
Robert 216
William 164
Thorne
Roger 194
Thornton
Richard 74
Thorpe
Roger 146, 147, 159, 164, 165, 175, 182, 183, 197, 198
Tidd
Josiah 181, 182
Tiler
Robert 162
Tiles
Robert 210
Tilghman
Mary 45, 134, 179
Richard 15, 20, 31, 45, 68, 134, 179
Tippin

Martha 126
Tison
William 192
Toat
Robert 6
Todd
Anne 187
Lancellot 215
Lancelot 169
Sarah 171, 194, 200
Thomas 171, 175, 181, 186, 187, 190, 194, 196, 200
Toulson
Anne 176, 199
William 175, 176, 199
Tovey
Samuell 160
Tovy
Samuell 169, 198, 206, 221, 222
Towell
David 145, 206
Towers
John 53, 72, 74
Rachael 53, 72
Rachell 73
Towlson
Anne 158
William 25, 27, 53, 66, 75, 80, 85, 107, 127, 129, 146, 152, 158, 159
Townehill
Edmund 19, 215
Townhill
Maudlin 19
Townill
Edmond 20
Magdalene 20
Towning
Edmund 20
Toyson
Thomas 211
Tracey
Samuel 84
Samuell 85, 144
Trasck
James 69
Trasey
Samuell 63
Trask
James 22
Travers
William 95, 111, 115, 117, 119, 197
Traverse
William 140
Trent
Henry 38, 44
Trewent
Richard 15
Robertt 15
Tripp
Henry 54, 131, 151, 197
Trippe
Henry 168
Trivett
Robertt 15
Truelock
Henry 54, 177
Trueman
James 158
Nathaniell 93
Thomas 7, 79, 96, 136, 158
Truman
Nathaniell 169, 196, 198
Thomas 169, 198
Tuberfield
Lidia 56
Tucker
Benjamin 157
Tully's Delight 4
Tully
Stephen 46, 134
Turberfield
Gilbert 64
Turberfile
Lidia 64
Turbervile
Gilbert 216
Guilbert 80, 105
Lidia 64
Lydia 220
Turner
(N) 85, 86
Edward 16, 17, 24, 75, 136, 188
Elisabeth 24
Henry 191
John 38, 76, 140

Richard 24
Robert 177
Robertt 54
Thomas 24, 26, 52, 132, 217
William 115
Turpin
John 146, 147, 179, 181, 193
Turpinne
Jane 49
John 8, 77, 79, 134, 162
Robertt 49
Symon 49
William 49
Twisse
(N) 98
Mr. 122
William 98
Two Good 37
Tydings
Richard 86, 111, 124, 208
Tyer
James 76
Tyler
Elisabeth 3
Grace 122
Joane 3, 5
John 122
Robert 84, 147
Robertt 3, 68, 76
Tyre
James 92
Tyson
William 211

Underwood
John 192, 211
Peter 133, 153, 179, 193
Utie
Bernard 173
George 97, 173
Uty
Bernard 8
Elisabeth 36, 60, 90
George 61, 80, 134, 209
Nathaniell 8, 36, 60, 90

V. Derheyden
M. 164
Van Heck
John 146
Vanheck
John 11, 17, 26, 27, 32, 43, 60, 69, 146, 159, 193
Sarah 26, 27
Vansweringen
Garrett 30, 32, 33, 36, 37, 50, 55, 119
Geritt 204
Varing
Edward 96, 108
Varloe
James 132, 157, 204
Vaughan
Tho. 12
Thomas 1, 13, 137
Vaux
Charles 54
Vearing
Edward 106, 204
Veitch
James 47, 71, 76, 87
Venall
John 128
Vigrios
John 210
Vine
John 135
Vineyard 28
Vyne
John 22
Vynes
Mary 76
Samuell 75, 76, 79, 94

Waas
John 34
Wachop
John 109
Wacop
Archiball 16
John 18
Wade

Zachary 137, 142, 145, 154, 156, 174, 177, 206, 216
Wadswoorth
Joanna 24
Richard 15, 24
Susanna 15
Wadsworth
Richard 15
William 15
Waghop
John 41
Wagstaffe
(N) 165, 182
Wahob
Achiball 34
Wahop
Archibald 117, 174, 177
Margueritt 39
Rebecca 39
Thomas 39
Waikfield
Ellen 9
Richard 9
Wakefield
(N) 86
Wakes
William 85
Wale
Edward 50, 54, 108, 210
Walker
Alice 6
George 22
James 6
Thomas 24, 210
Walkup
Archibald 122
Wallace
James 163
Wallstone
John 84
Walstone
John 133
Walter
Richard 148
Walters
John 19, 83
Richard 10, 88, 113, 210
Walterton
John 23
Walton's Neck 144
Ward
Andrew 144, 166, 183
Henry 13, 45, 56, 66, 67, 69, 71, 109
John 78, 93, 116, 140, 175
Margaret 144
Margarett 166
Margrett 118
Mary 221
Mathew 15, 22, 45, 46, 71, 74, 86, 89, 91, 104, 109, 134, 135
Matthew 162, 176, 177, 181, 190, 195, 196, 199
Thomas 118
William 212
Warde
Henry 223
Matthew 198, 221
Wardener
Christopher 153
Wardner
Christopher 109
Ware
Mary 221
Robert 114
Warhop
Joane 18
John 18
Warhope
John 18
Waring
Sampson 205
Sarah 205
Warren
Humphrey 75, 161, 171, 189, 190, 201
Ignatius 102
John 9, 102
Sarah 169, 206
Thomas 16, 69, 81, 169, 206
Waterland
Jonathon 54
Waters
Alexander 153
Humphrey 38

John 95
Watersworth
Humphrey 75, 76, 132
Waterton
John 8, 13, 47, 52, 53, 59, 62, 70, 73, 82, 85, 97, 98, 118, 178, 216
Watkins
Francis 129, 169
John 9, 62, 65, 85, 86, 90, 111, 112, 115, 140, 213
Walter 63, 69, 72
Watson
John 135, 139
William 133, 139, 153
Watts
George 5
Mary 40, 46
Peter 39, 40, 45, 46, 65, 77, 78, 81, 91, 94, 107, 134, 213
William 39, 40, 45, 46, 50, 57, 58, 74, 81, 89, 99, 110, 145, 221
Wattson
John 109
Wawhub
John 3
Way
Richard 109, 153
Wayd
Richard 11
Weather
John 82
Webb
Benjamin 124
Edmund 4
William 95
Webber
Lenard 61
Leon. 165, 182, 183
Leonard 80, 108, 183
Wedge
John 60, 169
Weecks
Joseph 30, 56, 88, 94
Weekes
Joseph 160
Weeks
Joseph 31, 68, 71, 75, 114, 130, 191
Welbourne
Thomas 54
Weller
Richard 78
Wells
Geore 79
George 7, 36, 62, 93, 100, 124, 127, 134, 135, 157, 162, 173, 179, 193, 211
John 15, 102
Mary 55, 105, 107
Richard 92
Tobias 5, 55, 98, 105, 107
William 117, 174, 220
Welsh
Anne 51
John 9, 51, 65, 85, 111, 112, 115, 186
Mr. 85
Wesbury
William 59
West
Elisabeth 133, 155
John 2, 12, 98
William 99
Westcott
John 99
Whackfield's Covenant 85
Wharton
Elisabeth 100
Jesse 99, 100, 116
Wheeler
John 76, 114, 117, 154, 174
Paul 146
Robert 137, 145
Wheellock
Edward 220
Wheelock
Edward 53, 68

Wheelocke
Edward 186
Whetstone
Mary 114, 153
Stephen 114, 153, 222
White
Alexander 9
Anne 145, 176, 177
Casea 105
Guy 48, 102, 122, 157, 207
John 50, 54, 108, 192, 211
Josias 62
Kesia 75
Martha 39
Robertt 4
Rowland 75, 105
Sarah 122
Stephen 26, 145, 176, 177
Whitle
George 78
Whittington
John 113, 210
Whittle
Dorothy 172, 183
George 172, 183, 195, 196, 201
Whitton
Richard 2, 14, 23, 67, 69, 87
Thomas 164
Wickes
Joseph 160
Wigfield
John 36, 72, 218
Wild
Abraham 2
Wilde
Abr. 2
Abraham 11, 12, 14, 23, 53, 67, 74, 89, 112
Wilkinson
William 142, 156, 158
Willcocks
Henry 87
Willen
Grace 49, 122, 123, 126
Willett
(N) 86
Williams
David 216
Edward 71, 92, 175
Harman 8
Henry 40, 41, 86
Hugh 2
James 7, 96, 97, 111, 178, 195
John 57, 73
Joseph 44
Lodowick 59, 62, 97, 220
Morgan 82, 149
Ralph 88, 107, 119, 150
Richard 33, 43, 69, 73
Samuell 163
William 209
Williamson
Christopher 41
Willmore
Luther 103
Willoby
William 133
Willoughby
William 153
Wilmer
Thomas 24
Wilmoth
John 179, 208
Wilson
George 53, 74, 127
James 74
John 98, 99
Mary 14
Peter 74
Robert 178, 194
Robertt 94, 129
William 6
Winchester
Isaack 160
Isack 55, 56, 80, 81, 106, 107
John 132, 149
Wincles
Edward 206
Winders
Joseph 150
Winfield
Thomas 23, 60
Wingfield
Thomas 216

Winles
Edward 190
Winley
Richard 47
Winne
John 180
Winnell
John 184
Winsmore
Alexander 135
Catherine 131
Katharine 198
Robert 131, 178, 196, 198
Robertt 36, 43, 44, 55, 72, 115
Winson
Alexander 120
Winsore
Alex. 35
Alexander 38
Mr. 34, 125
Wintersell
William 167, 200
Wiseman
John 2
Wismore
Alexander 36
Withers
Samuell 19
Witt
Peter de 146
Witthan
Richard 112
Wollman
Richard 1, 12, 62, 120, 131
Wood
John 57, 77, 82, 129, 175, 177
William 13
Woods
Mathias 53
Woodward
John 117
Woollman
Richard 210
Woolterton
Robert 206
Woolverton
Robert 188
Wootton
Simon 148
Worbelston 47
Word
Patrick 137
Worgan
(N) 138
William 122, 135, 138, 151
Worgin
William 168
Workman
Joane 179
Wotton
Symon 75
Wright
Abigail 149, 171, 191, 210
Anthony 146, 164, 165, 175, 181, 182, 183
Arthur 43, 99, 149, 166, 170, 171, 191, 210, 213, 217
Catherine 104
John 5, 21, 104, 128, 142, 174, 177, 180, 208
Katharine 180, 217
Mary 5
Mr. 164
Thomas 99, 166
William 76
Wyatt
Damaris 84, 85
Nich. 111
Nicholas 9, 75, 83, 84, 85, 86, 88, 101, 113, 151
Wyn
John 40
Wyne
Francis 75, 94, 212, 213
Wynne
Elisabeth 49
Francis 114
John 17, 109
Margueritt 49
Thomas 22, 28, 32, 33, 42, 49, 89, 98

Yaile
Clement 108

Yates
John 15, 20
Yeo
John 132, 157, 204
Yieldhall
William 193, 205
Yorcke
William 131
Yorke
William 8, 13, 53, 59, 97, 220
Yorkeshire
John 17
Young
George 33, 110, 130, 219
Mary 109
Mr. 2, 164
William 33, 110, 219
Younger
Alexander 93, 124, 132, 134, 156
husband 123
Mrs. 125
Sarah 123, 124, 125, 132, 134, 156, 157

Index of Equity Cases

www.ingramcontent.com/pod-product-compliance
Lightning Source LLC
Chambersburg PA
CBHW061004280326
41935CB00009B/834

* 9 7 8 0 8 0 6 3 5 2 8 9 3 *